The Withering Away of the Totalitarian State

The Withering Away of the Totalitarian State...
and other surprises

Jeane J. Kirkpatrick

The AEI Press

Publisher for the American Enterprise Institute
WASHINGTON, D.C.

1990

Distributed by arrangement with

National Book Network
4720 Boston Way
Lanham, Md. 20706

3 Henrietta Street
London WC2E 8LU England

Library of Congress Catalog Card No. 90-20789

ISBN 0-8447-3727-5 (alk. paper)

1   3   5   7   9   10   8   6   4   2

AEI Studies 498

The AEI Press
Publisher for the American Enterprise Institute
1150 17th Street, N.W., Washington, D.C. 20036

Printed in the United States of America

ʈP

Contents

PART TWO

SUMMITRY: MEN AND ARMS

PART THREE
THE UNITED STATES AND ITS ALLIES

PART FOUR
THE LAST COLONIAL EMPIRE

PART FIVE
REFLECTIONS ON THE NEW SOVIET REVOLUTION

Preface

The essays and columns included in this book track changes in the Soviet Union and Eastern Europe and related issues in foreign policy as they have developed over the past five years. They constitute a kind of journal of these momentous changes—written as the changes occurred. I have added comments when that seemed appropriate.

As almost everyone now understands, events in the Soviet Union have moved with dizzying speed during the past year. Major developments continue as this book goes to press. What happens after that cannot be taken into account here.

Most, but not all, the essays included here have benefited from the work of my principal editor at the *Los Angeles Times* Syndicate— Steve Christensen, from whom I have learned a great deal (though never enough) about clear, direct writing. I am appropriately grateful to him.

I also wish to thank Mark Salter, Tim Goodman, Winnie Peterson, Audrey Weg, and Mary Purdy for their help in various phases of the research, writing, and preparation of this manuscript.

Inevitably, the responsibility for errors is mine.

The Withering Away of the Totalitarian State

Abandoning the Totalitarian Project

When it [the state] ultimately becomes really representative of society as a whole it makes itself superfluous. Government over persons is replaced by administration of things and the direction of procuring production. The state is not abolished; it withers away.

FRIEDRICH ENGELS
The Origin of the Family, Private Property,
and the State

The replacement of the bourgeois by the proletarian state is impossible without a violent revolution. The abolition of the proletarian state . . . is only possible through 'withering away.'

V. I. LENIN
The State and Revolution

When people say that this is the 'collapse of socialism,' we ask in turn: 'What sort of socialism?' The kind that was essentially a version of the Stalinist authoritarian and bureaucratic system which we ourselves have rejected?

MIKHAIL GORBACHEV
July 3, 1990

Having failed, the biggest, boldest, most daring and ruthless social experiment of this or any other century is now being abandoned by its heirs. The Soviet Union was founded by a band of men who believed they had the key to history in a "scientific" doctrine that explained how everything was related to everything else and ultimately depended on property. With this "key" they were—they believed—in a position to transform society and human nature. Their doctrine and their conviction reverberated around the world.

For many, the Soviet Union seemed Promethean—the very embodiment of the dream that extraordinary persons can transcend history and mold a society and the human beings in it to their will. It was never a country like others. Books like John Reed's *Ten Days That Shook the World* tell us what this first twentieth-century utopia meant

1

to so many of the best and brightest of the time. Evolution, will, inevitability, redemption, utopia—each had a place in the post-Victorian imagination, and each had a place in the first Marxist revolution. In the imaginations of those who shared the dream, the Soviet Union quickly became the country of the fresh start, the country of the good plan, the homeland of philosopher kings.

The Soviet Union was also the inventor of modern totalitarian-ism—of the Party-state, which sought centralized political control of all society and the lives of all those in it. With Stalin it became as well the first terror state that relied heavily on terror for all aspects of government. It developed great military power and spread its doc-trine around the world, attracting converts and followers. It devel-oped colonies on five continents. It held supreme power in half of Europe. It stimulated fear, alliances, and a great arms race that lasted nearly half a century. Then, suddenly it all changed.

The world has watched with fascination the abandonment of the totalitarian project in Europe. It is not happening as Engels and Lenin predicted, but it is happening—in full view and at an accelerating pace.

Nineteen eighty-nine was the year the Soviet Union liquidated its Eastern European empire, ended the division of Europe, acceler-ated the dismantling of its totalitarian state, transformed the Com-munist party, and undermined the world Socialist system.

These developments were a great surprise to us all—scholars, statesmen, financiers, Europeans, Americans, everyone. There was a general recognition that under the policy of *glasnost,* launched in 1986, censorship of the Soviet media had been relaxed, famous political prisoners released and permitted to emigrate, and some important official "errors" in Soviet history "corrected." The West had also become aware of a chronic Soviet economic crisis. But no one expected the sweeping changes that took place in 1989. Western governments and intellectuals had—with few exceptions—long since persuaded themselves that Eastern European governments were "le-gitimate," acceptable to their populations and that Eastern European economies were reasonably successful. Almost everyone overesti-mated the amount of indigenous support for Eastern European Communist regimes and underestimated the extent to which they rested on force alone. And so we did not expect they would simply collapse when force was not used to sustain them. We may never know whether Mikhail Gorbachev himself intended his original re-forms to become the peaceful revolution that is still under way as I write. But that is what they became.

Like the dog that did not bark, the most important event of 1989

2

was a nonevent: the fact that Soviet troops were left in their barracks while the people of Hungary, Poland, the German Democratic Republic, and Czechoslovakia took control of their governments and their lives. "Internationalist duty" and the Brezhnev Doctrine were not invoked to crush 1989's Hungarian revolution, Prague summer, or Berlin fall.

No modern empire has been liquidated more rapidly than the Soviet Union's East European empire. From its founding, that empire had symbolized the cold war—the stark evidence that successive Soviet leaders would use force to extend and maintain control over reluctant peoples beyond their borders.

What began as an opening became a revolution in which the Soviet government and the world Socialist system were dramatically altered. The revolution that began in Moscow in 1917 with the Bolsheviks' seizure of the Russian government has been transformed from Moscow, its essential doctrines and practices revised. No one yet knows what the Soviet Union will become or what economic and political institutions may emerge. Clearly, though, the world revolution launched in 1917 is no longer in progress.

In February 1990, Gorbachev once again assured the Central Committee Plenum, saying, "We remain dedicated to the choice made in October 1917, the Socialist idea, but we are coming away from its dogmatic interpretation and refusing to sacrifice people's real interests to schematic constructions."

But it is not clear that the Soviet leader and his colleagues have remained true to the choice made in 1917. Instead, they have step by step abandoned key aspects of Marxist philosophy and the ideology built on it by Soviet leaders from Lenin forward.

In 1990, Soviet officials still cited Marxism-Leninism but now linked it to new policies, remote from those this orthodoxy had always supported. New principles of legitimacy, closer to the democratic tradition, had made their appearance. Public opinion was consulted; elections of a sort were carried out. The idea of government by consent of the governed was invoked, though not yet practiced. Force was renounced as a legitimate method of government. The Marxist-Leninist language of earlier years disappeared from speeches.

When Mikhail Gorbachev signaled Eastern European clients that Soviet troops would not be available to maintain them, those governments collapsed. Force and the threat of force were starkly exposed as the keystone of an Eastern European Soviet empire; the debate on whether Eastern European people had "chosen" or "accepted" the

Soviet model was settled forever. The people of Eastern Europe had submitted to force.

Reform created its own momentum. Each move toward opening the society brought to light deep fissures in the totalitarian edifices. The rush of Germans through the hole in the Hungarian border and through the Brandenburg Gate and the sweeping electoral defeat of Communist candidates in the Soviet Union, Poland, Czechoslovakia, Hungary, and East Germany revealed the failure of decades of indoctrination and repression and the vulnerability of Communist parties to change.

At the same time that the success of market-oriented societies revealed the full extent of socialism's failure, the survival of pre-Bolshevik identifications and attachments to nationality and religion established the failure of totalitarian controls to produce desired feelings. Estonians, given the chance to express their feelings, revealed themselves to be Estonians; Lithuanians, Lithuanians; Latvians, Latvians; Georgians, Georgians. Jews, given the opportunity to emigrate, signed up to emigrate. Russians, given the chance, voted for candidates opposed by the Party, elected Boris Yeltsin, and overwhelmingly supported independence for Russia. Totalitarianism had produced external conformity but not internal conviction. It had produced a centralized, comprehensively planned and controlled economic system that operated on the basis of force, not on either altruism or self-interest.

The Soviet Union is still not a country like others. Nor is it certain that its great military power will be used in constructive ways. But it is clear we are at the end of an era: the end of the Soviets' East European empire, the end of the Socialist world economic and military systems, the end of totalitarianism in Europe, the end of the Socialist world revolution. We have arrived at the end of a twentieth-century, Western version of utopianism to which perhaps 100 million people have been sacrificed in a merciless search for the good society.

We are also at the end of the era of international relations associated with this world revolution: the end of the cold war, the end of a divided Europe, and the end of an American stint as a superpower in a bipolar world.

No one knows what economic and political institutions could replace the Soviet state. It could become an authoritarian rather than a totalitarian state, with a Communist party that holds dominant but not exclusive power. It could become an authoritarian state in which the military effectively governs—no matter who appears at the top of the government. It could become a democracy. It could become a multinational federal state, or a dozen states.

What is clear is that the Soviet Union will never ever be the same. Many further changes will be required before the Soviet state relinquishes control over the economy, the culture, and the lives of citizens and permits the reconstruction and expression of society. But the earnest quest for total control by the Party, in the service of its vision, is finished.

The Perestroika Revolution

Introduction to Part One

Sakharov and Gorbachev—
A Challenge
May 15, 1985

The death of Andrei Sakharov in December 1989 deprived the nascent opposition group in the Soviet legislature—the Inter-regional Group—of a dynamic and eloquent leader. It deprived the Soviet Union and the world of a living symbol of courage and commitment in the face of repression and exile. And it deprived Mikhail Gorbachev of a nettlesome critic, one whose warnings he greatly needed to hear.

When Gorbachev ordered Sakharov's release from internal exile in December 1986, he showed himself to be a new kind of Soviet ruler. Liberating Sakharov foreshadowed the later remarkable departures of the Gorbachev era.

From time to time a man and his work and his choices assume mythic proportions, embodying in themselves the whole human experience for their times. Andrei Sakharov became such a man: a man of science in a century of science; a man of weapons in a century of weapons; a man of peace, human rights, moral clarity, and courage in a century of relativism, nihilism, holocaust, and gulag.

Sakharov was a Soviet superscientist. While still very young, he wrote articles on theoretical physics. In 1945 he began graduate studies at the Institute of Physics. In 1948 he was included in the research group that developed thermonuclear weapons. In 1952 he initiated important work on magnetic explosive generators and a year later, in 1953, was elected to the USSR Academy of Sciences.

But about the same time he began to think more and more about human rights and peace. Having involved himself deeply in the creation of weapons and bombs, horrified at the product of his own

9

nuclear research, he began to dwell on the threat to mankind and to our world of nuclear weapons and to advocate nuclear test bans and limitations on nuclear testing. He worked hard to promote the 1963 Moscow Treaty banning nuclear testing in the atmosphere, outer space, and under water. From 1967 forward Andrei Sakharov devoted himself progressively to the well-being or lack thereof of victims of repression in the Soviet Union.

In 1968, Sakharov expounded his ideas in a classic essay, "Progress, Coexistence, and Intellectual Freedom," ideas that he reiterated seven years later in his Nobel speech entitled "Peace, Progress, and Human Rights." From that point in July 1968, Sakharov was barred from secret work, his thoughts having become too dangerous. He was excommunicated from the Soviet establishment. In January 1980 he was deprived of all his official Soviet awards, including the Order of Lenin, the State Prize, the Hero of Socialist Labor, the Lenin Prize, and the Second State Prize for Peace. Pressure on his family and friends increased. Andrei Sakharov worked hard and lived under very constrained circumstances, under continual surveillance of the Soviet police.

Yet, Sakharov wrote, "I am inclined to believe that moral criteria, together with uninhibited thought, provide the only possible compass for these complex and contradictory problems. I believe in the power of reason and in the human spirit."

Reason, science, morality, human rights, and peace—these are the definitive preoccupations of the great, creative, constructive minds of our century and our age. The relations among them have been spelled out in the philosophic works of such figures as Morris Cohen, John Dewey, Jacques Maritain, Karl Popper, Raymond Aron, Sidney Hook, and Max Lerner.

The relations among these are also illustrated in the great political dramas and disasters of the century, in the theory and practice of such consummate totalitarians as Adolf Hitler, who in *Mein Kampf* and in his Third Reich demonstrated the consequences of repression and war, of making reason subordinate to will; science subordinate to race; freedom subordinate to power; dignity and democracy subordinate to slavery; and peace subordinate to conquest.

Sakharov wrote about the relations among inquiry, human rights, totalitarianism, and peace:

> Two contradictory, opposing trends in the development of society characterize our epoch. One leads toward economic, cultural and ideological pluralism, the other toward totalitarianism, dictatorship and cruelty. The expansion of totalitari-

anism is a cruel and present danger. I believe the main thrust in the struggle against totalitarianism lies in the international defense of human rights where those rights are violated.

Sakharov's insistence on speaking about the relations among science and human rights and totalitarianism and peace made him the target and victim of the Soviet state. He was silenced, exiled, isolated. One of the great minds of our century was subjected to mind altering drugs. He was attacked through those whom he loved. He was tempted, and he survived. The strength of his spirit was heroic.

Now there is a new ruler of the Soviet Union. There has been wide speculation in the United States and in the world about what manner of man this new ruler is. We have heard about his style, his dress, his new look, his charm, his wife, his power. We have heard about his supporters within the Politburo. The world has combed his records for his public utterances. What kind of man is Mikhail Gorbachev? There is a very simple test of the manner of man Premier Gorbachev is.

We have heard from Premier Gorbachev that he is concerned with economic development in the Soviet Union, that he is interested in raising productivity and establishing higher standards of living for the Soviet people.

Naturally, we welcome that concern. We share with him the hopes of a better life for the Soviet people. We regret the poor living conditions of the Soviet people. We regret the declining living standards of the Soviet people and the pervasive deterioration that affects all aspects of the economy and society of the Soviet Union. It has affected agriculture, industry, public health, life expectancy, housing, and communications. It has been said of the Soviet Union that it is a third world economy with first world weapons. Only the weapons seem to work.

The London Times noted that in 1981 the Soviet Union had still not met the housing standards established in 1928. As of 1984, more than 30 percent of all Soviet adults lived in communal housing with persons to whom they were unrelated by blood or marriage. Deaths from alcohol poisoning continue to rise. In 1980 they stood at 16 per 100,000, more than eighty-eight times the rate of death by alcohol poisoning in the United States.

Abortion in the Soviet Union is so high it has become a standard form of contraception and family planning. Food is rationed. Public health has so deteriorated that Soviet medical publications tell us

11

today that the incidence of measles is just below the epidemiological level, as are five other of the most common diseases, including polio, diphtheria, scarlet fever, and whooping cough. Infant mortality is rising in the Soviet Union; life expectancy, falling.

The Soviet people deserve better. The lack of freedom of Soviet life is pervasively destructive in its effects on all aspects of Soviet society.

The cycle of repression, stagnation, and violence denies the Soviet people the possibilities for a good life. It denies peace for the rest of us as well.

Will Mikhail Gorbachev change the situation? What manner of man is he? Is he the manner of man who will dismantle the structure of stagnation and repression that denies freedom to just such men and women as Sakharov, Yelena Bonner, Anatoly Shcharansky, and Yuri Orlov? Today in the Soviet Union the structure of totalitarianism stands not only between Sakharov and his freedom but also between the Soviet people and their aspirations, between Soviet leaders and their hopes. It breeds scarcity, corruption, and failure in a vicious cycle.

Claims of infallibility and total power by the state lead to the denial of free inquiry, and the denial of free inquiry leads to reliance on state power as a substitute for reason, then to repression of the reasonable. Reliance on power and denial of freedom lead to a pervasive search for control over everyone and everything, and that search for control leads to the denial of law and to more reliance on power. But there is never enough power to stifle all the freedom of all the people. And so more power is needed and more weapons and more territory, to protect the political doctrine that underlies the claim to total power—and more power and more weapons and more territory and more war, and more, and more, and more. And in this situation there is no freedom, no creativity, no science, and no progress.

Andrei Sakharov reminds us that one man *can* make a difference. Imagine what one man at the top of the pyramid of power could do in the Soviet system.

Is Premier Gorbachev the kind of man who will decide to free Andrei Sakharov, Yelena Bonner, Anatoly Shcharansky, and their comrades? Is he the kind of man who will bring hope to the Soviet people and peace to the world? That would be a remarkable man, indeed. Sakharov wrote:

> I am convinced that international trust, mutual understanding, disarmament, international security are inconceivable

without an open society with freedom of information, freedom of conscience, the right to publish, the right to travel, the right to choose the country one wishes to live in. I am also convinced that freedom of conscience, together with other civic rights, provides both the basis for scientific progress and a guarantee against its misuse to harm mankind.

If one man named Gorbachev were to understand the relations between free individuals, reason, science, progress, human rights, and peace, our world would be transformed.

New Men in the Kremlin
September 15, 1985

I was impressed from the outset by the bold self-confidence with which Mikhail Gorbachev assumed direction of the Soviet Union, changed personnel and policies, and launched an energetic campaign to make his presence felt in world affairs.

Gorbachev's energy and vitality contrasted sharply with the moribund style of his predecessors and dramatized the fact that a new generation was in charge—a generation that differed in some important ways from previous Soviet elites.

I did not at all anticipate the sweeping changes that have occurred, but I had learned from Plato that even closed systems cannot protect themselves from the different perspectives of different generations. Therefore, with the arrival of the first new Soviet generation to power, I tried to identify some differences in experience that might affect their perspectives.

It is useful to recall the style and substance of Gorbachev's early period when his tone was much harsher than it later became. We are reminded that he did not spring a full-blown reformer from the forehead of Yuri Andropov but that he and his reforms evolved with experience.

The most interesting and important political event of the summer, surely, has been the ongoing transformation of the Soviet Union's ruling elite. Like so many other developments during the brief tenure of Premier Mikhail Gorbachev, this one was set in motion by his patron and predecessor, Yuri Andropov.

13

With confidence and skill reminiscent of Joseph Stalin's consolidation of power in the 1920s, Gorbachev is unceremoniously retiring rivals and replacing the Chernenko generation with younger men who have more reason to be loyal to him. New ministers and managers have been appointed to direct foreign affairs, defense, the economy, and education. And most significantly, the Party itself is being "renewed" with personnel changes extending from the Politburo to the local parties.

In his interview with *Time* magazine (Sept. 9, 1985), Gorbachev described these changes as a "natural process of replacement" devoid of political significance. But from his acceptance speech on March 11 forward, Gorbachev has asserted his determination to take "resolute measures" against Party members, bureaucrats, and workers who lack adequate discipline and zeal.

It is all wrong, he said, to think that "antisocialist" individuals no longer exist in Soviet society because the class struggle has been eliminated. Some Party members have themselves become "antagonistic to socialism" and "must be dealt with." Such people, Gorbachev promised in an article in *Kommunist*, "will get what they deserve."

All "alien phenomena" will be removed from Soviet life. All "manifestations of showiness and idle talk, swagger and irresponsibility" must end. Alcoholism, absenteeism, laziness, waste, and theft are to be eliminated. Even in his interview with *Time*, Gorbachev asserts, "Everyone has got to restructure things, restyle his whole way of working and thinking."

We cannot really tell yet whether Gorbachev is mainly interested in creating a new "new Soviet Man," in promoting Socialist morality, in enhancing efficiency, or in building a reliable political machine to support his personal power. Whatever his motives, the principal consequence of Gorbachev's campaign is to hasten the process of generational change set in motion by death and disease and to advance a younger, better-educated generation of persons who more closely resemble Gorbachev himself. It is too early to be certain what these changes in the ruling elite portend for the Soviet people or for the rest of us. But there are certain things we can know about the new rulers of this closed society:

• We know they are products of the Soviet system, born and educated after the Bolshevik revolution, and that they have had no experience with freedom or with alternative ways of organizing life.

• We know they did not experience the great Stalinist purges. They did not need to fear the knock on the door in the middle of the night.

They did not achieve their positions over the bodies of dead or disappeared comrades. They missed the full impact of World War II— the Hitler offensive, the battle of Stalingrad, the struggle for survival.

• We know their most important professional experience has occurred in the past fifteen years, during the period of relative Western decline and Soviet success, the period in which the "world correlation of forces" shifted away from the West.

While none of these background facts enables us to predict with certainty the behavior of the new Soviet team, they provide some clues. Because the new leaders did not experience the terrible internal and external threats of the Stalinist period, they may feel less vulnerable, more confident and less cautious than their predecessors who emerged during a time of U.S. superiority and Stalinist paranoia.

Because they have risen to the top in the Soviets' vast interlocking, overlapping bureaucracy, they must be skilled in bureaucratic politics. Gorbachev, having achieved the pinnacle of power at the young age of fifty-four, has proved himself a virtuoso at internal bureaucratic politics, presumably displaying the same "charm" and tactical skill obvious in his dealings with Britain, France, the United States, and the editors of *Time* magazine.

The evidence so far available suggests that the new leaders are much better than their predecessors at both interpersonal and international politics. Gorbachev has already demonstrated that he is a master chess player capable of pursuing a complicated global strategy. Already he has moved to assert clear Soviet leadership over the Eastern bloc, to cement relations with third world client states, to woo America's allies, and to carry an appeal directly to the American public.

Thus, he has launched an *"offensive de charme"* in Europe that includes a projected meeting with France's President François Mitterrand in Paris one month before he sees Ronald Reagan in Geneva. His Asian moves include a stepped-up courtship of China, new aid for India, new threats and promises for Pakistan, continuing war for Afghanistan, a medal for Philippine President Marcos, some complaints against Japan's "resurgent militarism," and an intensified Soviet naval buildup in the north Pacific.

So it has gone around the world. Soviet diplomacy under Gorbachev has shown variety, complexity, and skill. In dealing with Americans, Gorbachev has demonstrated a flair for utilizing politics, diplomacy, and military might in pursuit of Soviet goals. He not only restored arms control talks in Geneva but also talked arms control to an array of congressmen, senators, and journalists, offsetting rigid formal proposals with promising informal hints and suggestions.

As the interview with *Time* magazine showed, Gorbachev and his colleagues understand that the open politics of the United States and the democracies are open to them and offer promising possibilities for directly and openly influencing public opinion and policy decisions. By now, they have made an all-out effort to influence the German elections and to prevent deployment of Pershing and cruise missiles. Soviet representatives have learned to work the U.S. Congress like skilled lobbyists. They have found spokesmen who can mix it up with Ted Koppel on "Nightline." There were no grounds for surprise that Gorbachev granted to *Time* magazine an interview with the clear purpose of influencing the U.S. arms control position at the upcoming summit.

As the interview confirmed, the Soviet Union does not want the United States to develop a defense against Soviet missiles. Aware that they have a clear superiority in offensive weapons, they want to maintain the advantage and U.S. vulnerability. They seem to have understood that most Americans hate and fear war, are sick of high defense budgets, and long for meaningful arms control agreements.

Gorbachev offered *Time* magazine an opportunity in exchange for an opportunity: *Time* would have its scoop; Gorbachev would have a credible means of direct communication with the American public.

Gorbachev's performance in that interview was impressive in the various ways commented upon by the American media. One disturbing aspect has been less noted.

To appeal to the American public's dread of war, Gorbachev emphasizes and, I believe, exaggerates the level of tension and conflict between the United States and the Soviet Union. "Relations between our two countries are continuing to deteriorate," he says, "the arms race is intensifying, and the threat of war is not subsiding."

What threat of war? Gorbachev tells us the Soviet Union will "never start a war." Anyone who knows Ronald Reagan knows *he* will not start a war.

Gorbachev comments, "[The] situation [in the world] today is highly complex, very tense. I would even go so far as to say it is explosive."

Why is it explosive? Nowhere in the world are the United States and the Soviet Union confronting one another directly as they did in the Berlin blockade or the Cuban missile crisis.

What is Gorbachev talking about? Surely, he is not suggesting that the American desire to defend itself against Soviet missiles creates an "explosive" situation.

It is not the first time the new Soviet leaders have invoked the

fear of war in the effort to influence Western publics and governments. In the German elections, in the campaign against missile
deployments, in the efforts to diminish Ronald Reagan's electoral
chances, the level of East-West tension was first exaggerated by the
Soviets and then by the American media—who hyped the Soviet
hype.

One hopes it will be the last time the fear of war is invoked to
persuade Western nations that it is too dangerous to defend themselves. One hopes the new leaders will abandon this verbal brinkman-
ship as they grow more accustomed to Western-style politics.

In fact, U.S.-Soviet relations have not deteriorated in recent
months; tensions are surely not explosive. Even if the Soviets were to
break off arms control talks in Geneva as Gorbachev hints, there
would be no crisis. Arms control talks are desirable, but we have lived
without them. Their absence could not endanger the peace. Obviously, however, it would be far better to continue the talks till
progress is achieved.

We have Gorbachev's word that the new Soviet leaders desire
nothing so much as the opportunity to cut military expenditures and
concentrate on internal economic development. "The main thing,"
he says, "is to make life better for the people."

It is possible that the new Soviet elite will give priority to internal
development over external expansion. Generations do differ; goals
do change. We do not know whether the new rulers will be more
reckless or more peaceable, more rigid or more pragmatic. We do not
know their priorities. There is room for hope.

New Thinking in the Kremlin
February 16, 1987

*I wrote this piece after my visit to Moscow with other former officials, a
visit organized by the Council on Foreign Relations.*

*I was impressed—as everyone was—with Mikhail Gorbachev's
personal force and vitality and with how different he seemed from his
predecessors. Usually there is a "fit" between a political system and its
top leader; yet Gorbachev seemed to me a "sport" in the Soviet system—
more expressive, more colorful, more persuasive and interested in persuasion. I watched his much grayer colleagues listen as he spoke for*

hours and asked myself when they would grow bored with listening to him and watching him perform.

The Soviet Union was a bureaucratic dictatorship, and Gorbachev is a personalist-style leader. He is, I thought, the kind of man who would be successful in any political system. I was especially impressed with Andrei Sakharov's support for Gorbachev as the best chance for reform in the Soviet Union.

I was ready to believe the situation was, as Sakharov said, "complicated and contradictory." Indeed, Gorbachev himself expressed an interesting mixture of orthodox Leninist clichés and new departures.

One thing was clear. Our Soviet hosts wanted us—the small group of former U.S. government officials visiting Moscow—to understand that changes were taking place in the Soviet Union. The day we arrived, they presented to each of us a copy of the speech Mikhail Gorbachev had delivered January 27 to the powerful Plenum of the Central Committee of the Communist Party of the Soviet Union. "Comrades," it began, "we have begun reorganization and will not look back. . . ."

Gorbachev, who became general secretary only two years ago, has launched a campaign for sweeping changes of Soviet society, apparently even before he has fully consolidated his own power.

Our group watched and, especially, we listened to a series of top Soviet officials. We listened to Gorbachev, who, during a three-hour conversation with our group, appeared vigorous, intelligent, charming, manipulative, and supremely self-confident. Wherever we went, we heard the themes of Gorbachev's eighty-four-page speech: criticism of ineffective management, of "scholastic" dogmatic thinking, and of a failure to understand the "full need for change" and a demand for self-criticism and for "new thinking."

The new thinking features such words as "restructuring," "reform," "participation," "democratization"—words Americans automatically associate with our kind of system. But Gorbachev and others warned us repeatedly against imagining that the Soviet Union was abandoning socialism, planning a Western-style democracy, or emulating any other country. The democracy the Soviet Union seeks, they explained, is Soviet-style democracy with one-party elections and socialism.

The new thinking takes aim at problems created by the "old thinking" of this centralized society in which decisions are made at the top and handed down through many layers of bureaucracy. So reforms seek to eliminate some of those layers—giving factories more power over the conduct of their affairs and giving enterprises interested in export an opportunity to be in direct contact with foreign markets.

What Gorbachev and his colleagues want is a more efficient, creative, one-party Socialist state. So he is prodding the leadership of this top-heavy, bureaucratized society to overcome stagnation with "openness" and "reform." He and his associates speak of stimulating worker participation in the decisions of the work place.

What is one to think of these efforts? Is Gorbachev sincere?

The answer is that a real campaign for change has been launched by the Soviet leader. We cannot know Gorbachev's innermost thoughts and feelings, and we do not need to. We do know that he is now publicly committed. His future and his political fortunes are firmly identified with this campaign for change.

Will it work? We do not—and cannot—know.

Gorbachev is not the first Bolshevik leader to attempt sweeping reforms in the management of Soviet society. V. I. Lenin, whose photograph hangs like a holy picture in every public room we visited, undertook sweeping reforms when he launched the New Economic Policy. The last man to undertake sweeping changes of this heavy-handed bureaucratic despotism was Nikita Khrushchev, who in 1956 launched the de-Stalinization campaign that opened the doors of the gulag and relaxed the grip of the KGB. But when Khrushchev turned his reforms on the Communist party itself, the Party turned on him and unceremoniously removed him from power.

Gorbachev and his colleagues do not forget this experience. Carefully, they distinguish their efforts. Khrushchev's speech to the twentieth Congress was "lacking in a positive perspective," one official told us, while Gorbachev's speech to the twenty-seventh Congress stressed "positive" aspects of development. Meticulously, they place their reforms in the Bolshevik tradition. Punctiliously, they cite Lenin's views in support of new projects.

Gorbachev's bold personal style contrasts sharply with his careful move from theory to practice. Nowhere is this clearer than in the field of human rights. Where thousands of political prisoners were released in Khrushchev's era, the doors of Soviet prisons have been opened only a crack to permit the release of some 140 political prisoners. A thousand others remain incarcerated for such crimes as teaching Hebrew, distributing Bibles, or criticizing the government.

The present situation, Andrei Sakharov told us, is complicated and contradictory. Some people are in prison, he said, because in the past they said the same things that today are printed in *Pravda*. Most of those recently released have been forced to "repent and recant" as a condition of winning their freedom, Sakharov said. A new restrictive emigration law has been passed and is being narrowly applied. Rumor has it that of 100 applicants for visas, only 1 was judged eligible to leave. Time, Gorbachev and others told us, is needed to deal with these old problems.

If Mikhail Gorbachev's intentions for his own society are not entirely clear, his plans for the rest of the world are even more uncertain. Is it possible, he asks, for the current generation of Soviets and Americans to develop positive relations? Maybe. That depends.

Reykjavik, Gorbachev said, was a missed opportunity. But he said it still might be possible for the United States and the Soviet Union to reach agreements on armaments, trade, and regional conflicts. During our stay, however, no new Soviet proposals were offered for arms reductions or for a Soviet withdrawal from Afghanistan or for settlement of any other conflict in which the United States and the Soviet Union find themselves on opposite sides.

Clearly, the new thinking has produced fewer ideas in international relations than in internal management and trade.

New thinking in foreign affairs is hampered by Gorbachev's lack of accurate information about the United States. His thoughts about us are distorted by stereotypes—the military industrial complex, the munitions makers. It would be useful if Mikhail Gorbachev knew us better. One hopes he will accept Ronald Reagan's invitation to visit the United States and try a little "new thinking" about America.

Is He a New Kind of Communist?
December 13, 1987

Is Mikhail Gorbachev a new kind of Communist? George Shultz thought so early on. Ronald Reagan came to think so, and after meeting Mikhail Gorbachev I thought so, too, but I was not certain the substance of his intention and policies was as different as his personal style.

I was disturbed by the conventional Marxist-Leninist thinking of his book, Perestroika, *and I believe it is a mistake to ignore the books of would-be rulers—as the world ignored Adolf Hitler's* Mein Kampf *until it was too late.*

I was bothered by the hostility to the United States expressed in Perestroika *and by the hostility to the United States and Ronald Reagan*

that Gorbachev expressed when he spoke with our group.
The book is more conventionally Leninist than the views Gorbachev
later expressed. But certain themes, including his insistence that he
would "deprive" the West of the Soviet threat and his insistence on a
"common European home," have never changed.

Ronald Reagan believes Mikhail Gorbachev is a different kind of man
from his Soviet predecessors, and this belief enables our president to
set aside a lifetime of caution concerning what Communists are like
and how we should deal with them.

The president is not alone in his view. Underlying the euphoria
of the summit week was a widespread notion that Gorbachev is a
new kind of Soviet ruler, with new goals for his country and new
views about how to achieve them. This optimistic belief is based not
only on our national character but also on Gorbachev's style and on
the fact that he represents a new generation of Soviet leadership.

The style is that of a modern man. Gorbachev does not sound
like a man who threatens anyone's security. So many of his Western
hearers, including the American president, conclude that the country
ruled by Gorbachev is less aggressive and expansionist than in the
past. Months ago, George Shultz argued that Gorbachev was a new
type of Soviet ruler. Reagan then resisted this view; now he believes
it.

The belief is not implausible. We regularly assume that style is
an external reflection of internal realities, and, as far back as Plato,
discerning people have believed that political generations sometimes
differ in fundamental ways and that the arrival of a new generation
in power may mark the beginning of a new political era.

Moreover, we Americans have wanted desperately to believe in a
transformation of the Soviet Union and of U.S.-Soviet relations. We
think it would be good for them, good for us, and good for the world.
Most Americans have, therefore, been enormously gratified and
encouraged to hear of Gorbachev's campaign for *glasnost* and *perestroika* and "new thinking."

People rethinking their view of the Soviet Union, including
Ronald Reagan, would be well advised to actually read Gorbachev's
new book—dull as it is—which casts great light on his conceptions of
where the Soviet Union is, where it is going, and why. The Gorbachev who wrote *Perestroika* is a classical Leninist—flexible, adapta-
ble, skillful in the pursuit and use of power, absolutely committed to
"the revolution," to socialism, to a one-party state, and not unduly
disturbed about the high human cost of past Soviet policy.

The book rejects utterly the common American view that economic difficulties have prompted Gorbachev's campaign of reform and that these reforms constitute a retreat from socialism. Again and again, Gorbachev insists that his goal is the consolidation and perfection of socialism, not its modification.

"We will proceed toward better socialism rather than away from it," he writes. "We are saying this honestly and without trying to fool our own people or the world. Any hopes that we begin to build a different, non-socialist society and go over to the other camp are unrealistic and futile. Those in the West who expect us to give up socialism will be disappointed."

Concerning democratization (a word that Gorbachev uses as frequently in his book as in his speeches in the United States), he says it is indeed a goal. But, as he has emphasized in Moscow conversations and makes clear in the book, the democracy he seeks is not American-style, Western-style democracy in which rulers are chosen in periodic, competitive elections under conditions of free press and assembly. The democracy Gorbachev seeks means decentralization and broad participation in society. It does not and could not mean competitive elections, for, as Gorbachev remarks without embarrassment, "We have no political opposition." The Party rules.

If *perestroika* is not a retreat from socialism and not a drive for liberalization caused by Western pressures, then what is it?

"It is a revolution. A decisive acceleration of the socioeconomic and cultural development of Soviet society which involves radical changes. . . . It is a jump forward in the development of socialism." he writes.

There are few surprises in this book. From it we learn that Gorbachev is a Soviet national who clings firmly to Leninism and the one-party state. We also learn that his foreign policy approaches are the same as would have been assumed by any close observer.

There are the familiar justifications. The Soviet Union went into Afghanistan "because its leaders asked the Soviet Union to help." There is no mention here of the murders of those same Afghan leaders at the hands of their Soviet "benefactors" within hours of the Soviet army's arrival.

There is the familiar theme that "Europe is our common home," a Europe that "stretches from the Atlantic to the Urals." Russians then are European. Americans are not. Russians seek to realize closer bonds with their "common family."

There are harsh, familiar complaints about America's role in the world. U.S. foreign policy is depicted as being dominated by a "caveman" mentality that sees the Soviet Union as a persistent threat to the world. "We have the impression that the United States needs regional conflicts to maintain its confrontation with the Soviet Union," Gorbachev says.

The United States is charged with attempting to build relations on the basis of violence and command. It is charged with causing the cold war. It is charged with grandiose conceit.

"What motivates the United States?" Gorbachev asks and answers. The old villain, the military-industrial complex. American foreign policy is based on illusions of technological superiority and the belief that "the economic system of the Soviet Union is about to crumble," that it will be possible to restore American military supremacy.

America is not the only target. Gorbachev reaffirms Soviet opposition to "any manifestations of nationalist narrow-mindedness and chauvinism, parochialism, Zionism and anti-Semitism in whatever forms they may be expressed."

His conception of the Soviet past is conventional, orthodox, and unembarrassed. He describes the collectivization policy that killed 5 million as "a great historic act, the most important social change since 1917."

The book lacks the charm and flexibility that characterize Gorbachev himself. It is dull; he is not. Perhaps he did not write the book at all. Gorbachev describes *perestroika* as a revolution. But the book testifies that Gorbachev is no revolutionary within the Soviet tradition.

I hope the president reads it before the next summit.

Four Questions about Gorbachev's Reforms
February 23, 1987

Much of Gorbachev's "new thinking" resembled V. I. Lenin's New Economic Policy. Even that, however, seemed to me hopeful since it began from a realistic appraisal of the Soviet economic situation and recognized that free-market incentives and practices would help.

By February 1987, Gorbachev had spelled out his new thinking and accompanied it with the release of several of the more famous prisoners, including two of the three I had focused on in my Christmas column.

I was enormously interested in these developments but uncertain

23

about their meaning for the future. Were they one more twist in the shifting line of the Kremlin, or did they represent a desire for more basic change?

I began to try to identify some criteria for evaluating this new-style Soviet leader and his program of reform.

It was spring 1989 before I firmly concluded that Gorbachev did in fact desire sweeping internal reforms of the Soviet system and also that he "needed" international peace to pursue them. Nonetheless, I noted, the Gorbachev regime showed no signs of reducing its support for its overseas empire. And the Soviets remain tough and wily in conversation and arms reduction negotiation.

In Moscow, there are more visitors and more assurances. "Revolutionary changes are under way," Mikhail Gorbachev assures an international audience of hundreds. "Broad democratization" of Soviet society is now "irreversible." There is talk not only of "opening" Soviet society but also of "restructuring" it. And we should all understand by now this is not just a line for foreign consumption. The Central Committee hears it. *Pravda* prints it.

The general secretary has assured a worldwide audience that the "new thinking" has already passed from theory to practice: "Our new approach to the humanitarian problem is there for all to see." The presence of dissident Soviet scientist Dr. Andrei Sakharov at international discussions, the release of Josef Begun, and rumors of the impending release of Anatoly Koriagin seem to illustrate his point—even though most Soviet political prisoners still languish in their cells.

Obviously, Americans welcome indications of a liberalizing trend in this society whose citizens have been deprived so long of rudimentary freedoms. Americans desire the liberalization of the Soviet Union for their sake and for ours.

Americans are therefore an eager audience for Gorbachev's campaign of change. They would rather applaud the general secretary's declarations than analyze them. But because the Soviet Union has great military power and is an extremely dangerous potential adversary, it is important that we approach the Soviets' "new thinking" with some straight thinking of our own.

There are questions which simply must be asked:

1. Do the "sweeping reforms" proposed by Gorbachev represent a change of heart or direction in the Soviet system, or are they only a tactic designed to help Gorbachev consolidate and expand power at home and abroad? Some specialists, especially those in France, have

been quick to note that proposed election "reforms" calling for multiple candidacies and a secret ballot would provide Gorbachev a needed procedural mechanism for replacing the Brezhnev team with his own men while leaving the system of one-party bureaucratic dictatorship intact.

That is doubtlessly true if all candidates are handpicked by the leadership and the results are rigged. But if open discussion and criticism are permitted and real competition occurs, even restricted elections could be an important step toward democratization of the ruling party. We cannot know which will occur. We can only wait and see whether election reforms provide a contest or only a device for purging rivals.

2. Does Gorbachev "need" international peace in order to concentrate on economic modernization in the Soviet Union? Americans who see our own high defense costs as a terrible economic burden are inclined to think so. As French Foreign Minister Jean Bernard Raimond observed, however, "The Soviet leadership is not as gloomy about that country's economic and political prospects as Westerners believe they ought to be."

Gorbachev's own statements indicate that while he desires a more efficient economy, harder work, and higher productivity, he is also confident of the Soviet capacity to meet any challenge. When the United States imposed a grain embargo and blocked the sale of computers to the Soviet Union, the Soviet Union responded by working to develop its own industries. Now Gorbachev claims his country is self-sufficient in grain and has a major computer industry.

3. Does Gorbachev's campaign for change foreshadow a less expansionist Soviet foreign policy? In fact, there has been an increase in the quantity and quality of weapons provided to third world client states during Gorbachev's tenure. There has been no move toward internal reconciliation of violent regional conflicts. And although the Soviet government affirms a desire to withdraw from Afghanistan, no withdrawal has taken place. No progress has been made in UN negotiations toward a diplomatic settlement of the Afghan war.

4. Will Gorbachev's desire for more constructive relations with the United States lead to new negotiations and actual arms reductions, or is his interest in arms control limited to a desire to stop the development of a U.S. defense against Soviet missiles? At Reykjavik, he seemed interested only in stopping the Strategic Defense Initiative. But before the Iceland meeting, Soviet negotiators had displayed an interest in agreements on other subjects. At Reykjavik, it seemed clear that real, even dramatic, reductions in arms would not be too difficult to negotiate—if Gorbachev were interested.

He likes to say the ball is in our court, but the decision on deep, verifiable arms reductions is, in fact, his to make. As Raimond said, "If they [the Soviets] want to join the new global industrial revolution, they should cut defense spending, agree to truly effective arms limitations and liberalize their economy and society."

Raimond warned that all this might take time and that therein lay the historic Soviet advantage over the West: the West is too impatient.

Finally, however, the Soviet Union seems to have acquired a leader whose impatience matches our own.

Communist Contradictions

April 6, 1987

The analysis of Communist contradictions by a young Czech émigré, Jiri Pehe, foreshadowed the publication of similar analyses by Soviet officials.

It explained how the Soviet economic system could have achieved its basic goals in the early stages of industrialization but fell further behind in the information age. It argued that a centrally controlled totalitarian state is peculiarly ill suited to the requirements of the information age. In a totalitarian state skills and information are a tightly controlled monopoly, but growth in the information age requires sharing both.

Pehe also offered the interesting insight that Marxist leaders will have increasing difficulty believing in their own legitimacy if they see they cannot deliver the promised good life to the workers.

Can *glasnost* and Mikhail Gorbachev last? Or will he—like Nikita Khrushchev—be dumped by the same bureaucracies that brought him to power? Can reform survive in China? Or will Deng Xiaoping's "opening" be shut tight by "traditionalists" who insist on strict Marxist orthodoxy and tight centralized control? A large question mark hangs over the futures of these two leviathans, whose top rulers are ready to risk a degree of "Western" liberalism in order to enjoy the benefits of "Western" technology and economic success.

We do not know what will happen in either country because we do not know much about the transformation of totalitarian states. American and European experts on the Soviet Union and China know a great deal about how those societies are organized and work, but experts did not predict the appearance of Khrushchev and his dramatic de-Stalinization campaign, nor his sudden removal from power. Experts did not foresee the murderous ferocity of China's cultural revolution nor Deng's dramatic "opening" of Chinese society nor the demotion of Deng's heir apparent, Hu Yaobang, and the strong pressures to return to Marxist orthodoxy.

The small ruling groups that govern these great bureaucratized societies operate in secrecy. Their power struggles are shielded from public view. It is impossible to estimate the relative strengths of factions except as we see their consequences.

The world has had the opportunity, however, to observe efforts to transform totalitarian systems in Hungary, Poland, China, and Yugoslavia. A very interesting article by Jiri Pehe in this month's *Freedom at Issue* magazine examines the experience. Pehe, a Czech émigré and journalist, argues that totalitarian states are under heavy pressure to change. He believes their total control over economics, culture, and politics produces bureaucratization and stagnation that are incompatible with the requirements of computer and communications technology in this information age.

Without that technology, Marxist regimes cannot compete militarily or economically with the West or fulfill their own claims to represent "the future." But utilizing this technology requires sharing control over information and communications. It also requires decentralized economic decision making. Thus, the ruling elites of these societies are confronted with the need to dilute either their control or their claims.

Pehe notes that so far change has occurred "either by a takeover by the army and police [Poland] . . . or by fundamental changes initiated by the elite itself and reflecting the needs of the post-industrial age [Hungary]."

The Hungarian "road" away from totalitarianism features elements of market economy, decentralization of economic management, sharing of information, and acceptance of a degree of economic and political competition. In Poland, economic stagnation and rigidity produced first a revolt of the workers and then a takeover by the army and police.

Hungary is the first Communist state in which a member of the opposition has been permitted to run for a seat in parliament. Poland is the first Communist state in which a military leader has assumed power and totalitarianism has been "transformed into a common dictatorship run by the army."

Now, Pehe observes, the "Socialist fatherland" itself is confronted with the same internal contradictions that have produced change elsewhere.

"It must modernize if the prestige and the might—above all, the military might—of the state is to be saved," he says, "and it is afraid to modernize because post-industrial modernization is possible only if the regime relaxes control over the economy." It seems possible, even likely, that the small ruling elite that governs the Soviet Union does not agree about which of these roads to take.

Pehe's analysis does not tell us what will happen next in China or the Soviet Union, but it identifies the hard choices that confront the fifteen or twenty men who govern these countries. It also illuminates the motives of Marxist "modernizers" such as Deng or Gorbachev, who take most seriously the need to "compete" in the modern world, and the motives of Marxist "conservatives" or "traditionalists," who are more interested in maintaining control than in competing short term with capitalist countries.

Pehe's analysis tells us that resistance to the modernizers is most likely to come from the military, which has the option of establishing a "classical" military dictatorship. Most important, Pehe urges us to look for the "internal contradictions" of Communist regimes and to expect changes in Marxist as well as non-Marxist states.

His analysis takes no account of the Khrushchev experience or the recent Chinese backlash, both of which illustrate that reform is also not "irreversible." It does, however, offer a fascinating insight into the "gray" character of established Marxist leaders and contains a strong implicit warning for Gorbachev. Classical dictators are "the creators of their systems; totalitarian rulers, creations of theirs," Pehe says. Not only did Khrushchev try to open the Soviet "prison house of peoples," but also like Gorbachev, he was a much more interesting, distinctive personality than his colorless bureaucratic colleagues in the Politburo.

Obviously a man well-trained in Marxist analysis, Pehe believes internal contradictions make "real change" in totalitarian systems inevitable: "Both the absolute state and the petrified doctrine are doomed from the moment the totalitarian state decides to catch up with developed post-industrial countries. But they are also doomed if the state elects stagnation."

His analysis is a welcome reminder that we are not the only ones with problems, caught in the double bind of changing circumstance.

Crisis of Communism
December 5, 1988

The New Class established (and subsequent writing confirmed) the Yugoslav writer Milovan Djilas as one of the most brilliant and penetrating analysts of communism. In a wide-ranging interview with George Urban published in Encounter *magazine, Djilas argued that the crisis of communism was not limited to one or a few Communist states but extended from Belgrade to Beijing and derived from flaws intrinsic in the system.*

Djilas believed—as I believed—that perestroika *would lead to a less expansionist foreign policy and therefore was very much in the interest of the West. He also believed it important that the West not bail out the Soviets, thus reducing the economic pressure driving reform.*

The crisis of Communism from Belgrade to Peking is continuous. . . . Every Communist country suffers from the inbuilt inadequacies of the system," the brilliant Yugoslav writer Milovan Djilas said in a long interview published in the current *Encounter* magazine.

This crisis—simultaneously economic and political—is manifest in economies that have failed to grow and governments that have not managed to win the loyalties of the people they rule. It can be observed in the economic stagnation of entrenched Communist societies and the ethnic strife that has become endemic on the borders of the Soviet Union and inside its Eastern European empire.

The crisis is clearest in the countries where Marxist-Leninist governments have ruled the longest and so have had the greatest opportunity to achieve their economic, social, and political goals. But living standards in the Soviet Union remain the lowest in Europe, infant mortality rates are rising, and life expectancy is falling.

The crisis in communism can be observed in the contrast between economic development in the People's Republic of China and in the non-Communist Chinas: Taiwan, Hong Kong, and Singapore. It can be observed in the "reform" programs of the People's Republic of China, Hungary, and Poland. Above all, it can be observed in the Soviet Union of Mikhail Gorbachev.

Though Gorbachev insists in his book and in public commentaries that the Soviet revolution has been a great success, which *perestroika* will only enhance, his speeches to Soviet party congresses and other official Soviet bodies indicate otherwise.

Djilas, a former vice president of Yugoslavia, then a political prisoner, and today one of the world's most astute observers of communism, has no doubt about what has stimulated the urge for reform in Gorbachev and his colleagues.

"Let us be quite clear about one thing," he writes. "The Soviet leaders' attempt to reform the system is not inspired by some noble realization that the system is unjust or poorly regarded abroad, but by strict necessity. They have come to realize what other Communists in Yugoslavia, Poland, Hungary, Czechoslovakia and China realized much earlier—that Communism doesn't work."

Djilas says they seek only to reform the methods of Communist rule, not the rationale or character of the rule itself, whose essence is "the possession of totalitarian power."

But the democratization and decentralization that Gorbachev is now urging involve the system as well as its methods. Moreover, the prospects for reform in the Soviet Union are diminished by the absence of a Russian democratic tradition and the lack of a democratic tradition within the Soviet Communist party. They are also diminished by the danger that loosening central power over the "constituent republics" may lead to chaos.

The Baltic states have been in open rebellion. Soviet troops have been dispatched to put down riots in Azerbaijan. Meanwhile, Georgians continue to organize public protests.

Still, Djilas is not wholly pessimistic. He anticipated all these problems: "The arrival of Mikhail Gorbachev demonstrates what some of us have long suspected—that indigenous Communist parties, notably the Yugoslav and the Soviet parties, have sufficient inner resources left in them to shed the Stalinist incrustation and make a fresh start."

Today the Soviet, like the Yugoslav, Communist party is "vaguely groping for a reconceptualization of the whole Communist experiment." And Gorbachev pursues a path of "cautious de-Stalinization," including careful steps toward a full reckoning with the terrible reality of the Soviet past.

Cautiously, Gorbachev permits the filling in of the blank pages of Soviet history. Cautiously, he permits correction of the gross lies in Soviet official accounts. Cautiously, he tries simultaneously to take the lid off the pent-up outrage of captive peoples and to keep the lid on—understanding both the necessity and the danger.

Already Gorbachev's regime, pledged to restructuring, is using force against Armenians to maintain the structures imposed from above by a central government he has pledged to weaken. Already Soviet peoples are demanding the self-determination guaranteed by the Soviet Constitution. What is Gorbachev to do?

Gorbachev, Djilas believes, is a transitional figure who cannot achieve his economic goals without transforming his political system. But Djilas predicts the entire party bureaucracy—the ruling class of the Soviet Union—will eventually resist political pluralism, understanding that it would end their privileges.

Were Gorbachev's reforms to succeed, the West's problem with the Soviet Union would disappear, Djilas believes: "If restructuring is to be seriously pursued . . . the Soviet Union will have neither the will nor the energy to embark on expansionist policies."

Nonetheless, the Soviet Union remains far more skillful than the United States and the West in political and psychological competition, even while it is in economic crisis.

Today, Djilas believes, the Soviet Union looks to the West to take the pressure off the Soviet system. It is dealing from a position of weakness, a fact that gives the West a great opportunity to extract from the Soviet state "a whole strain of political guarantees of the most tangible and enforceable kind, that the international civil war which they declared on the rest of the world in 1917 has ceased to be their objective."

And thus, skillfully managed by the West, the crisis in communism may be made to serve the cause of freedom.

Rectifying History—Then and Now
July 13, 1987

An early indicator that there really was something new in Gorbachev's new thinking was his interest in correcting the record in some cases of the blatant miscarriage of justice.

The effort to set the record straight involves a break with totalitarian ways of thinking. Its inarticulate premise is that there is an "objective" history about which it is possible to know the truth and that justice takes account of this.

Halfway through 1987 I posed a test: When current Soviet rulers permit living citizens to criticize today's leaders and policies, then we will know they share the core values of democratic Europe.

I should have known better. The ability to criticize leaders is important, but safety in dissent requires laws and institutions that protect the individual's right to free speech. The personal decisions of a

31

simple ruler are not a safe basis on which to rest civil liberties—no matter how benevolent or far-seeing the ruler.

In Europe last week one man was declared guilty and one man innocent for "crimes" committed more than forty years ago. Klaus Barbie, SS chief in Lyon during the Nazi occupation of France, was found guilty of "crimes against humanity" and sentenced to life imprisonment. Theodor Raskolnikoff, a Soviet diplomat who denounced Stalin's crimes, was posthumously and informally "rehabilitated" in a Soviet publication for the letter he wrote denouncing Stalin in August 1939.

Both cases raise fundamental questions about the relation of citizens to their governments. What are the limits of a citizen's obligation to his government? When can obedience to a brutal government be judged a crime? These are, of course, questions encountered again and again in history and in political philosophy. They are the questions of Socrates, Antigone, Martin Luther, and the men who signed the American Declaration of Independence. They are relevant not only to the past. They are urgent questions in confronting current horrors.

Nazis like Klaus Barbie and Adolf Eichmann claimed that not only were they obeying orders from their government but that their obligation to obedience had no limits. Their prosecutors—at Nuremberg, in Jerusalem, in Lyon, and wherever Nazis are tried for such crimes—argue that there are some things no government has the right to require and some things every citizen has the obligation to refuse: the cold-blooded murder of civilians and the elimination of "inferior" races. Such acts cannot be excused or justified—not during wartime or by oaths of obedience. A citizen is neither obliged nor permitted to commit "crimes against humanity."

But is a citizen permitted to protest massive violations of human rights by his government? Governments that claim total power over their citizens do not think so, and except for the brief "Moscow spring" of Nikita Khrushchev's de-Stalinization period, the Soviet government has considered it a crime to criticize its human rights violations.

Theodor Raskolnikoff knew this and sought refuge in France at the same time he released his open letter to Stalin on August 17, 1939. After years of dishonor, Raskolnikoff was "rehabilitated" by Khrushchev only to be again denounced for Trotskyism and treason under Brezhnev and now to be once again informally "rehabilitated." These two events have interesting implications. Does Klaus Barbie's reclassification from Nazi official to French criminal mean that it is all relative, that law and morality are merely a function of power, that—as Socrates' antagonist Thrasymachus of Chalcedon argued—justice is merely the interest of the stronger?

No. It means that the Nazi regime was vicious precisely because it did not respect the human rights that Klaus Barbie was found guilty of violating.

Does Raskolnikoff's "rehabilitation" mean that the Soviet government is now willing to accept limits to its power and to accept that its citizens have the right to criticize government excesses? Does it mean that the Soviet Union is now ready to respect the human rights of its citizens in theory as well as in practice?

Not necessarily. Raskolnikoff, like Boris Pasternak (also again being mentioned in the Soviet press), is long dead. So is Joseph Stalin. The right of a long-dead man to criticize a long-dead ruler is hardly the equivalent of the right of living persons to criticize incumbent power holders. Last week a living Soviet, Anatoly Koriagin, was stripped of his Soviet citizenship for criticizing the use of mental hospitals and mind-altering drugs to punish dissidents.

When current Soviet rulers permit living citizens to criticize today's leaders and policies, then we will know that they share what French Prime Minister Jacques Chirac described as the core values of democratic Europe: "a certain idea of liberty, of democracy and of the rights of man."

Everything is easier to face forty years later. Terrible as it is to hear Barbie's victims describe his crimes, how much more difficult it is to think about such terrible contemporary "crimes against humanity" as Ethiopia's "village-ization," described recently in *The New Republic* (July 6, 1987):

> The basic outlines of the program are not in dispute. The army moves into a group of villages, and forces the inhabitants to tear down their huts piece by piece. Then the peasants are force-marched, with the remnants of their homes on their backs, to a new, central location previously selected by party cadres. The new site usually lacks a mosque, a school and an adequate nearby water source, but it comes equipped with a guard tower and Workers Party banners.
>
> By the end of 1986 close to 4 million Muslim Oromos . . . had been forcibly uprooted through this nightmarish scheme. And 29 million others are slated for the same fate by the mid-1990s.

When will someone, somewhere, try Ethiopian Col. Mengistu Haile Mariam for his "crimes against humanity"?

Rectifying History—The Uses of the Past

February 15, 1988

The rehabilitation of Nikolai Bukharin struck me as a most important break with Bolshevik orthodoxy, because the reputation of the Old Bolsheviks—Trotsky, Bukharin, et al.—is part of the "founding myth" of the Soviet Union and also because correcting the record strikes at the Party's claim of infallibility. If Bukharin was innocent, then not only Stalin but all his successors have been wrong about Soviet history.

Such issues have special importance in governments that rest their legitimacy on an official myth and an official party—both of which claim infallibility.

The most interesting of Gorbachev's reforms thus far came last week with the rehabilitation of Nikolai Ivanovich Bukharin, one of the old Bolsheviks who helped engineer the Soviet revolution only to fall prey to Stalin's Great Purge.

Bukharin, who served on the Politburo at the time of Lenin's death, was charged with "espionage," "counter-revolution," and "plotting with foreign powers" to destroy the Soviet government. He was arrested, isolated, mercilessly interrogated, and framed, and eventually he "confessed" in the great Moscow show trial of 1938.

Like five of the other nine Politburo members at the time of Lenin's death, Bukharin was sentenced to death and entered Soviet history as a traitor to the revolution he had devotedly served all of his adult life. Because Bukharin was brilliant and outstanding within the Politburo, he was made a kind of arch villain in official Soviet demonology.

Though serious observers never believed Bukharin's manifestly false confession, not even Khrushchev attempted to set the record straight. After Khrushchev's fall, interest in rehabilitating Stalin's victims ended—until recently, when Mikhail Gorbachev indicated his intention to reopen the question of Bukharin's guilt.

Now, fifty years after Bukharin was executed, a commission of the Communist party of the Soviet Union has overturned the verdict of treason against him. The commission's decision was published a week ago on the front pages of *Pravda* and *Izvestia* without comment. But no one who is interested in the evolution of Soviet government under Gorbachev can let this event pass without further attention.

Beginning with Stalin, Soviet leaders have made the writing and rewriting of history one of their spoils of victory. They incorporate history into politics and rewrite as they go, granting and withdrawing honor, dropping some leaders down the Orwellian "memory hole," reinterpreting the past to make it serve current policies.

To understand why Nikolai Bukharin has been rehabilitated, we must understand what he stood for in Soviet politics and how that relates to the current rulers of the Kremlin.

Bukharin was one of the Politburo members who, during the crucial period after Lenin's death, favored the continuation of the New Economic Policy (NEP) in agriculture and industry. Like Lenin, Bukharin and his allies sought to win the peasants' cooperation by concessions to individual farmers and by utilization of free market devices. They opposed forced collectivization and forced industrialization and reliance on terror as a principal instrument of social control. These eminently sensible views that had guided the NEP were rejected by Stalin as "right deviationism."

The reader may already have noticed that these views bear a striking resemblance to Mikhail Gorbachev's *perestroika*, or "restructuring." By rehabilitating Bukharin and his fellow "right deviationists," Gorbachev has given his ideas a pedigree and has reinforced his link to Lenin.

Meanwhile, he has moved to delegitimize the policies of his immediate predecessor, Leonid Brezhnev, a man who clearly ruled in the Stalinist tradition. Brezhnev's statue has disappeared from a Moscow square in which it stood, and his name has disappeared from the square itself.

All this has happened during the same period that Gorbachev's associates have been reexamining and publicizing a major Brezhnev legacy—the war in Afghanistan. Doubtless the attack on Brezhnev makes it easier to reject his judgment that the control of Afghanistan is vitally necessary to the Soviet Union.

It is all very interesting. Lenin used force when he deemed it desirable, but never relied on terror as a major instrument of domestic or foreign policy.[1] All this revisionism in Lenin's name may presage a broad evolution toward less reliance on force in internal and external affairs—if Gorbachev lasts.

And he just may. As George Orwell wrote in *1984* of just such a totalitarian society, "To control the present is to control the past. To control the past is to control the future."

---

1. This comment elicited a pained and outraged and probably correct letter from my friend Arnold Beichman, who reminded me of the times Lenin had used force to achieve political goals. I was thinking of persons who had used force genocidally like Adolf Hitler; Joseph Stalin, Pol Pot, and Colonel Mengistu.

The New Styles of the New Bolsheviks
November 23, 1987

When I first met Victor Tirado Lopez, the Sandinista director of foreign affairs, he was gaunt, his hair halfway down his back. He sported faded jeans, work shirt, and field jacket. This "Che Guevara" look persisted until 1984, at which time I did not recognize him. He was twenty to thirty pounds heavier, wore gray flannels, a gray cashmere sweater, and a navy blazer, and had a fashionable haircut. When I finally realized it was he, the word embourgeoisement *took on a new, more concrete meaning for me.*

Later I was struck by Daniel Ortega's changed hair style, glasses, and manner of dressing. I had also been impressed by the more open, relaxed Western style of Gorbachev and Zhao that permitted them to answer questions and engage in give and take.

I did not think the new style necessarily meant new substance, but I did think it meant something. It illustrated at least that these Communist rulers had understood that personal style can be an important political tool. That meant understanding that culture is more important in politics than classical Leninists and Marxists understood.

In the early years after the Sandinistas came to power in 1979, Nicaraguan President Daniel Ortega would come to the United Nations in full military uniform, with slicked-down hair, steel-rimmed glasses, and harsh language punctuated by karate chops. Now Ortega sports the blow-dried look, fashion glasses, a cashmere sweater, and a well-cut civilian suit. His rhetoric has changed as much as his appearance. Today he speaks softly and sometimes attempts wry jokes.

Ortega has learned to look and sound like the new style of Communist ruler, like a Gorbachev or a Zhao Ziyang. These well-tailored new Bolsheviks look like modern men and often sound like them as well. When they speak to the outside world, they avoid the Marxist jargon and polemics that once marked the Leninist style of politics. They no longer speak—to us, at least—of "burying us." Nor do they publicly counsel others to "cast off the shackles of imperialism."

More and more often, as they discuss arms reductions or the Central American peace plan, they sound like reasonable men committed to building a safer world. They have become expert practitioners of image politics. And more and more it seems downright churlish to doubt the good will of these manifestly reasonable men—especially since we Americans want so much to believe them.

Almost every American longs to end the state of mutual distrust and disrespect that has characterized U.S.-Soviet relations since World War II. Americans hate spending large amounts of money on armaments. We dislike permanent alliances and are dismayed at the thought that we have real enemies. And so we welcome with enthusiasm every evidence that Soviet or Nicaraguan leaders are "mellowing" with time. The smallest move to free-market strategies in economics, to liberalization in domestic affairs, to a less expansionist foreign policy is greeted with relief and optimism.

The fact that we believe in change and embrace it makes it much easier to believe that other countries will change as well. While Marxists think history is governed by inexorable laws, we believe men (and sometimes women) make history and can change it. So we take every change in leadership seriously, especially when generational change is also involved and is accompanied by a change in style.

Whether a new generation has come to power, as in China or the Soviet Union, or the same leaders speak in new tongues, as in Nicaragua, we explain to each other that "the pressures of reality have had their impact"; that the responsibilities of power have "mellowed" the leadership; that revolutions and revolutionaries "always moderate" given time and experience. We applaud and magnify the evidences of change, and we wonder aloud and obsessively how we can help.

We try not to notice when such events as the demotions of reformers Hu Yaobang or Boris Yeltsin suddenly call into question our hopes for imminent democratic transformation and for greater openness and tolerance.

Our optimistic reactions to welcome trends are manifestations of the American national character. They are shared by both parties, by Ronald Reagan as well as Jim Wright. And the danger that imprudent decisions will be based on our hopes is also bipartisan.

In thinking about arms agreements and Central American peace plans—as policy makers are these days—responsible people in both parties urgently need to face the harsh facts that we do not really know Mikhail Gorbachev's intentions vis-à-vis his country or our own, that we do not really know how great his power is within his government, how long he can maintain it, or by whom he might be followed. We do not know why there were sudden shifts in his decisions on a summit meeting in Washington or why he so harshly attacked his close associate Yeltsin. We do not know if his new line on war, peace, and capitalist evolution and on the relations of the Soviet Union with Eastern Europe presage permanent changes in policy or are only shifts in verbal tactics.

With regard to Central America, we do not know if the Ortegas and the FSLN have any serious intention of providing to their people the freedoms they have promised or if they are merely maintaining a facade of liberalization until the U.S. Congress has forced the dismantling of the contras.

These are extremely important questions. Americans should not permit themselves to make substantive decisions on the basis of style.

There is finally only one way to judge the promises of the new Bolsheviks. It is how they use force against those weaker than themselves. Rulers who use force to subdue opponents, conquer neighbors, and intimidate allies can hardly be expected to treat the rest of us differently.

Moscow's Anti-American Reformer
October 17, 1988

Alexander Yakovlev presents a most interesting contrast: on the one hand, he has written long, bitterly anti-American diatribes—as recently as 1985; on the other hand, he is Mikhail Gorbachev's close associate and supporter in the campaign for internal reform. He has even been called the father of glasnost.

Although the explanation of such apparent contradictions is still not clear, I think they are worthy of note.

Quiz time:

1. Who said, "The origin of the American desire to possess the world lies deep within the country's social system"?

(a) Donald Trump, explaining why he was bidding on Buckingham Palace, or

(b) Alexander Yakovlev, explaining why Donald Trump was trying to buy Buckingham Palace.

2. Who said, "All of Ronald Reagan's actions are steeped in fanaticism and personal hatred for socialism and all progressive changes"?

(a) Manuel Noriega, speaking to the Panamanian National Guard, or

(b) Alexander Yakovlev, telling why Ronald Reagan had signed the INF Treaty.

3. Who said, "Marxists have never forgotten that violence must inevitably accompany the collapse of capitalism in its entirety and the birth of socialist society. That violence will constitute a period of world history, a whole era of various kinds of wars, imperialistic wars, civil wars. . . . This epic of gigantic cataclysms has begun . . . and is only the beginning"?

(a) Mikhail Gorbachev in an interview with Tom Brokaw, or

(b) Alexander Yakovlev, approvingly quoting Vladimir Lenin.

The answer to each question is leading Soviet "reformer" Yakovlev, who sits at Gorbachev's right hand, advising him on American affairs and—since the most recent shakeup—overseeing the conduct of foreign policy.

Yakovlev, like Gorbachev, emerged from the Kremlin's power struggle with his own power significantly enhanced. Even before Anatoly Dobrynin's retirement, Yakovlev had established himself as Gorbachev's principal adviser on North America, frequently sitting in on Gorbachev's conversations with high-level Americans, traveling with Gorbachev to the Washington summit. In Dobrynin's absence, he becomes the Kremlin's unchallenged authority on matters American.

It is time we know more about this man who studied at Columbia University, worked in various Soviet Communist party schools and publishing houses, and served as Soviet ambassador to Canada from 1973 to 1983. Yakovlev is also author of a book on the United States suggestively entitled *On the Edge of an Abyss: From Truman to Reagan, the Doctrine and Realities of the Nuclear Age.* The English-language version of this book, published by Progress Publishers in Moscow, appeared in 1985 and includes coverage of the 1984 U.S. elections.

Even if we acknowledge that Yakovlev is first a party man and only second a historian and that he may have had political motives for writing the book, it is recent enough and relevant enough to his current role that it should be taken seriously. Presumably, it reflects with reasonable accuracy the author's atitude toward the United States and the world.

It matters, therefore, that the book is unremittingly hostile— even contemptuous—in its attitude toward the society, culture, politics, and foreign policy of the United States. From John Wayne to Jimmy Carter, Yakovlev finds Americans simple if not primitive, often violent, and regularly malevolent in their dealings with the world.

39

Yakovlev dismisses American society and institutions as corrupt and fraudulent.

"Reality," he writes, "is such that we must deal with a country where freedom is suppressed, where violence flourishes, where trade unions are persecuted, where the press services big business and where basic rights of individuals are hampered."

The United States, in Yakovlev's view, is governed by a military-industrial complex that seeks only its own greater profits. Elections are mere facades: "The election routine is a familiar and rather boring theatrical performance put on for people who are not quite aware of what true democracy really means."

It is not surprising to Yakovlev, then, that an actor should win out in 1980 and 1984 and even less surprising that he should have been handpicked for the job by California millionaires.

In Yakovlev's view, all of Ronald Reagan's actions are characterized by "fanaticism and personal hatred of socialism." The Republican platform confirmed his opinion that Reagan's "peace rhetoric was nothing but shameless hypocrisy and primitive demagoguery." The American people are brainwashed. Those who inform them are too corrupt to do their job honestly. American history and historians, politics and political scientists, journalism and journalists are servants of a corrupt system:

> Bourgeois political science is distinctly oriented to serve the capitalist system and is conscientious about its social duty. . . . Indifference, egoism and individualism are cultivated under the slogan of defending "freedom of the individual". . . . Everything is done to spawn selfishness, greed, accumulation of wealth, and the cult of money and property.

Yakovlev's hostility to the United States is implacable, unrelieved, splenetic. His analysis and interpretation of U.S. "imperialism" is as orthodox and about as benign as Joseph Stalin's. Yakovlev does not say, "We will bury you," in the manner of Nikita Khrushchev, but he just as clearly predicts our "inevitable downfall" and asserts that bourgeois society is already in its "death throes." Most significant perhaps, he emphasizes the "absolute incompatibility" of capitalism and socialism.

There is no "new thinking" in Yakovlev's book, no hint of revisionist ideas about the existence of common values or a common human destiny: only dogmatic repetition about the coming defeat of capitalism.

Maybe Yakovlev has changed his mind about some of the matters discussed in *On the Edge of the Abyss*. Maybe he hasn't. Maybe it doesn't matter much since making policy and writing books are two quite different activities.

But by their rehabilitation of Nikolai Bukharin and their reverent citations of Lenin's text, the "new thinkers" in the Kremlin—including Gorbachev—indicate that ideas do matter to them. If they do, it will be important for Americans dealing with Soviet leaders to have read and digested the book written by the man who sits at Gorbachev's right hand.

Gorbachev's Tricky Task in Eastern Europe

July 18, 1988

Like a good many other observers of the Soviet Union, I believed (and believe) that the Soviet relationship with Eastern Europe was crucial to the question of Soviet intentions. The Brezhnev Doctrine was also crucial not as an idea but as a justification of action to maintain Communist dictatorships in Hungary and Czechoslovakia and to keep those countries in the Warsaw Pact bloc.

As long as the Soviets used force—or were prepared to use force— to maintain Communist governments integrated in the Soviet empire in Eastern Europe, there was no reason to suppose they would not use force to extend Soviet power.

Previous Soviet leaders were content to *control* the countries of Eastern Europe. But Mikhail Gorbachev wants to be popular as well as powerful in this region. His visit to Poland demonstrated again the Soviet leader's skill in international public relations, and also his daring. Throughout Eastern Europe Gorbachev is raising hopes. His talk of reform, of relationships based on equality, his compliments and near apologies have diminished fear in the Warsaw Pact countries.

Le Monde correspondent Bernard Guetta wrote last week, "In three years of Gorbachevism, the fear of Soviet military intervention has been totally eroded in the peoples' democracy."

This could be dangerous. For, as Guetta also notes, fear of the Soviet Union has prevented bloodshed by discouraging revolts and repression of the kind that took place in Hungary (1956) and Czechoslovakia (1968).

41

The suppression of those movements carried its own message about relations between Eastern European states and the Soviet Union. After Soviet tanks had crushed the Prague Spring, the Brezhnev Doctrine spelled out flatly the Soviet view of the limits on Eastern European development:

There is no doubt that the peoples of the Socialist countries and the Communist parties have and must have freedom to determine their country's path of development. However, any decision of theirs must damage neither socialism in their country, nor the fundamental interests of other Socialist countries, nor the worldwide workers' movement, which is waging a struggle for socialism.

The *language* of the Brezhnev Doctrine is not so very different from that of Mikhail Gorbachev, who also speaks of each country's being free to make its own way to socialism. But what made the Brezhnev Doctrine important was not the claim but the fact that it had been backed by brutal force.

Gorbachev, to the contrary, has said in Yugoslavia and has implied elsewhere that the use of force between Socialist countries is "unthinkable."

It is possible that Gorbachev does not understand the role of brute force in the governments of Eastern Europe or in their relations with the Soviet Union. Historically Poland, Czechoslovakia, and Hungary have been closer to Western Europe than to Russia. They have had more experience than Russia with liberalism, nationalism, pluralism. Independence lives on in memory and desire. Gorbachev may not understand their strength.

Glasnost and "reform" mean something very different in Warsaw from what they do in Moscow. The declaration issued by a Polish-Czech group last weekend (on the twentieth anniversary of the Soviet invasion of Czechoslovakia) spelled out what "equality" among members of the Warsaw Pact would mean to opposition leaders such as Adam Michnik, Vaclav Havel, and Zbigniew Bujak. It would mean "the right to sovereignty," "the right of religious and national development, and an end to religious repression," "the right to an independent judiciary," "the right to travel," the right to develop relations with countries outside the Warsaw Pact. And the right to rectify their own history.

Perestroika has been welcomed in Poland by Solidarity leaders and defined to encompass aspirations not compatible with any known Communist system. These aspirations are also probably not compatible with Gorbachev's idea of reform. They are certainly not compatible with Jaruzelski's Poland, which is widely and openly detested by Poles.

Gorbachev is a cool, high-stakes poker player. Doubtless he wants to maintain the Communist governments of Eastern Europe and also their subordination to the Soviet Union. But he also wants to create the impression that the Warsaw Pact is an alliance of equals and to dispel the image of the Soviet Union as a threat to the independence of its neighbors.

The nations of Western Europe will be persuaded to cut their links with the United States, dismantle NATO, and disarm only if and when they perceive no threat from the Soviet Union to their freedom or independence.

Any use of force by the Soviet Union against an Eastern European state would be deadly to Gorbachev's efforts to dismantle NATO.

Perestroika in Eastern Europe will almost certainly encourage movements opposing the one-party dictatorship that has for so long denied those people freedom. The use of force to put down such movements would severely undermine Gorbachev's goals in Western Europe.

This contradiction in Soviet policy could create a moment of rare opportunity for the people of Eastern Europe.

The Limits of Pluralism under Perestroika

May 16, 1988

How rapidly events have moved! Midway through 1988 the rulers of Poland were unwilling to permit organization of an independent, unofficial labor union.

The issue of "unofficial" organizations has always been crucial to Communist states because those states seek to absorb all organizations and associations and adapt them to the purposes of the state. This is the very opposite of pluralism. The fact that Lenin himself had forbidden factions put the very idea of "Socialist pluralism" at risk.

By 1990 it has become increasingly clear that one-party rule is incompatible with the "Socialist pluralism," which Gorbachev has championed.

"It is easy to make the best of both worlds while living safely in a regime of liberty; to let oneself become enchanted by the notion that the promises of the Providential State can be reconciled with the blessings of freedom," Walter Lippmann wrote in the years before World War II, at a time when apologies for collectivism—Fascist, Nazi, Communist—were nearly as widespread as they are today.

It is easier for those living in New York or Washington, Paris, Bonn, or London to be optimistic about the "expanding freedoms" of communism than it is for residents of Gdansk.

In Gdansk and Nowa Huta, Polish workers once again pitted their courage and faith against the power of the state dictatorship. Once again they lost. And in struggling and losing, they again exposed the tyranny the West would much rather forget.

By the time police had crushed the steel strike in Nowa Huta with a predawn raid and blocked the delivery of food to striking workers in Gdansk, they had forced the world to notice that General Jaruzelski's dictatorship was still unwilling to permit workers to organize independent unions. The demand for legalization of Solidarity, therefore, was flatly rejected.

To Poland's rulers, the workers' initiative seemed to threaten the whole social order. "I do not see the possibility of dealing with those who propose to Poland chaos and the return of a new phase of self-destruction," Politburo member Mieczyslaw Rakowski commented, as if free association were the equivalent of anarchy. It is not, but it *is* incompatible with the drive of rulers to control the whole of society.

In their view, if a society is to be planned by its rulers, then members must conform with the plan. Alternative views about ends and means threaten official plans, and associations independent of the state are the most threatening of all. This is why force is used in such states to crush nascent associations.

Jaruzelski understands that his government's economic plan is not acceptable to many Poles. "Part of the population," he said, "cannot reconcile itself to the hardships, and they react painfully." When he uses force to protect the plan, Jaruzelski's response is typical of the ruler who, like Mussolini, believes, "All in the state: nothing outside the state. Nothing against the state."

In Managua and Moscow, Communist rulers have made the same choice for the same reasons. Sandinista rulers used force when labor unions protested the government's Draconian economic policies. Daniel Ortega commented that the "revolutionary process" is "not up for discussion."

In Moscow, Soviet police moved against a hardy band of dissidents who dared to meet and dream aloud of an opposition party that would work openly for an end to one-party dictatorship.

So much for pluralism under *perestroika.* There is none. Pluralism means competing centers of power, but a party that claims the right to direct the society can tolerate no opposition. Mikhail Gorbachev has given no indication of any intention to forgo the monopoly of power established by Lenin soon after the Bolshevik revolution. Gorbachev's criticisms of Stalin and his rehabilitation of Bukharin et al. do not imply an endorsement of pluralism.

After all, it was Lenin, not Stalin, who made the decision to suppress competing parties and opposition groups. It was Lenin who described independent trade unions as a "syndicalist and anarchist deviation." It was Lenin who urged the Tenth Party Congress in 1921 to destroy "all groups without exception that have been formed on the basis of various platforms" and to "secure the complete elimination of all factionalism." It was Lenin who denied even fellow members of the Communist party the right to express political differences or to question party policy.

The notion that pluralism is incompatible with socialism is not Stalinist heresy. It is as old as the Soviet state.

It is easy and comfortable to forget these unpleasant facts, easier to be hopeful about pluralism in Washington than in Gdansk, about *perestroika* in Paris than in Moscow.

Relaxing the Totalitarian Grip
October 31, 1988

The key sentence in this column is the last—but it is a question: "Is it possible that we are now watching the early stages of an evolution of totalitarian states into authoritarian regimes?" We now know the answer was yes.

I concluded that Gorbachev had determined that Soviet society and the Soviet economy could be modernized only if more cultural and social freedom were granted. As soon as he granted that freedom, the survival of ethnic and national identifications and of religion and other unauthorized beliefs became clear. Obviously these beliefs could become the basis of multiple parties. Mikhail Gorbachev's reiterated intention to maintain a one-party system, however, suggested his reforms were headed not to democracy but to an authoritarian system in which the Communist

45

party would retain a political monopoly but would allow cultural and social pluralism.

This point had special significance for me, since I had argued that while there was no historical example of a totalitarian state evolving into a democracy, there were many examples of authoritarian states making the step. If the Soviet government was becoming an authoritarian state, then that authoritarian state might become a democratic one.

In Lithuania, Latvia, and Estonia people are speaking their own languages, singing their own songs, flying their own flags. They are meeting and speaking of autonomy, even of independence. They are publicly recalling the Hitler-Stalin Pact, which led to the forcible incorporation of their countries into the Soviet Union.

In Moscow the announcement comes of plans for a new center for Judaic studies to train rabbis and promote the study of Judaism.

In Warsaw the Polish government offers the Roman Catholic church unprecedented powers and freedoms in exchange for full diplomatic recognition.

A Hungarian delegation makes overtures for a papal visit.

A Soviet literary journal discusses the Soviet role in the Katyn massacre of Polish officers in World War II. And another announces that the writings of Leon Trotsky will be published in Moscow next year.

These moves to relax government's iron grip on key aspects of society and culture give new meaning and importance to Mikhail Gorbachev's plans for reform. *They suggest that Gorbachev and his colleagues may be ready to abandon the efforts at total control, the distinguishing characteristic of the totalitarian state.*

Totalitarian governments claim the right to control all aspects of society and seek to absorb all social institutions into the state. A totalitarian state recognizes no limits to its power and no rights against the state. Individual rights and free association do not exist in the totalitarian context.

Religion is always a special target of Communist governments because they admit no interpretation but their own of human life, duty, and destiny and because they tolerate no competing claims on the consciences or energies of citizens. This is why Communist governments have outlawed many religious sects, closed churches, sought to eliminate religious education, and imposed heavy penalties on religious observance. This is why the teaching of Hebrew, the circulation of Bibles, and the participation in unauthorized religious gatherings have been made criminal offenses. It is why religious belief is judged incompatible with membership in the Communist party, where party membership is a prerequisite for advancement in most professions.

It is therefore extremely interesting that the government of the Soviet Union—which has so recently outlawed education in Judaism—has now announced that it will create an institute devoted to its study. And it is extremely interesting that the Polish government has offered to recognize formally the right of the Catholic church to publish magazines and form youth organizations in exchange for full church recognition of the Polish government. These moves toward limited pluralism suggest that it may prove possible to transform totalitarianism peacefully from within.

It is extremely interesting that the Polish government has agreed to discussions with representatives of Solidarity, providing that all members of Solidarity's delegation agree to "respect the constitutional order"—that is, that they acknowledge the legitimacy of the Communist party's claim to govern the country.

The government is willing to grant economic status on condition of political submission. Solidarity has rejected the government's demand, but Lech Walesa is distinguishing between economic pluralism, which means free markets; social pluralism, which means the right to form organizations freely; and political pluralism, which means the right to compete for political power. He thinks they can leave political pluralism for last.

No type of pluralism exists in a totalitarian society, certainly not in the Soviet Union or Eastern Europe. So far, the government is still seeking to intervene in the internal affairs of nongovernmental organizations. Nonetheless, we are watching the Marxist governments of the Soviet Union and Eastern Europe relinquish control over some domains and begin to share power in others. We are watching them give ground to their own societies and people.

No longer are Polish soldiers required to swear allegiance to the Soviet Union and the Warsaw Pact. Now they are asked to swear allegiance only to the Polish government. No longer are Soviet Jews arrested for studying Hebrew.

Why is this happening now? The most likely reason, I believe, is that Gorbachev has decided that totalitarian control is not compatible with modernization and is not necessary to continued political control by the Communist party.

He is surely right about the former proposition. Time will tell whether the monopoly of political power can be maintained if control over the economy and culture is relinquished. Is it possible that we are now watching the early stages of an evolution of totalitarian states into authoritarian regimes?

Let Them Eat Cake
November 28, 1988

Central control of recipes is a kind of reductio ad absurdum *of the Soviet totalitarian state—the kind of regulation that is the enemy of tradition, innovation, self-expression, and ethnic identity. No wonder the people of Estonia demanded change.*

On November 29, 1988, Mikhail Gorbachev promised the Soviet republics that his proposed political reorganization would bring them more independence. "The strength of the union," he said, "must rely on the strength of its constituent republics as sovereign socialist states." At the same time he asserted that the changes were needed to "exclude the possibility of any part of the state machinery getting beyond the control of the people and their representatives," that is, the Soviet Communist party. These statements illustrate the double bind that Gorbachev faces in domestic political reform: the success of perestroika *depends on opening up the political system but risks unleashing the USSR's suppressed nationalities.*

Dissent in the Baltics grew throughout 1988. In October the Popular Front of Estonia demanded that the central authorities give Estonia more autonomy in economic and cultural affairs, called for exemption of Estonians from compulsory military service, and demanded constitutional protection of private property and punishment of those who participated in Stalinist abuses.

In November, the Supreme Soviet of Estonia asserted that it had the right unilaterally to veto national laws affecting the Estonian republic. The Kremlin condemned the Estonian measure as unconstitutional, and on November 27 Gorbachev mentioned Estonia and Transcaucasia in his speech denouncing the "disastrous" rise of nationalism throughout the Soviet Union.

As soon as the grip of totalitarianism loosened and the fear of the Soviet state diminished, the Baltic peoples demonstrated that they still had a strong taste for independence. And they communicated something of the nature of the problem the Soviet Union would face if and when it granted enough freedom that people could express themselves.

48

"Estonia should be allowed to decide for itself . . . its cake recipes."
"Cakes for export?"
"No, for the cakes we make ourselves and eat ourselves. Permission to use our own recipes was not granted [by the central government]. Just imagine," Dr. Reyn Otason, chairman of the Estonian SSR economic planning council, told the editor of the *Literaturnaya Gazeta*.

"But there are also more serious matters in our lives on which the republic should make autonomous decisions. . . . It is not only the quality of cakes that is affected by the dictatorship of the central departments," he said.

Each level of government, Otason said, "is forced to play the part of a supplicant, a dependent. And dependence is death to initiative. It is more important to know how to beg money, food, feed, goods than to know how to make them."

Otason's criticisms of overcentralized decision making are not so different from those of Mikhail Gorbachev. But the inferences Estonians have drawn from these and other criticisms go far beyond anything the architect of *perestroika* had in mind.

Gorbachev's proposed constitutional reforms were both disappointing and offensive to Estonians. Now Estonia—of all places—has virtually declared its independence from the Soviet Union. By overwhelming majorities, the Estonian parliament has claimed the right to veto Soviet laws and has asserted that the new Soviet constitution would not be binding on Estonia unless it is first "registered" by the Estonian parliament.

As if this revolutionary "right of veto" were not enough, the Estonian parliament has drafted a number of other amendments (scheduled to be adopted next week) that are manifestly incompatible with the Soviet constitution. These Estonian proposals would recognize the right of private property. They would declare the land, air, minerals, forests, and natural resources of Estonia to be the exclusive property of Estonia (although the Soviet Constitution makes them the property of the Soviet Union). They would declare major enterprises that operate in Estonia—including banks—to be Estonian property.

"No one is seeking a collision course with Moscow," said Estonian Popular Front leader Marju Lauristin, but no one doubts that Estonia has created an unprecedented constitutional crisis with the Soviet Union.

Gorbachev's proposed constitutional reforms were widely regarded in the Baltic states as a giant step backward toward a more unitary, centralized state. Dr. Igor Gryazin, chief of the Estonia SSR

Academy of Sciences, expressed the view of many when he said of the proposals:

They would turn the Soviet Union into a less democratic state. For instance whereas we currently elect people's judges, it is now envisioned to have them appointed by the local Soviets. . . . Hitherto neither Estonia nor other union republics have enjoyed real sovereignty—that is a fact. But formally it has existed. Now if the amendments to the U.S.S.R. constitution are accepted, it can be confidently stated that there will be no Soviet socialist republics left and the Soviet Union will cease to exist as a union of republics.

The most remarkable aspect of the events in Estonia was that the *official* bodies acted to challenge the Soviet Union. The Estonian parliament, the Estonian Communist party leadership, the Estonian Academy of Sciences led the way—demonstrating in the process that the institutionalization of Soviet rule in this Baltic republic has not been accompanied by the internalization of Soviet identifications and norms. Estonians do not feel like Soviet citizens.

Parallel to the action of official Estonian bodies came even stronger demands from unofficial groups, one of which held a press conference denouncing the "abnormal accumulation of Soviet troops" in the area. Economic reform, it declared, has "no chance to succeed under the conditions of the power monopoly of the Soviet army, the state security apparatus and the Communist Party."

These unofficial groups demanded the withdrawal of the Soviet "occupation forces," free elections under United Nations supervision, and admission of Estonia to the United Nations—a body which, of course, is just now considering similar declarations of the Palestine Liberation Organization.

Manifestly the Estonian moves are part of broader ethnic assertions throughout the Soviet Union. Thousands took to the streets in Georgia and more thousands protested the Lithuanian parliament's failure to follow Estonia's example. The greatest turmoil of all broke out in the Azerbaijani and Armenian republics, where Soviet troops were rushed to put down an uprising.

Meanwhile, Mikhail Gorbachev denounced those seeking to exploit *glasnost* and personally announced that the presidium of the Supreme Soviet, the Soviet Union's highest state body, had formally invalidated Estonia's declaration of home rule. Still, he indicated willingness to compromise on the proposed constitutional amendments that were most objectionable to the Baltics.

None of this means that the Soviet Union is falling apart, but it is a sharp reminder that many of the peoples who constitute the Union of Soviet Socialist Republics were incorporated into that union by force. And apparently force is still required to maintain what V. I. Lenin once called "the prison house of peoples."

Transforming Soviet Communism from Within
December 12, 1988

In thinking about radically new important phenomena such as Gorbachev's reforms, I find it useful to look at the news and analyses of previous writing from somewhat different perspectives and traditions.

Soviet scholarship is strong in France. For example, Michel Tatu, Jean François Revel, and Alain Besançon have an excellent knowledge of the Russian and Bolshevik cultures.

Can totalitarianism transform itself from within? Is the Soviet Union doing so today? These are the questions of the hour.

Two articles in France's leading quarterly on foreign policy, *Politique International*, illuminate present and future developments in the Soviet Union.

One by Michel Tatu—editor of the Paris daily, *Le Monde*, Sovietologist, and author of a new book on Gorbachev—asks, "Will Gorbachev survive until 1994?" A second by brilliant French intellectual Jean François Revel asks an even more fundamental question: "Is communism reversible?"

Both of these distinguished scholars believe current changes constitute new departures that should be taken seriously.

"The great originality of Gorbachev by comparison with his predecessors," writes Tatu, "is not to have undertaken economic reforms, but to have understood that they will not produce the desired results unless they are accompanied by political reform." Tatu argues that, even though the Soviet Communist party still enjoys a monopoly of power, "a relative but real democratization" of the Soviet Union would be possible providing that the leadership is willing to give up "the dogma of democratic centralism" that forbids the existence of all factions and tendencies inside the Communist party. Democratic centralism, not multiparties, are crucial, in his view.

51

The "dogma of democratic centralism" was born in 1921, when Lenin—who had crushed the opposition—urged the tenth Congress of the Communist party to "destroy all groups without exception that have been formed on the basis of different platforms" and "to secure the complete elimination of all factions."

Gorbachev has not challenged this doctrinal "sacred cow," but Tatu believes he has fuzzed the issue by suggesting that "democratic centralism" should be translated as "decentralization."

One good reason for Gorbachev's caution, Tatu argues, is the continued existence within the Communist party of three important layers of opposition to change: first, the inertia of a population that is not enthusiastic about working harder or drinking less or paying higher prices; second, the opposition of the 18 million bureaucrats who have a vested interest in the current sluggish system, who feel both their places and their privileges threatened by change, and who find it easy to sabotage reforms with passive resistance; third, ideological opposition from those convinced that Gorbachev's reforms threaten the entire system. This group, which is headed by Gorbachev's chief rival, Yegor Ligachev, profits from all the problems encountered by *glasnost* and *perestroika*—such as the current ethnic strife in Azerbaijan and the Baltic states.

Tatu does not answer his own question: "Will Gorbachev survive?" But he seems on balance doubtful that Gorbachev or any other reformer of this monolithic system can avoid falling victim to his own reforms—that is, to the opponents he must tolerate if he is to democratize the Party.

For Revel as well, political reforms are crucial because "socialism has never been an economic system." It is a way of governing that gives a monopoly of power to the Communist party, then centralizes that power in the hands of a general secretary. As Revel sees it, the process of centralization is still under way, and "supreme power, embodied in Gorbachev, is reinforced by his reforms, not decentralized."

The Soviet empire, says Revel, is in no greater jeopardy than the power of the Communist party. He says Soviet leaders' political skills have enabled them to avoid the political consequences of military defeats in Afghanistan, Nicaragua, Angola, Cambodia, and elsewhere. Thus with brilliant politics and Western economic aid, he argues, the Soviet Union has avoided the consequences of "imperial overstretch."

Gorbachev is not the architect of Soviet retreat. To the contrary, with "prodigious Machiavellian charm"—as Revel puts it—he is succeeding where his predecessors failed, in separating Germany from the rest of Europe and Europe from the United States. Thus he attains by seduction what the heavy-handed threats of Leonid Brezhnev failed to achieve. And Western aid permits the Soviet Union to survive its internal crises and remain Communist.

If the West sought seriously to promote the reversibility of communism, argues Revel, it would refuse to rescue the system. But the West lacks the necessary restraint, so there remains today no example of communism transformed from within.

Sakharov's Fear of Benevolent Despotism

November 7, 1988

As usual, the late Andrei Sakharov was right about his homeland. Although he had decided to support Mikhail Gorbachev as the best and the only existing hope for reform of the Soviet system, he was deeply disturbed by the concentration of power in Gorbachev's hands.

Like the U.S. Founding Fathers and most other proponents of constitutional government, Sakharov understood that a people's liberty is secure only under a democratic constitution. He knew that no man, no matter how wise or virtuous, is an adequate substitute for a government of laws.

As usual, Andrei Sakharov has gone to the heart of the matter. The trouble with the Soviet Union's new electoral laws and constitutional amendments, he says, is that "once more, everything boils down to one person, and that is extremely dangerous for *perestroika* as a whole and for Gorbachev personally. This is an extremely important question on which the fate of the country depends."

In theory, the new laws transfer a good deal of power from the party bureaucracy to the government—presumably part of a plan to make the Soviet Union a "government of laws." The new laws establish a Congress of People's Deputies and a new two-chamber Supreme Soviet, which will meet almost continuously. Their members are to be elected. In fact, however, Party leaders in each district will present themselves for election to the Soviets, and candidates for the Congress of People's Deputies must be drawn from official organizations and approved by local party officials.

The result will be thorough interpenetration of Party and government bureaucracies, with Mikhail Gorbachev at the apex of both. The new laws, says Sakharov, create a leader with "absolute power."

Although Sakharov has been a vocal supporter of Gorbachev ever since the Soviet ruler released him from exile, Sakharov insists that too much concentration of power is dangerous no matter who is in office. He knows as clearly as the American Founding Fathers that you cannot always count on the virtue or restraint of the man at the top: "Today it is Gorbachev, but tomorrow it could be somebody else. There are no guarantees that some Stalinist will not succeed him."

Moreover, the absence of opposition will enhance the rulers' temptations of power.

"This is *perestroika* only from above," he says. The new "popular front" organizations that have grown rapidly in the Baltic states will not be permitted to present candidates under the new laws. Neither will any other "alternative" organizations. The Communist party retains its monopoly of power.

Sakharov says the proposed changes constitute "a time bomb." His wife, Yelena Bonner, goes further, commenting that she is "increasingly disbelieving in *perestroika*."

The new Soviet electoral laws are one of several recent developments that underscore the limits of Gorbachev-style "democratization." Recent decrees regulating public demonstrations and granting emergency powers to Soviet police have already been invoked to break up demonstrations in the Ukraine, Byelorussia, and the Baltic states.

Alexander N. Yakovlev, Politburo member and close Gorbachev associate, clarified in a *New York Times* interview the limits of reasonable hopes of nationalities: "We believe a new status should be elaborated for the constituent republics and we are working on this." But he described some of the nationalist ideas now circulating—such as separate currency—as "out of touch with reality" and "simply unrealistic." (California does not have a separate currency, he notes without recalling that California also was not incorporated by force.) Most unrealistic of all, Yakovlev makes clear, are notions about independence for constituent republics.

The Yakovlev comments, the new electoral laws, the Polish demand that Solidarity's delegates "respect the constitutional order," the crackdown on demonstrators celebrating Czechoslovakia's independence day, all communicate the same message: the character of the regime and the right of the Communist party to a monopoly of power are not to be questioned. The structure of power is nonnegotiable.

Perestroika does not mean sharing power with non-Communists, and it does not mean giving them a voice in government. The new electoral laws do not mean legitimizing opposition to the regime. There can be competition for office, but it must be competition among Communists who accept the regime. There can be nationalism and manifestations of nationalist feeling in Latvia, Lithuania, Estonia, and the Ukraine, but there can be no questioning the status of these territories as an integral part of the Soviet Union.

In fact, questioning the legitimacy of the Communist party's right to rule is not legitimate in any Communist country today. Such questioning may be tolerated, as in contemporary Poland, but it is not regarded as legitimate, and questioners are not accepted as participants in an ongoing dialogue concerning the country's future.

Acceptance of the Communist party's legitimacy of rule is a prerequisite to participation in the politics of all Communist countries. Daniel Ortega made this point last spring, at a time when he was presumably committed to democratization of Nicaragua via the Central American Accords:

> They think we are willing to discuss whether there is going to be a revolutionary process or a counterrevolutionary process here. That is not up for discussion. What we are discussing is how the mercenary forces, who are already defeated, can lay down their weapons. They should be grateful that we are not offering them the guillotine or the firing squad, which is what they deserve.

If under Gorbachev socialism remains "irreversible" and centralization of power in the hands of a single man its characteristic structure, then there has been precious little "new thinking" about the most basic question.

Human Rights—The Essential Element
January 23, 1989

This column insists that human rights are more important than arms control and that international treaties in which governments promise to respect their citizens' rights are more important than international treaties in which they promise to limit some category of arms.

I believe it. I therefore believe very deeply that the traditional Soviet view of individual rights as subordinate to the state is profoundly wrong and that all the apologists for tyranny who have argued that people must forgo freedom while they concentrate on bread are utterly mistaken. Those who enjoy freedom also have bread. Those without freedom are, alas, all too often also hungry, cold, and lacking basic necessities. The testimony on everyday life now coming out of the Soviet Union and Eastern Europe will set the record straight once again.

If the promises are kept and the commitments honored, the East-West Accord on Human Rights signed in Vienna this week by the United States, Canada, and all European countries except Albania will prove far more important than the INF and START treaties combined.

After all, INF and START reduce only the numbers of certain kinds of nuclear weapons. In this violent century, more millions of people have died at the hands of their own governments than in war.

The lack of great marches and the absence of international campaigns make it easy to miss or to forget that the greatest mass murders have been conducted by governments against their own unarmed populations: in the man-made famine of the Ukraine, in Stalin's gulag, in the Holocaust, in Pol Pot's murderous "utopia," in China's Cultural Revolution, in Ethiopia's "villagification" program. Additional thousands more have been slaughtered by Uganda's Idi Amin, by the Syrians at Hama, by the Ayatollah Khomeini, by the Argentine generals in the "dirty war."

Human rights violations have created more dead, more homeless, more human misery than all the weapons of mass destruction.

Moreover, as Andrei Sakharov has emphasized, the relationship among human rights, democracy, and war is integral and crucial. Where people enjoy the right to criticize their government, to form associations, and to emigrate, governments become responsive to their citizens. Democracies do not start aggressive wars.

Still, the impression persists that weapons of mass destruction—nuclear, chemical, biological—are more threatening than repressions. As a result, more excitement is generated by an agreement between two powers to eliminate only one category of weapons than by the solemn promise of thirty-five to permit free speech, press, association, and emigration.

Of course, the Vienna agreement—like the INF Treaty—may be violated. Indeed, Czech police used force to put down a peaceable demonstration before the ink was dry on Czechoslovakia's pledge to permit free association. Soviet and Eastern European governments repeatedly violated the promises contained in the Helsinki Final Act and then arrested Helsinki monitors for commenting on the violations.

It can be argued that promises solemnly repeated and systematically violated breed cynicism rather than progress. Nevertheless, it is potentially important that the Soviet Union has agreed in principle to honor political and civil rights in these accords.

Communist governments are not the only ones that violate human rights in the modern world, but today the most systematic, pervasive denial of free speech, press, association, emigration, and due process are found in Eastern Europe, Cuba, Nicaragua, Vietnam, Afghanistan, Mozambique, Ethiopia, and other members of the "world Socialist system."

Individual freedom has never been conceived as part of "the revolution" carried out in the name of Marx, Lenin, and the Socialist fatherland. Until recently, the Soviet Union has persistently rejected the very idea that citizens could have rights against their governments.

When the United Nations in its early years drafted the Universal Declaration on Human Rights, Soviet delegate V. T. Teplialiov sought to delete as unnecessary and undesirable most of the rights found in the French, American, and British constitutions. These rights, he argued, might be appropriate enough for a capitalist state, but were inappropriate in Socialist states—where the division between the individual and society had been overcome.

At that time, Soviet Deputy Foreign Minister Andrei Y. Vishinsky put it this way: "The rights of human beings cannot be considered outside the prerogative of governments. The very understanding of human rights is a government concept."

This approach did not die easily. In his early meetings with Ronald Reagan, Mikhail Gorbachev aggressively sought to avoid any discussion of human rights, and in these conversations (as in his book, *Perestroika*) Gorbachev expressed disdain for Western conceptions of civil and political liberty.

Soviet "democracy" is not the same as that of the West, he said. Soviet rights are not the same: they are superior. The very existence of socialism guarantees the rights of citizens, he argued.

"In the USSR, freedom of speech and the press are primarily guaranteed by the fact that the media all belong to the people and are not owned by private individuals or companies," said Gorbachev, ignoring the undoubted fact that state ownership of media guarantees the expression of only official opinions.

The Soviet Union's new endorsement of political and civil liberties is potentially important because each new affirmation makes repression more embarrassing, harder to defend. Each conference that focuses on these commitments can become a demonstration that tyranny is even more dangerous than war and becomes an opportunity to remind the world that, as Father Morrison of Guyana wrote, "No country is so poor it cannot afford freedom of expression."

The Logic of Freedom
March 14, 1989

Gorbachev's reform program picked up dramatic momentum in early 1989 when he turned to elections and agricultural reform. One of the most interesting and important aspects of both was the debate that surrounded them, exactly the kind of public debate that had been prohibited in the Soviet Union for seventy years. Although these reform processes were flawed, I believe freedom has its own dynamic, making it very unlikely that one-party rule can last long where there is public debate and electoral choice. I believed this dynamic would bring multiple parties to the Soviet Union itself regardless of the intentions of Soviet rulers.

In Poland, Hungary, China, and especially the Soviet Union, taboos that have protected official Marxist ideology since the revolution have lost their power. Now a new stage of the reform process has begun.

About 2,000 Muscovites gathered in Gorky Park last week to honor the victims of Joseph Stalin and to let their views be known. They shouted "Shame on Ligachev" and "Yeltsin is the son of the people" and punctuated speeches with demands that Mikhail Gorbachev's principal rival and critic, Yegor Ligachev, resign and that deposed reformer Boris Yeltsin be restored to power.

Forced out of the Politburo last year for pressing too hard for reforms judged too sweeping, Yeltsin has become a folk hero to reform-minded Soviet intellectuals and has attracted an enthusiastic following. His recent appearances on Soviet television and radio indicate that some of his supporters are influential as well as fervent.

Meanwhile, evidence accumulates that the split within the Politburo is deep and the balance of power uncertain. If those who brought down Yeltsin do not have the power to eliminate him from public life, they demonstrated last week that they do have the power to block Gorbachev's proposed agricultural reforms—at least temporarily.

Faced with chronic shortages of grain, meat, and consumer goods, Gorbachev has been pressing for basic changes in Soviet agriculture. He argues that unproductive farms and state enterprises should be dissolved in favor of cooperatives and a new system developed for "leasing" land to individual farmers.

To maintain these state farms longer at the expense of the state "through credits they don't pay back is not only impossible, but makes no sense," he has said. Gorbachev's close associate and official ideologist, Vadim Medvedev, says the experience in China and Hungary shows that leasing collective property to individual farmers "ensures explosive growth in agriculture and services."

Noting that the 1.6 percent of arable land now farmed in private plots produces 30 percent of the Soviet Union's food, Medvedev does not flinch from the implications of the Chinese, Hungarian, and Soviet experiences.

"The key to reform is restructuring property relations and ending the state of alienation between people and public property," he said. "We must now admit that our previous concepts of public property have proven untenable."

The first step is to end the ban on leasing imposed in 1930, Gorbachev and Medvedev have recommended.

"It was not for this that we established Soviet power," Ligachev complained.

When a special two-day meeting last week on agricultural policy failed to produce a decision, most observers concluded that forces supporting Ligachev's position had been strong enough to block Gorbachev's plans.

Meanwhile, the case in favor of "privatizing" property was pushed still further in articles by Soviet writer Alexander Tsipko, who has argued recently that socialism cannot be democratized in the absence of a free market.

In an analysis that could have been borrowed from Milton Friedman, Tsipko argued that centralization of economic power and management leads directly to dictatorship and terror.

He noted that terror developed soon after centralized controls over the Soviet economy were imposed in 1919 under Lenin, before Lenin restored free markets with the New Economic Policy.

Ligachev is right that arguments such as these call into question the ideological foundations of the Soviet system. Permitting individuals to manage their "leased" property and to profit personally from their labor is more compatible with the views of Adam Smith than those of Karl Marx.

Gorbachev's advocacy of both restructuring and openness (*perestroika* and *glasnost*) makes him the premier reformer among Communist leaders. But, although centralized control of the Soviet economy and culture have come under fire from him and his closest associates, the Communist party's monopoly on power is still sacrosanct. *Glasnost* is used as another justification for a one-party state.

"The party respects the right of non-Communists to have an opinion and to defend their interests. Under such conditions, there are no grounds for creating any alternative parties to oppose the policy of the Communist Party," Medvedev wrote in an echo of Gorbachev.

In insisting on the exclusive, central role of the Communist party, no Soviet leader has yet addressed the question of where it will all lead. French Sovietologist Michel Tatu believes opponents left inside the Politburo to fight another day will eventually depose Gorbachev. Other observers believe intraparty democracy will eventually accustom Soviet leaders to tolerating differences.

We should be clear that, reforms to the contrary notwithstanding, the Soviet Union, Eastern Europe, and China remain today what all Communist governments have been—one-party states. They still repress dissidents—as when the Soviet government cracked down in Azerbaijan or when the Czech government imprisoned Vaclav Havel, Jaromir Nemec, and Pavel Dodr last week, and as the Chinese government harshly represses free expression in Tibet.

But the logic of freedom is already at work in these societies. One-party rule is not democracy. But one-party rule with public debate and choice probably cannot last long. At a minimum, the Party will change internally, even though its outer shell remains the same, as Chinese dissident Liu Binyan predicted.

Gorbachev vs. Lenin

April 3, 1989

In June 1988 the Soviet Communist party convened its nineteenth All-Union Conference, the first held since 1941. Mikhail Gorbachev chose this dramatic forum to unveil a program for sweeping political reorgan-

ization of the Soviet state, designed to shake up the huge Soviet bureaucracy and to win popular support. On that occasion, Gorbachev called for reorganization of the Supreme Soviet into a more representative two-chamber legislature, comprising a 2,250–member Congress of People's Deputies and a 400–450–member Supreme Soviet; 1,500 Congress deputies would be popularly elected by secret ballot at the local and regional levels, and the remaining 750 would be chosen by Party organizations, youth groups, unions, and popular fronts. Multiple candidates would be allowed for the contested seats, but all would require Party approval.

The elections were held on March 26, 1989. Voter turnout was heavy, even in the districts in which only one candidate was on the ballot (25 percent of the total). Gorbachev had sought a popular vote of confidence in perestroika, *but the results reflected an overwhelming rejection of the status quo and a demand for even more radical change.*

I believed the Soviet elections were extremely important, even though incomplete. They involved a new, non-Leninist conception' of both the Party and the people. They endorsed the ideas that the people should participate in government and that the Party should listen to the people. The elections introduced a new conception of legitimacy into the Soviet polity. In suggesting that officials must win the approval of the people, Gorbachev tacitly abandoned the claim that Communist leaders derived their legitimacy directly from history.

It is true that the nominating process for Soviet elections was severely restricted and partly rigged and that it excluded important opposition groups. It is also true that in nearly one-fourth of all districts the official candidate ran unopposed and that about 80 percent of all candidates were Communist party members. It is true too that these elections were only one stage in the selection of one governing body and that the final outcome is stacked in favor of the Communist party.

Still, these Soviet elections were extremely important. For the first time in seventy years Soviet citizens had an opportunity to express their views about those who govern them. Since Vladimir Ilyich Lenin and his band of Bolsheviks ignored the outcome of legislative elections and seized power in 1917, the Communist party of the Soviet Union has claimed its right to rule is based on iron "laws of history" and does not require popular approval.

While claiming that they spoke for "the people," successive Communist leaders never found it necessary to ask "the people" about who should rule or to what broad ends. They have governed instead by force and imposed policies that stifled Soviet society and the economy. By force they incorporated formerly independent nations into the USSR. By force they eliminated opposition parties, silenced critics, and blocked all the channels through which the Soviet people might have expressed their views. Dogs, fences, and guard towers have prevented emigration—denying the people an opportunity to vote with their feet. Elections have been staged plebiscites in which the government scored 99 percent of the votes. Public opinion polls have been strictly forbidden. Control consolidated under Stalin by terror was maintained by his successors, who jailed or banished refuseniks, philosophers, whistle-blowers, evangelicals, dissidents, poets, and musicians.

So thoroughly did the Soviet leadership control expression and stifle dissent that no one, including Soviet leaders themselves, could say what the Soviet people thought about anything. No one knew for certain what the Soviet people wanted, what they opposed, for whom or what they were willing to work. No one could say how the Soviet people felt about the Communist party, religion, art, Afghanistan, *perestroika*, Ligachev—or anything. Anyone could and did claim to represent the people—as long as the people could not speak for themselves.

One step at a time Mikhail Gorbachev has provided the Soviet people opportunities to express their views: in media, books, meetings, and now in a campaign and elections.

Gorbachev could not have known the outcome of this unprecedented experiment in free expression. Probably he is disappointed by some of the results. Probably he did not guess the strength of the popular movements in Estonia, Latvia, and Lithuania. Probably he did not foresee that party chiefs would lose elections in six major cities or that a nonvoting Politburo member whose election was uncontested would nonetheless be defeated, or that Boris Yeltsin would win nearly 90 percent of the votes against the designated Party candidate, or that dissident historian Roy Medvedev would run first in a field of six, or that so many official candidates might lose even though they were unopposed.

Medvedev was probably right when he said it must have been "a very sobering day for the Communist Party and for Mikhail Gorbachev." It is impossible at this stage to guess the consequences of this fascinating Soviet experiment with limited choice. But certain conclusions almost leap out of the experience.

First, the campaign and elections demonstrated that seventy years of repression have not deprived the Soviet people of a capacity to form independent views and to express them. They are neither too apathetic nor too brainwashed to think or act for themselves.

Second, in spite of seventy years of official propaganda, the Soviet people have not been persuaded that the Communist party necessarily represents their views or interests. Both the campaign and the outcome reveal a good deal of explicit distrust and dislike of Party officials.

Third, the campaign also made clear that the Soviet people do believe their society is rent by a class struggle but not the one described by Karl Marx. Rather it is a class system created by Marxism, which pits a small privileged party elite against the people. Boris Yeltsin based his campaign on popular resentments of this elite.

Fourth, while the outcome was far worse for Party conservatives such as Ligachev than for Gorbachev himself, Gorbachev had an opportunity to learn the same lesson the U.S. government was taught in El Salvador a few weeks ago: given a choice, people cannot necessarily be counted on to vote as their leaders wish. The election results provide strong proof of the persistence of intense national identifications of Baltic peoples and the Ukraine. The Estonian popular front won twenty-five of thirty-six seats, Latvia's popular front won twenty-five of twenty-nine seats, and in Lithuania the nationalist Sajudis took thirty-two of the forty-two seats. In the Ukraine several official candidates running unopposed were defeated when an electoral boycott deprived them of the 50 percent needed to win.

Finally, and most important, there is the fact of the elections and of Gorbachev's promise that those lacking Party support might lose their jobs. When Gorbachev says officials should have public approval, he is moving toward the view that government should be based on the consent of the governed. That is a big step toward the democratic view of legitimacy that Lenin rejected. The biggest news of all is that Mikhail Gorbachev has reopened the question about the appropriate relations between people and their rulers.

Is the Brezhnev Doctrine Dead?
March 20, 1989

By 1989 the idea of "captive" nations had been revived. Hungary and Poland were pushing against the limits of autonomy believed to be available to Warsaw Pact countries. The Baltic states were raising questions about their own relations with the Soviet state.

Would Mikhail Gorbachev, who insisted that it was "unthinkable" to use force against a Socialist nation, use force to keep them Socialist? No one knew, and in the absence of certain knowledge, Hungary and Poland pressed cautiously but doggedly forward toward self-government.

The last time a Hungarian government seriously questioned that country's Socialist regime and its ties to the Soviet Union, Soviet tanks rolled into Budapest to end the discussion. Today, thirty-three years later, the Hungarian government is again promoting sweeping economic and political reforms and planning for a new "humanist" constitution that will provide freedoms and competition never before permitted in a Communist state.

Already there is open discussion of Hungarian membership in the European Economic Community and a general expectation that Hungary will be granted "observer" status in the European parliament at Strasbourg. Meanwhile, some Hungarians are looking closely at Austria's constitution as a model of neutrality.

The Soviet Union is making it clear that it will not regard it as a defeat if Hungary continues to move toward closer relations with the European community. And already the word had been passed by Gorbachev adviser Oleg Bogomolov that "a neutral Hungary would constitute no threat to the Soviet Union."

Do these and other developments in Eastern Europe mean that the Soviet Union has abandoned what is called the Brezhnev Doctrine (though it was actually invoked long before Brezhnev took power)? That doctrine claims for the Soviet Union the "internationalist duty" to act—by force if necessary—to prevent people from "damaging socialism" in their own country or "weakening the Socialist bloc" by separating their country from the "commonwealth of European Socialist countries."

As if to avoid a direct test of the doctrine's current status, Hungarian spokesmen have offered public assurances that contemplating neutrality does not imply a rupture with the Warsaw Pact. "There is no question of leaving the system of alliances to which we belong," said Hungary's vice-minister for foreign affairs.

In fact, no one knows how much freedom or independence Soviet leaders will tolerate. But in Hungary, Poland, and Lithuania, governments and dissidents are testing the limits.

In Hungary and Poland, as in the Soviet Union itself, two categories of reformers have emerged: the "moderates," like Mikhail Gorbachev himself, who spearhead reforms that, while producing important limited changes, will preserve the one-party system and the powers of the Communist party; and the "extremists," who seek to use the new freedom to end the Communist party's rule and to restore independence to their people. Distrust and bitterness have already emerged between these two groups.

Seeking to relax control while preserving the Communist party's monopoly on power, "official reformers" are offering free elections, but in rigged systems.

For example, the government of Poland has proposed elections and an "elected parliament" in which Solidarity may hold no more than 40 percent of the seats. Hungary's official reformers will permit opposition parties to contest local and national elections with the understanding that if successful, they may win a place in a coalition dominated by the ruling Socialist Workers party. In Lithuania, the popular opposition group Sajudis is fielding candidates for the March 26 elections of a new national congress with full understanding that, even if Sajudis candidates win a sweeping victory, they will have no impact on the composition of the next government.

In all these areas opposition parties are willing to compete on unequal terms.

Sajudis leaders may have stepped over the invisible but real line that separates permissible from impermissible opposition when they announced that an independent Lithuania was their eventual goal.

As in the case of Solidarity, some Sajudis leaders fear that demands for a genuine democracy and for independence from the Soviet Union or the Warsaw Pact will provoke repression and endanger the entire reform process. Such a "counterrevolution" against "plurocommunism" would please only the die-hard defenders of the *status quo ante*, those who are less concerned with economic development than with political power, less interested in ending the Soviet "threat" than in preserving the "Socialist commonwealth."

They are men like Yegor Ligachev, who last week traveled to Czechoslovakia in search of a "Socialist" model for Soviet agriculture to counter Gorbachev's proposed reforms. He found it. In Czechoslovakia, he said, "There has not been a single deviation" from the system of collective and state farms as has taken place in Hungary and China, yet the farms are productive.

Where will it end? What are the limits of Gorbachev's tolerance and of his power? How is it possible to be a "neutral" member of the Warsaw Pact? Will Leninist "socialism" be supplanted by posttotalitarian regimes of which no example yet exists? Will nationalism prevail over socialism? Will democracy prevail over the dictatorship of the Communist party?

We do not know. What we do know is that decades of repression and control culture have not produced a monolithic "Soviet man" and that any stable solution in Eastern Europe must take account of the persistence of strong ethnic and national feelings.

Poles *will* be Poles. Hungarians *will* remember that they are above all Hungarians. And Lithuanians *will* insist on speaking their language, flying their flag, singing their songs.

Can Communism Transform Itself?

June 19, 1989

In June 1989 the answer to whether Mikhail Gorbachev would permit self-government in Eastern Europe was still unknown. Would he permit non-Communists to win power? Would Solidarity be permitted to win Polish elections? No one knew, least of all Solidarity's leaders. There was, as I say here, still no example of a Communist state transforming itself into another type of regime. But the prospects looked better and better.

Once again a leader of the Soviet Union committed his country to "respect for the right of peoples to self-determination"—this time in a joint declaration with West Germany. But the same document permitted each state "the right to choose freely its own political and social systems." So the pledge remains ambiguous. Moreover, Mikhail Gorbachev did not respond at all to Helmut Kohl's appeal to help heal the "open wound" that is the division of Germany or to bring down the Berlin Wall, which symbolizes a divided Germany and a divided Europe—and the Soviet will to maintain both, by force if necessary. One step forward. One step back.

Meanwhile, in Poland the government is just now making a public response to its defeat in the Polish elections. Of thirty-five government leaders who ran unopposed in the June 4 elections, only two obtained the 50 percent necessary for election. Last week, Premier Mieczyslaw Rakowski joined several other defeated colleagues in announcing the intention to resign their government posts. The same day the Polish government announced that—in keeping with its agreement with Solidarity—the next president must be a member of the Communist party, probably Gen. Wojciech Jaruzelski. A spokesman for Solidarity immediately asserted that the accords made no such provision. Two steps forward. One step back.

Meanwhile in China the government continued a relentless search for leaders of the democracy movement, extracted confessions, displayed bloody and bowed demonstrators on national television, and spoke endlessly of "counterrevolutionaries" and "traitors" and their determination to take Fang Lizhi into custody. No steps forward. Two steps back.

Can totalitarianism be transformed from within? It is the question of the decade. No one knows the answer. But now is a good time to consider the evidence.

There is still no example of a Communist state transforming itself into another type of regime or of the Soviet Union permitting an Eastern European state to be so transformed. That doesn't prove it can't happen, only that it hasn't happened.

The bloody purges under way in China testify to the limits of reform in that place at this time. The fact that Communist party candidates so often lose elections in Hungary, Poland, and the Soviet Union without the party's losing control of the government reminds us of the limits of reform in these Marxist societies. The anxiety in Poland that Solidarity should not win too many votes tells us how fragile Solidarity supporters believe their gains to be. The ease with which the Chinese military put down the massive demonstrations at Tiananmen Square is a fresh reminder of how unequal is the balance of forces between citizens and their governments.

It is probably true, as Italian writer Curzio Malaparte argued in his book *Coup D'Etat*, that successful popular revolution is impossible in our times—without at least the passive acquiescence of the government in power. And it is probably true that a modern government can stay in power as long as its leaders are willing to massacre civilian demonstrators. But not all leaders are.

The Hungarian revolution was put down because Nikita Khrushchev gave orders to shoot to Soviet troops willing to obey them. The Prague Spring ended when Leonid Brezhnev gave the same orders. No man acts in a vacuum, but it seems reasonable to suppose that either might have decided otherwise. Deng Xiaoping and his associates chose to fire on students massed in Tiananmen Square. Conflict within Chinese leadership circles makes clear that he might have made a different decision.

In the modern state, leaders decide. In Communist states especially, the leaders control the guns, the tanks, the communications, the food—or, as Lenin would have put it, they control the decisive means of production and the instrumentalities of the state.

The question, "Can communism transform itself from within?" can be more accurately posed: Have Communist states produced rulers who are willing to relinquish power?

Deng proved unwilling to share power or relinquish it or even to discuss the question.

Will Jaruzelski submit his power to competitive elections? Will he leave office if defeated? Will Gorbachev and his colleagues permit a man who is not a party member to be elected president of Poland? Will they permit such a man to be elected president of the USSR?

Will Gorbachev permit Germans to heal the "open wound" of division? Will he take down the Berlin Wall?

Only as we learn the answers to these questions will we know whether communism can transform itself in our time.

Messages to China, from Hungary
June 26, 1989

June 1989 was a big month. Hungary opened its border with Austria, ending the division between Communist and non-Communist Europe that had lasted forty years. Hungary corrected its history, rehabilitated the leader of its 1956 revolt, Imre Nagy, and reburied him with high honors. Meanwhile, China's rulers falsified history—forcing public trials on the captured leaders of China's democracy movement, executing them, moving quickly to stamp out dissent and root out actual and potential dissenters.

The ultimate failure of such efforts was also becoming clearer and clearer. The return of some freedom to Hungary and Poland proved a prelude to the reemergence of truth about major events in the history of those countries—proving again the futility of relying on force to repress facts.

In Hungary, they are correcting history. In Beijing, they are falsifying it.

In Budapest, the government and people are liberating themselves from repression and lies. In China, the government is repressing the people and lying about it as it stamps out spring.

A great Russian writer still not fully "rehabilitated," Alexander Solzhenitsyn, noted that violence and lies go together. Both are part of the effort to make reality conform to ideology.

We know now that it cannot work. Reality will finally overcome ideology, as it has recently in Hungary, where hundreds of thousands turned out for the solemn ceremony in which Hungarians "rehabilitated" Imre Nagy and reclaimed their history.

In 1956, Prime Minister Nagy with his colleagues moved Hungary away from the dictatorship of the Communist party and the hegemony of the Soviet Union toward democracy and independence. The Brezhnev Doctrine had not yet been enunciated, but Nikita Khrushchev had no doubt that he had the right and the "internationalist duty"—as leader of the Soviet Union—to make certain that history moved in only one direction for the countries of Eastern Europe that had been incorporated into the Soviet empire after World War II.

Soviet tanks and troops already in Hungary crushed the Budapest Spring as brutally as the Chinese dictators cleared Tiananmen Square. Nagy, Pal Maleter, and their colleagues were arrested, tried, and executed as "traitors" and "counterrevolutionaries."

Now, thirty years later, Janos Kadar—the man who reestablished order and protected the official (Soviet) version of events—helps to dismantle the machinery of repression and tells us that the execution of Nagy was a great "personal pain and problem" for him.

Of course, the rehabilitation of Nagy indicts his executioners and the regime built on those executed. But that regime has already been supplanted by reform.

One hopes that, as he was tried and executed, Nagy knew he eventually would be exonerated and celebrated by his countrymen.

One hopes the Chinese workers and students who have been captured or already sentenced understand that they eventually will be celebrated as the leaders and martyrs they are. One hopes these arrests, trials, and executions will be a great "personal pain and problem" for Deng Xiaoping, himself once a victim. One hopes he understands that the violence and lies that emptied Tiananmen Square will someday be swept away by truth. One hopes the hunted, haunted, hollow-eyed young Chinese who are the victims of today's violence and lies know there will once again be celebrations of freedom and truth in the square.

We know now that Orwell was wrong about certain details. It isn't true that "who controls the present controls the past." Perfect truth and objectivity are not possible in history.

All the details of the deal between Hitler and Stalin may never be known, but too much is known about how Stalin conquered and incorporated Latvia, Lithuania, and Estonia for the truth to be ultimately suppressed. Too much is known about how the Soviet army murdered Polish officers in the Katyn Forest. Too much is known about what Nagy and Maleter did for Hungary for the official lies to have been maintained indefinitely.

The truth will come out—about Stalin's great show trials, about the gulag, about the Nazi-Soviet pact and its victims, about the Katyn massacres, and about the "premature" democrats in Hungary who sought to lead their people toward democracy and independence before leaders in the Kremlin were ready.

One day there will be monuments in Czechoslovakia to the leaders of the Prague Spring. And in China to the democracy movement in Tiananmen Square.

One day, as the future is claimed, the past will be reclaimed.

Gorbachev's Double Binds
September 18, 1989

The task Mikhail Gorbachev has set for himself may be impossible to accomplish. How can he grant free speech and be sure the freedom will not be used to demand more freedom? How can he grant free elections and be sure the Communist candidates will not be defeated? How can he quiet fears of Soviet force and still maintain control of Eastern Europe? How can he limit the power of the Communist party and still maintain his own position? He cannot. Students of political change know that relaxing repression is often more dangerous for the rulers than intensifying it.

The debate about Mikhail Gorbachev's motives and intentions has been narrowed by the changes that have already occurred this year in the Soviet Union, Poland, and Hungary. So far the changes are in policy rather than in personnel.

The pace and scope of change have surprised almost everyone. No one expected that contested elections would be held in which Communist candidates would be overwhelmingly defeated. No one expected that the Soviet government would acknowledge the Secret Protocol of the Nazi-Soviet pact, which delegitimizes the Soviet incorporation of the Baltic states. No one expected the Kremlin would acknowledge the Soviet role in the massacre of Polish officers in the

Katyn Forest during World War II. No one believed that strikes in a basic industry would be tolerated or permitted to spread. But it all happened.

And it is now obvious that Mikhail Gorbachev not only wants to rule the Soviet Union and to enhance its international power but also seriously seeks broad reform of his own society.

Gorbachev is, manifestly, a man with a vision of a different kind of Soviet socialism—more successful, less coercive, and more partici- patory. He calls it "Socialist pluralism." If he succeeds, we will speak henceforth of Marxism-Leninism-Gorbachevism. What his success or failure will mean to the United States and the rest of the West is still an open question.

Success, of course, is not ensured. The experience of the past year has illustrated how difficult it is to change a great bureaucratic society in which everyone works for the government. Each aspect of the system reinforces the rest. Centralized political power reinforces the centralization of economic power and vice versa. So entrenched is state ownership that it is extremely complicated to privatize any- thing. The stagnation of the economy prevents the production of goods that could serve as an incentive to increased production. For seventy years private initiative and private enterprise have been discouraged at best or punished severely.

Le Monde correspondent Bernard Guetta has said the prerequisite for progress in the Soviet Union is for its citizens to believe in the possibility and durability of change.

Perhaps they are beginning to. The Soviet people have been quick to seize the opportunities for greater expression offered them in the past two years. Latvians, Lithuanians, and Estonians did not hesitate to vote for Baltic nationalists in local elections nor to oppose government policies and advocate independence. Elsewhere, Soviet citizens have voted overwhelmingly against Communist party leaders and office holders—showing little reticence about their opposition.

Indeed the Baltic independence movement and the unpopularity of Communist party candidates have become major problems for Mikhail Gorbachev. So strong are both that in dealing with domestic affairs, Gorbachev is caught in a double bind: he believes more freedom is necessary for a more successful Communist society—but when he grants more freedom, the people reject communism and Soviet rule entirely.

How can socialism be reformed, yet remain Socialist? How can Gorbachev limit the Communist party's monopoly of power, yet maintain it in power? How can he weaken the Party, yet consolidate his own power? How can he grant free speech and prevent the conquered peoples of the Soviet Union from demanding independence?

As if that were not bad enough, Gorbachev confronts a similar double bind in foreign affairs. His success is in large measure a consequence of persuading Europeans, Chinese, Americans, and assorted others that "there is no Soviet threat." He has sworn that the use of force by the Soviet Union against a fellow Socialist state, or by any European state against another, is "unthinkable." He has strongly implied that every Warsaw Pact country is free to choose its own allies and map its own future. Already the people of Hungary, Poland, and East Germany have made clear that given a choice they prefer a non-Communist future.

If Gorbachev accepts the progressive independence they seek, the Warsaw Pact dissolves. If he holds them by force, he revives the Soviet threat—in technicolor.

His situation is extremely difficult. His problems are probably insoluble. Socialism is not a successful economic system, anywhere. And it is probably impossible today to hold on to an empire except by force.

Will Mikhail Gorbachev be in power a year from now? Personally, I hope so. But don't bet on it.

Bad Bargain in Poland
September 11, 1989

The final disintegration of Communist rule in Poland began in December 1988 when, after months of unrest and industrial strikes, Communist party chief Wojciech Jaruzelski agreed to Solidarity's demands for talks centering on political liberalization and the legalization of Solidarity. In early February 1989 the talks finally began, and on April 5, 1989, Communist and opposition leaders signed an agreement mandating sweeping political reforms, including the legalization of Solidarity. In the elections of June 4, Solidarity won virtually all the Senate seats as well as its allotted share of Sejm seats, while most Communists nominated for the remaining parliamentary seats failed to secure the required majority. In a runoff election for the remaining unfilled seats, Solidarity won all but one of those open to non-Communists.

On August 18 during my visit to Poland, Jaruzelski named the long-time Catholic activist and Solidarity adviser Tadeusz Mazowiecki to lead Poland's first non-Communist government in more than forty years. While in Poland, I spoke with leaders of both Solidarity and the Communist party, including General Jaruzelski. The atmosphere was electric; there were excitement and apprehension. No one knew how much Polish independence the Soviet Union would tolerate. No one wanted to risk finding out.

Change had come so fast that members of the Communist party could hardly believe it. They could not imagine sharing power. Solidarity leaders could hardly imagine that those who had so recently been the jailers were willing to admit them into government.

But the word was out: Mikhail Gorbachev wanted a coalition government. So the same government that had so long tolerated Soviet demands for one-party rule now accommodated his demand for coalition government.

"Can we do it?" Solidarity leaders ask one another. "Can we do it?" they ask sympathetic foreigners.

The task looks easier from Washington than from Warsaw.

In the United States, commentators speak as if the transition from Marxist dictatorship to parliamentary democracy has already been made, as if Poland's national independence were an accomplished fact. The leaders of Solidarity know it is not.

The experience of martial law and imprisonment sensitized Solidarity's leaders to what the Soviets call "the correlation of forces" in Poland. They do not forget that, although Solidarity candidates won virtually every election they were permitted to contest, Gen. Wojciech Jaruzelski is president of Poland and commander in chief of Poland's army and police. They do not forget that the same Soviet force that has guaranteed control to Poland's Communist government for forty years is still there—like a 400-pound gorilla—reinforcing the demands of Poland's Communist party for power it cannot win in elections.

Solidarity leaders do not forget that the possibilities of a democratic transition depend ultimately on Soviet restraint in the use of that force. So they are exceedingly circumspect when they speak of these matters.

"Is communism finished in Poland?" a *Time* magazine reporter asked Poland's new prime minister, Tadeusz Mazowiecki.

"The transformation now taking place would not have been possible if it were not for the support of [reform-minded] Communist party members," he replied. "I told President Wojciech Jaruzelski last week that the success of my government will depend on his help. I

73

don't think communism will disappear, but I believe it will undergo a transformation."

Solidarity's leaders weigh their words and their decisions—careful not to provoke unnecessarily their reluctant Polish coalition partners, careful not to offend the 400-pound gorilla, uncertain about how far they can go.

They demonstrate the "new maturity" about which Jaruzelski spoke when he contrasted the confrontations of 1981 and 1982 with the present collaboration between government and opposition. "The situation is very different," he told several of us in a private conversation as the process of selecting a government got under way. "In 1981 the opposition lacked experience. They made mistakes. The government lacked experience. It made mistakes. I myself made mistakes. Now we have matured." And though Jaruzelski doesn't mention it, the 400-pound gorilla has also "matured."

The "mature" Polish government permitted elections in which the Communist party was clobbered. The "mature" Solidarity leaders offered the Communist party the key ministries of defense and interior, thus giving it continued control of the police and military.

Moreover, Lech Walesa found it possible and prudent to announce that Poland would continue as a member of the Warsaw Pact, and other Solidarity spokesmen have offered assurances that Communist party members will not be purged from ministries under Solidarity control.

But all this was not enough for Poland's Communist party. Even before Mazowiecki was named prime minister, the word was out in Warsaw that the Communist party would demand five or six ministries, including defense and interior. U.S. officials in Warsaw were quietly predicting the demands would largely be met, even as Walsea insisted that "the government must be one of reformers and not one full of seats reserved for the *nomenklatura* [top party bureaucrats]." Now it appears that Mazowiecki has accepted the demand for additional Communist ministries, including foreign affairs, defense, interior, and communications, leaving Solidarity with responsibility for the economy. Even if this is the only bargain available, it is a bad bargain.

The Polish economy is in acute crisis. It is obvious that the Communist leadership hopes that Solidarity can attract immediate Western assistance, which the party could not obtain. It is just as obvious that the Communist leadership hopes Solidarity will take the responsibility and the wrath for adopting needed but unpopular economic reforms. Probably the Communist leadership is right on both scores.

It is true that the West has far more incentive to assist a parliamentary democracy headed by Solidarity than a Marxist dictatorship. We should, however, also make it clear (and Solidarity should make it clear) that our incentive to help diminishes as the Communist leadership uses tacit threats of force to increase its presence in the new government.

The transition to democracy in Poland is not yet complete. And communism is not yet "finished" in Eastern Europe. But a new order is struggling to be born out of the contradictions of the present.

The New November Revolution

November 1, 1989

Gorbachev's reforms have turned into a revolution. Almost no one presumes to know where it will end. Ideology—once invoked to justify everything—is now less and less mentioned. The confession of Eduard Shevardnadze concerning past Soviet sins was less remarkable for its substance—which was well known anyway—than for its style. The new style fit a planned trip to the Vatican and a new "peace offensive" to the United States and Western Europe. It did not fit as well the Soviets' continuing shipments of money and weapons into the Western Hemisphere.

As in any revolution, the ruling elites in Eastern Europe and the Soviet Union are changing both their composition and their vocabulary. Although the changes in rhetoric may appear less substantial than the emergence of new faces, they signal fundamental shifts in ideology and orientation.

Hungary's reform government makes clear its rupture with Marxism-Leninism—opening its border; changing its name from "Socialist Worker" to simply the "Socialist" party; removing the great statue of Lenin from Heroes' Square; honoring Imre Nagy; formally proclaiming (as its president did) that Hungary is henceforth an independent democratic republic.

It is the classic politics of rupture—bold, determined, shocking to those who believed the countries of Eastern Europe would need to walk slowly and on tiptoe toward greater independence.

The changing vocabulary of the "people's democracies" of the

75

East was nowhere more evident than in the speech by Foreign Minister Eduard Shevardnadze, who described the Afghan invasion not as a "mistake" but as "the most serious violation of our own legislation, of party and civic norms and ethical stands of our times." In this speech Shevardnadze violated the norms of Marxism-Leninism a second time when he spoke about "sorting out matters" to get to the "entire truth" about the Krasnoyarsk radar station.

In the matters of both Afghanistan and Krasnoyarsk, the news was in the rhetoric—public self-criticism is definitely not part of the Leninist lexicon.

Soviet troops are already out of Afghanistan, but it was the first time a member of the ruling elite had condemned the Soviet invasion in moral terms. Since 1983, evidence has been available that the Soviets were building an antimissile defense at Krasnoyarsk in Siberia. What's new is the public confession that the Soviet government had violated the ABM Treaty and lied about it, just as the Reagan administration first said in 1983 and the Soviets denied as recently as last November.

By the time Shevardnadze made his speech, Krasnoyarsk had become something of a moot issue. Moscow had informed Secretary of State James Baker in September of its intention to dismantle it.

Still, Shevardnadze's statement was most interesting. It was not only an example of the new style of Soviet self-criticism, but, when a Soviet official acknowledges that they "violated the norms of proper behavior" and engaged in a "open violation of the ABM Treaty," he cuts the ground from under residual denials and rationalizations of Soviet apologists around the world. Similarly, his characterization of the invasion of Afghanistan cuts the ground from under those who have continued to describe it as a somehow "understandable" response to a somehow "understandable" desire to ensure a "friendly" regime on the Soviet border.

What shall we make of these extraordinary public confessions? Both instances involve decisions made by predecessors of the previous government—men already dead. But Mikhail Gorbachev and his associates have affirmed and defended the policies they now describe as illegal, so Shevardnadze's speech should remind us of the evolution in Gorbachev's statements *since* he assumed power.

Nonetheless, events surrounding the statements also make clear we should not jump to the conclusion that the new Soviet rhetorical style is tantamount to an end of efforts to manipulate and exploit these issues for political advantage. The Soviets' belief that the invasion of Afghanistan was a violation of civilized norms does not prevent them from continuing their effort to control that country.

Soviet military assistance is still pouring into Afghanistan, and Shevardnadze made a point of describing puppet president Najibullah as a "true patriot."

It is just as clear the Soviet government is still attempting to get something for dismantling part of an antimissile defense it should never have built. With incredible chutzpah, Shevardnadze suggested that confessing a treaty violation that was already known was somehow tantamount to an extraordinary effort to preserve the treaty and that, because the Soviets proposed to dismantle the illegal station, the United States incurs a moral obligation to permit inspections of U.S. installations not in violation of the treaty.

Change in the East is real and important. But Soviet leaders do not (yet?) regard it as inconsistent with restless striving after advantage and power.

The End of Totalitarianism in Europe
November 20, 1989

Take the word of a participant observer about totalitarianism, Solidarity leader Jacek Kuron, who has lived through the claims to power of the Polish Communist party. He writes,

> *Totalitarianism is an attempt to command all social life. It is based on the exclusive control of the power center over the organization of all activities. This monopoly is so total that if citizens gather and discuss freely a matter as simple as roof repairs on a block of apartments, it becomes a challenge to the central authority. Accompanying this monopoly of organization is a monopoly of information, meaning that every printed word—not to mention the electronic media—is controlled by the central authority. And these monopolies in turn lead to a monopoly of decision making by the central authority. Obviously this totalitarian ideal cannot be fully implemented, but even the attempt to implement it destroys a nation's economic and political life.*

During 1989 it became clear that the leaders of the Soviet Union had themselves abandoned totalitarian goals. By the time it was clear,

77

the process of reconstituting civil society in Poland and Hungary was already advanced.

The governments of Kadar and Jaruzelski did not relinquish power except as they were challenged to. Then, step by dramatic step, the government gave way to reform.

The dramatic events of recent days confirm beyond reasonable doubt that Mikhail Gorbachev and his collaborators in Eastern Europe have abandoned the totalitarian project.

That project seeks comprehensive control of what is said and read, learned and taught, produced, bought, and sold in a society. It seeks a monopoly over the economy and culture. It requires saturating a society with coercion and closing it against heretical influences.

Sealed borders, armed guards, tightly controlled emigration are the means by which Communist rulers have sought to control the environments where—decade after decade—the Party has conducted a great experiment in human engineering designed to make human nature conform to its preferred model.

The failure of totalitarianism to produce the desired human product has been clear in defections, refuseniks, rising nationalism and church attendance, and resistance of many kinds. The failure of comprehensively controlled economies has been clear in economic stagnation, scarcity, and declining living standards. But until recently, Communist leaders have been unwilling to accept the evidence.

With *glasnost*, Gorbachev took a giant step back toward relinquishing control of Soviet culture—permitting criticism and debate of official policies and persons, establishing commissions to "fill in the blanks of history" and "rectify falsification," and largely ending censorship. Permitting emigration is another such step. Opening borders between the Communist East and the democratic West means accepting new limits on the powers of governments over their citizens. "Conform or die!" Big Brother tells his hapless subjects. "Conform or die or leave!" is a very different message.

What would a Communist state that had abandoned the totalitarian project be like? It would be less repressive than Yugoslavia, which is already less repressive than most governments in the Soviet bloc. It might resemble Pinochet's Chile, although Chile has privately owned and operated media and a more efficient economy.

The world has now had a good deal of experience with socialism. The evidence is in. The evidence indicates persuasively that socialism is an economic system that does not work. It does not work because it stifles, rather than liberates, human energy and creativity. Socialist systems vest economic decisions in bureaucrats who will neither gain nor lose by their decisions, and thus it builds in irresponsibility.

A comprehensively controlled economy is one in which natural connections are broken between talent and work, between effort, creativity, and reward. As Peruvian social scientist Hernando de Soto demonstrates in his brilliant book *The Other Path*, the union between ownership and state power (whatever it is called) protects and rewards inefficiency. This is the reason that structural reform is a prerequisite to improving the economic situation of Poland and the rest of Eastern Europe. It is also the reason it is not so simple to help those economies.

Solidarity leader Lech Walesa is an utterly unexpected world-class leader, a determined, charming, persuasive spokesman for the Polish people. His strength, commitment, warmth, and leadership were all manifest in his whirlwind visits to the White House, Congress, the AFL-CIO, and Radio Free Europe's conference on Eastern Europe. To each American audience he brought the same message: Poland needs help. Now. "There is a large supply of encouraging words and advice offered us," he said, "but there is no large demand for this rhetoric. Poland needs dollars and food."

"There is business to be done in Poland," Walesa told his RFE audience. "It will be mutually profitable. Come. Do business with us now." The moment is here, he insists. We must not lose it. "If things go on as they are, you'll give us a beautiful necktie and it will look wonderful in our coffin."

Walesa reminded his audiences repeatedly that he was an electrician, not a politician or diplomat. But he spoke politically and diplomatically about the failure of communism in his country and the misery it has caused.

"There is no point in pulling the bear by his mustache," Walesa observed. "It is better to tickle him."

Walesa is not interested in scoring debating points. Poland needs food and freedom. "This time," he assures us, "we will know how to use your help."

Solidarity leaders freely admit that last time great quantities of money were transferred from Western banks to the Polish government—in the 1970s—it reinforced repression and inefficient economic structures and left the country with little to show except a crushing debt. "This time," Walesa promises, "we have had experience. We must not make a mistake."

This time Western governments have also had experience—

enough to know that assistance assists only if it reinforces institutions of a free market and a free society.

What does a Communist state that has abandoned the totalitarian project look like? It looks about like Poland—freer than it has been for more than forty years and in desperate need of the right kind of help, help that will strengthen not undermine its own productive capacities, that will stimulate indigenous initiative, reward indigenous effort and help build needed frameworks for self-sustaining freedom and growth.

Walesa is surely right. The time is now. The West must not lose this opportunity.

Enough to Break an Old Bolshevik's Heart
January 8, 1990

Much has been written arguing that Communist regimes are legitimate because they satisfy the people's material needs. But the people did not think so. They decisively repudiated the Communists. Clearly some new scholarship is warranted.

In fact, legitimacy depends on consent. The events of 1989 remind us that, as Rousseau put it, "The strongest is never strong enough to be always the master, unless he transforms his strength into right, and obedience into duty."

Political scientists have written multivolume studies on how and why regimes change, studies that examine historical cases and make generalizations. But none of those cases and generalizations can help us in explaining the collapse of Communist regimes all over Eastern Europe, because nothing like this has ever happened before—not in the history of empires, not in the modern period, certainly not among Communist states. Not one such state had ever been toppled by military coup, or brought down by internal dissension, or overthrown by mass revolution, or transformed from within by evolutionary change.

Why did it happen?

It didn't happen because of the stagnant economies of Eastern Europe. Those economies had been stagnant for decades. Moreover, the states with the most productive economies—Czechoslovakia and

East Germany—were no more able to withstand the events of 1989 than those with the most stagnant economies.

Leave the economic explanations to the Marxists and look instead for a political explanation for a political phenomenon. Ask yourself: Of all those regimes, why did all but Romania's Nicolae Ceausescu turn over power without resistance? Why, of all the secret police and indigenous armies, did only Romania's fight (and they not very long nor very hard)?

All these governments were fashioned on the Marxist-Leninist model: interlocking bureaucracies held together by their own Communist parties and secret police, reinforced by thousands of Soviet troops. All were created at the initiative of Joseph Stalin in the shadow of Soviet armies after World War II and enjoyed a large continuing Soviet military presence.

Several of the rulers—such as Erich Honecker of East Germany, Janos Kadar of Hungary, and Ceausescu—had been in power for decades. They had used force against indigenous rebels on more than one occasion. They were men without scruples about firing into crowds of unarmed civilians, imprisoning thousands, stamping out dissent. They were tough, seasoned leaders in the Stalinist mode.

Why did they turn over power without resistance?

I believe these governments died of a broken heart and spirit. Honecker, Ceausescu, Kadar, and Milos Jakes of Czechoslovakia were such utterly disciplined Communists accustomed to following Soviet leaders that they had long since abdicated the power of independent judgment. Like the old Bolshevik in Arthur Koestler's *Darkness at Noon*, who confesses in Stalin's purge trials to crimes he did not commit, they performed one last service to the Communist cause.

These Bolsheviks of the previous generation must have felt that Mikhail Gorbachev had betrayed them with his talk of reform and openness, betrayed them when he tolerated strikes and criticism, and betrayed them especially when he spoke about how "unthinkable" it was that the Soviet Union would ever use force against the people of another state.

Had they not supported the Socialist fatherland in the use of force against their own people?

They were demoralized by Gorbachev's policies but were too disciplined to oppose them. And now they were left to confront their own countrymen without certain support from the Soviet troops they had welcomed.

It was too much.

The peaceful revolution in Eastern Europe began in Hungary and Poland, where in the beginning dissidents moved slowly, cautiously toward greater self-expression and self-government. When Soviet troops did not arrive to crush them, the people of Hungary and Poland began to lose their fear. And then so did the people of East Germany, Czechoslovakia, Bulgaria, and Romania.

What happened then made it clearer than ever that the Communist regimes of Eastern Europe have rested all these years on force, nothing but force. With the fear of force removed, the civil societies of Hungary, Poland, Czechoslovakia, and East Germany reasserted themselves.

The identity of the people had been suppressed but not eradicated. After all those years of indoctrination and repression, the people were demanding democracy right under the noses of Soviet soldiers. It was enough to break an old Bolshevik's heart.

Did Gorbachev intend to do it? It is said in Europe that Gorbachev personally approved Hungary's decision to open its border with Austria, personally requested the Polish Communist party's acceptance of Solidarity's entry into government, and personally engineered the resignation of Honecker and the changes of government in Czechoslovakia, Bulgaria, and Romania.

But we do not know these things for certain. We only know for certain that Gorbachev had put in place military commanders who did not fire into large crowds demanding freedom and that the removal of fear has revealed what we always thought was there—people who long to be themselves.

If They Ousted Gorbachev I
January 15, 1990

The liquidation of the Eastern European empire, the progressive restraints on the power of the Communist parties, and the revision of basic doctrines of Marxism-Leninism have aroused continuing concerns abroad about how long Mikhail Gorbachev's colleagues would permit him to continue the process of internal transformation of the Soviet state.

Uncertainty about Gorbachev's tenure has kept alive the question of how reversible are his reforms. This question of reversibility is dealt with in the next two selections.

Suppose Mikhail Gorbachev were brought down and replaced by Yegor Ligachev or some such man with the active backing of a KGB-military coalition. How many of Gorbachev's sweeping reforms could survive? For how long? And how many are irreversible?

Could a successor again close borders and restore a "dictatorship of the proletariat" in Eastern Europe? Could he send Czechoslovakia's Vaclav Havel back to jail and Lech Walesa back to the shipyards? Could he junk the new Hungarian Constitution, close the Brandenburg Gate, dig up Imre Nagy's body and rebury it? Could he make Hungary and Poland once again "people's republics"?

Not everything is reversible. Janos Kadar and Nicolae Ceausescu are dead. Erich Honecker is mortally ill with kidney cancer. But stand-ins could be found with the will to clamp down and the needed skills at repression to do the job.

The successor repressers would need to understand that an authentic, peaceful revolution had been under way for several years—that that revolution had already dramatically changed the vocabulary and composition of the ruling elite of the Communist world. An effective restoration would return to power a disciplined and ruthless Leninist elite, one not inhibited in the use of force, one that would govern without embarrassment in the name of the "dictatorship of the proletariat."

Imagine the arrival in power of such a tyrant. What would he do to restore totalitarian rule in the Soviet Union? It might go like this:

He quickly dismisses the new Congress of People's Deputies and Supreme Soviet and appoints a new Politburo, new editors at *Pravda* and *Izvestia* and other leading Soviet journals, and new directors for state radio and television.

He ruthlessly represses dissident and nationalist journals, cancels the publication of Solzhenitsyn, and terminates the Soviet tour of Mstislav Rostropovich and Washington's National Symphony. He outlaws factions, arrests leaders and editors who resist. The Party issues a long proclamation on doctrine that rejects critics and criticism and reminds the faithful that class conflict is inevitable and that the ultimate contest between capitalist and Socialist states is unavoidable. The proclamation denounces revisionism and revisionist doctrines concerning the role of the Party, sternly rejects bourgeois constraints on the Party, and reasserts its privileged and exclusive historical position.

This government arrests nationalist leaders as "counterrevolutionary agitators," restores censorship, jams foreign broadcasts, and strictly controls the importation and circulation of foreign publications. It reestablishes "proper" curriculums at universities, bans the teaching of Hebrew and other religious practices, and revokes visas for refuseniks.

It cancels joint economic ventures, confiscates Estee Lauder's Moscow store, outlaws cooperatives, and arrests any "profiteers" who had managed to accumulate gain. It formally expunges from the vocabularies of Marxism-Leninism the words "glasnost" and "perestroika" and informs the Communist parties of the world that these "unwords" should never be mentioned again.

At the request of the new leader, and under the personal attention of Fidel Castro, Cuba's representative to the UN Human Rights Commission—who also serves as its vice president—files complaints against the "excesses" and "abuses" of the previous government.

A new International Commission on Peace and Justice is established with the direct participation of Castro, Nicaragua's Daniel Ortega, North Korea's Kim Il Sung, Ethiopia's Mengistu, and Afghanistan's Najibullah. Its purpose is to intensify the global campaign against imperialism and find new ways to advance "peace through struggle."

To make amends, new announcements are issued on the grand monuments to be constructed to the fallen martyrs purged in the Gorbachev era—Ceausescu and Honecker are to be subjects of the largest. Leonid Brezhnev's bigger-than-life statue is restored to what is again called Brezhnev Square.

The new leader is helped in his effort to restore "order" in Eastern Europe by the fact that 700,000 Soviet troops are still in Eastern Europe as he takes charge. They move to arrest the leadership of the "revisionist counterrevolutionary governments" and restore reliable leadership recruited from the third or fourth echelons of the national secret police—personal protégés of Ceausescu, Honecker, and other reliable Bolsheviks. It does not take this new leadership long to restore the gun towers and guard dogs along the borders. The wall is mended overnight.

Western governments complain in the beginning. But almost everyone adapts. For some governments, there is a certain relief in having the question of German reunification retire from the European agenda and seeing the difficult issue of Eastern European membership in the European Community disappear.

NATO finds a lot to do in the new crisis, practicing for the thousandth time a coordinated response to a possible Soviet attack on Western Europe. American and Western European governments request large supplementary defense appropriations. Cuts in the SDI budget are restored. All this is needed because the Soviet Union's own military expenditures have quickly increased to a full 35 percent of its annual gross national product.

Everything, in sum, is back to normal—and a little more.

I don't think it will happen. But the fact that it could makes it enormously urgent to consolidate the changes and render them irreversible. Now.

If They Ousted Gorbachev II

February 1, 1990

Reforms could be reversed, repressive dictatorships could be reestablished, but whatever happens in Azerbaijan or Armenia, whatever is decided by the just-postponed meeting of the Central Committee of the Communist party of the Soviet Union, however long Mikhail Gorbachev remains in power, nothing will ever be quite the same in Eastern Europe or in Western Europe or in the Soviet Union.

Four major processes of change have seriously eroded the foundations of East-West relations in postwar West Europe: reform inside the Soviet Union, the democratization of Eastern Europe, the progressive integration of Western Europe, and the momentum toward reunification of Germany.

The length of Gorbachev's tenure is unpredictable, but at least some changes wrought under his leadership are already irreversible. A military dictatorship might reestablish tight control in the entire Soviet Union, but the Communist party's claim on power will not again be credible. The myth of Party legitimacy cannot be restored. Too many truths have been affirmed, too many lies exposed, and too many horrors acknowledged.

The myth of Soviet unity has been destroyed. Secessionist moves in the Baltic states and violence in Azerbaijan, Georgia, Armenia, and elsewhere have reminded the world and Soviet leaders that that country is an empire based on conquest and united by force.

The myth that the Soviet Union represents economic progress in the march of history cannot be restored. Economic failure is manifest to the whole world.

Liberalization and democratization in Eastern Europe are still less reversible. Political restructuring has proceeded with accelerating speed—pushed in most countries by new governments in which a majority of members are no longer under the control of Communist parties and by Communist parties that are themselves undergoing

85

rapid transformation. It would take a major war for the Soviet Union to reestablish former levels of control over Eastern European countries. And the Soviet Union is in no condition for such a war. Already these countries are indicating their desire to disengage from the Warsaw Pact and are expressing a longing for close connection with the democratic countries of Western Europe.

Inevitably, these dramatic changes have had a great impact on Western Europe, forcing the question of Germany to the top of the European agenda and driving the question of Eastern Europe into the carefully laid plans for the integration of the European Community. These changes offer undreamed-of opportunities for a unified Europe and unwelcome promises of a changed balance of power within the EC. But they cannot be deferred.

In Western Europe, the reunification of Germany is almost universally viewed as inevitable. Obviously, a unified Germany will have a major impact on the EC and NATO.

These fast-breaking, momentous changes shake to the foundations the structures through which international affairs have been conducted for the past forty years. An American administration with an avowed aversion to "big think" (as one administration official called it) will likely be confronted with the most sweeping reorientation of U.S. foreign policy since 1947. What should a U.S. government do in this unprecedented situation?

First, it should not be overly worried about instability. It should understand that instability is an essential precondition of an independent, self-governing, democratic Eastern Europe. Dismantling governments that have tried to control everything requires destabilizing those political structures.

Second, the United States should face the fact it does not and cannot control these events, and it does not need to try. The United States cannot control the Soviet future. Gorbachev's tenure will be decided by and within the Soviet government. The future of the Baltic people will be decided by Latvians, Lithuanians, and Estonians interacting with Russians. Germans will settle the future of Germany. A unifed, democratic Germany is no threat to the United States or to democracy in Europe. The Soviet Union has a powerful vested interest in preserving East Germany. The United States does not. The administration has already tilted too far in support of Gorbachev's position and away from that of West German Chancellor Helmut Kohl.

What the U.S. government can do is remain faithful to its own ideals. For forty years, the United States has refused to recognize the legitimacy of the Soviet claim to the Baltic states. There is no reason to change that position now.

Americans should not fear a reunified Germany, a shrunken Soviet Union, or a united Europe without a need for NATO. These have long been the goals of American foreign policy. Now, on the eve of their fulfillment, it is time to welcome change even when it rouses old fears and stirs new anxieties.

Bad News? What's Bad about It?

February 13, 1990

For years Communists have worked to make reality conform to the theories of Marx and Engels. When reality resisted this—when "kulaks" hid their grain and intellectuals published and distributed prohibited thoughts via samizdat and Ukrainians celebrated their banned liturgy in fields—the authorities redoubled their efforts to compel obedience.

But no longer. Gorbachev has addressed the contradictions between human nature, society, and Communist ideology, not by tailoring reality to fit a priori beliefs, but by modifying or rejecting the beliefs themselves. It is very good news indeed.

"It's hard to look at the Soviet Union over the past five years and be particularly sanguine about Gorbachev's future," a "senior official" of the Bush administration told *The Washington Post* on the eve of Secretary of State James Baker's departure for Europe. "It's almost all undiluted bad news."

Dismantling the world's longest-lived, most expansionist modern dictatorship—bad news? Ending religious persecution and diminishing censorship—bad news? Shelving the Brezhnev Doctrine and liquidating Europe's only empire—bad news? Permitting multiple parties, free elections, and independent policies in Eastern Europe—bad news? Ending the division of Europe, opening borders, tearing down the Berlin Wall—bad news? Halting the cold war—bad news?

Doubtless the "senior official" was thinking about economic disorganization, scarcity of goods, ethnic agitation, and instability in the Soviet Union—not about freedom and independence. Twentieth-century Americans often take these for granted. But of course the peoples of Eastern Europe and the Soviet Union do not.

They seize each new opportunity for self-expression. They press long-stifled demands and crowd into urban squares. The noisy chorus of calls for more democracy, for independence, for emigration do not signal failure. They testify that long-repressed peoples are no longer afraid.

Liberation, decolonization, and freedom are in themselves good, regardless of the associated problems. When Abraham Lincoln signed the Emancipation Proclamation, former slaves faced civil war, unemployment, and poverty, but few doubted that freedom was better than slavery.

In 1989 scarcity, inflation, and economic disorganization did not lead Poles, Czechs, Hungarians, East Germans, and other Eastern Europeans to look back with nostalgia on their previous condition of stable servitude.

I am certain the U.S. administration's "senior official" welcomes these changes. The president himself has expressed warm support for Gorbachev's reforms. Still, there is something skewed about the administration's response to the dramatic changes in Eastern Europe—as if it did not fully appreciate the importance of what has occurred. Key persons keep sounding as if they have confused stability with success.

Of course, there have been grounds for concern about Gorbachev's motives, and there are continuing grounds for concern about his vulnerability. But there is a time for caution and a time for celebration. Now is the time to celebrate the new freedom of Eastern Europe.

It is now fairly clear *what* has happened. Mikhail Gorbachev understood from within the Soviet government the need to transform the system of one-party dictatorship and to liquidate the world's last empire.

It is also clear *how* it happened. From the top of the system, Gorbachev adopted a policy of restraint in the use of force. As he recently told Lithuanians demanding independence, "We will follow the way of discussions. I myself have chosen this road. My destiny is linked to this choice." Gorbachev has also used the power of the general secretary of the Communist party to change the Party itself.

What is less clear is *why* it has happened. Joshua Muravchik offers the most plausible explanation yet of Gorbachev's own ideological evolution (in the March–April 1990 issue of *The American Enterprise*). The political scientist and policy analyst argues that Gorbachev's development is similar in important respects to that of other great Communist dissidents such as, for example, the Yugoslav Milovan Djilas.

On the basis of Gorbachev's writing and speeches, Muravchik makes a credible case that, like Djilas, Gorbachev began by noting significant discrepancies between Soviet reality and Marxist theory and moved step-by-step from criticizing and rejecting Stalinism and Brezhnevism to questioning and rejecting key elements of Leninism itself—including the doctrines of one-party dictatorship and democratic centralism.

I think Muravchik is right. His explanation fits the facts and removes the mysteries of how Gorbachev, who seemed a conventional Marxist-Leninist, has moved so far away from dictatorship and toward institutions and relations based on consent.

That he has maintained his position at the apex of the system while he reformed it reminds us that he is also a man of extraordinary political skill.

From the political point of view, it is a record of almost undiluted good news.

Decolonization: Opting Out
April 9, 1990

As force held the Soviets' Eastern European empire together, force holds the Soviet Union itself together. But economic and political reform requires freedom, and freedom offers opportunites to demand secession. Gorbachev faces insoluble contradictions.

Leaders of the Soviet Union have always understood the importance of the nationality question. On the very first day of its existence, the new Soviet government issued an official declaration. It was an affirmation of an absolute right of self-determination.

This conception of self-determination was promptly dropped in favor of a quite different doctrine reiterated by subsequent leaders that self-determination is "not an absolute" but must be subordinated to the class struggle and the interests of the Socialist camp.

As everyone understands, the self-determination question transcends the current showdown with Lithuania. All the nationalities are involved. According to the most recent census the Russians constitute 50.8 percent of the Soviet Union's total population. Many of the others have shown signs that—given a choice—they might well choose independence. Mikhail Gorbachev understands that in dealing with Lithuanians he is also dealing with Georgians, Ukrainians, Byelorussians, Uzbeks, Moldavians, Azerbaijanis, the Crimean Tartars, the Armenians, and various other nationalities who were incorporated by force and who ever since have been the intermittent object of great cruelty and cultural genocide.

The issue of secession will not only determine the size and shape of the Soviet Union but also determine the kind of country it can become.

"One thing is clear. Genuine democratization and the preservation of empire, however disguised, are incompatible," state the authors of a forthcoming book, *Soviet Disunion.*

I believe that Gorbachev desires to preserve the Soviet Union intact without using violence to do so. The history of the past four decades and the events of the past week indicate he probably cannot do so in the long run. But he can try.

The great show of force in Vilnius was clearly intended to send a message. But Gorbachev has said the message he wishes to send is not the same that Khrushchev sent to Budapest and Brezhnev sent to Prague. He is still insisting that secession is possible under the Soviet Constitution.

This crisis goes to the heart of Gorbachev's reform program. The great achievement of Mikhail Gorbachev has been that he kept the troops in their barracks while the people of Eastern Europe reorganized their governments and resumed control of their lives. He accepted the popular decisions and let go the Eastern European empire. Obviously he feels differently about the internal empire.

He does not desire to see the country he rules diminished by half. He desires that all voluntarily remain a part of the Soviet Union. He has been willing to admit past "mistakes" and past repression. He has offered assurances of change.

"We cannot continue in the old way," his close associate Alexander Yakovlev told the Latvians last winter and strongly implied that under the new plan the central government would control only foreign and defense policy and leave all else to the government of the constituent republics.

"We think it essential to ensure a democratic solution in line with the interests of both each individual ethnic group in the Soviet family and our Socialist society as a whole," Gorbachev declared.

But many of the nationality groups want no part of either the Soviet family or a Socialist society. They want out. Now the Soviet parliament has offered a five-year process leading to independence and including a referendum with a requirement for a two-thirds vote in favor of independence.

After a few days' show of Soviet force the government of Lithuania has said it is ready to negotiate, but not as part of the Soviet Union and not under the Soviet Constitution. Gorbachev has said there will be no negotiations until Lithuania revokes its declaration of independence and accepts the process leading to secession provided by Soviet constitutional law.

What are we to think of their situation?

First, we must note that with his show of force Gorbachev has demonstrated once again that while he prefers to govern by consent he will use force where consent is lacking. The Eastern Europeans were simply lucky.

Second, he has demonstrated willingness to honor the Soviet Constitution's provision for secession ignored by all his predecessors.

Third, while onerous, the proposed process for secession is not intrinsically unreasonable. What makes it seem so is the long years of brutal treatment and denial of identity that so many of the non-Russian people have endured. Two-thirds majorities are frequently required for constitutional revisions and amendments. So are waiting periods.

Fourth, we should be clear that the Soviet situation is not comparable to the U.S. Civil War (as some have suggested), because the Soviet Union's non-Russian peoples never petitioned to join the union and never decided to do so. It is also not analogous to Spain's situation with its Basque secessionists or to Puerto Rican *independistas,* because in those cases secessionists constitute a tiny minority of a large population that thinks otherwise.

Finally, we should remember that in politics hard questions are settled by power as well as by principle. The Soviets have the power. The deal the Soviet government has offered will probably turn out to be the only deal in town.

It is a way out. And it is a pathway available to all the "republics" of the USSR. With its passage, Gorbachev and the Soviet government have opened another Pandora's box.

The Costs of Empire

April 16, 1990

As Soviet officials became less interested in world revolution and global power, they became more interested in the costs of empire and less enthusiastic about paying the price.

The Soviet Union is not having a good year. The March economic report acknowledged that total production for the month was 1.5 to 1.7 percent less than the year before. Production of food, coal, and electric power had declined. So had output of textiles, footwear, and oil-drilling equipment. Meanwhile, the country was confronted with an unprecedented 600,000 refugees who desperately need basic necessities.

The pinch is causing Soviet economists to look for ways to economize. One obvious choice is trade relations with the Socialist bloc.

Western economists have long understood that empires are a political luxury that almost no one can afford. But Lenin and his disciples always believed that empires enrich the imperial power by impoverishing its colonies. Now at long last, Soviet economists have begun to examine and discuss the high cost to the Soviet Union of assisting Socialist countries on three continents.

An article in the March issue of a leading economic journal, *Ekonomika I Zhizn*, raises doubts about whether the "world Socialist economic system" is worth the price.

The whole question of Soviet aid to its associated states is obscured by secrecy and complexity, the authors warn. Part of the "aid" consists of the Soviet habit of paying inflated prices for goods readily available elsewhere: seven to nine times more for Cuban sugar, greatly swollen prices for Vietnamese cement. A second type of aid involves selling goods far below the market price, as Soviets sell oil to Cuba. A third form of hidden aid consists of providing services at virtually no cost, as when the Soviets commit 300 of their ships to transporting Cuban products, thus freeing Cuban ships for profitable engagements. A fourth form of aid is the provision of credit on fantastic terms, such as allowing Mongolia 200 years to reimburse funds for a poultry farm.

An article in *Argumenty I Fakty* (March 17–23) asserts that non-equivalent conditions of trade with Cuba currently cost the Soviet Union some $6–10 billion annually. The authors see no sign of lessening Cuban dependence, "not one sector of the economy fulfilled the plan quotas in 1989 (except for transport and sugar production). . . . The living standard of the population is declining. Unemployment has increased."

Soviet economists also note that their trade is disadvantageous not only with Socialist countries in the third world, but also with Poland, Czechoslovakia, and the German Democratic Republic, all of which profit from Soviet products delivered at discount prices. Under current practices the Soviet Union subsidizes the reorientation of the economies of Eastern Europe at a time it can ill afford to do so.

The answer to Soviet economic problems may lie in reordering its political relations as well as adopting a market approach to trade with other countries.

The solution, according to the authors cited above, is "to separate aid from commerce and trade from politics" and get fair prices for Soviet products. The fault is not with the debtors in the Soviet countries but with the bureaucracy that "sacrifices the interests of the country at home and abroad for the sake of high-sounding slogans."

Once the question, Who profits? is raised, it catches on.

Russians have begun to notice that as the Soviet Union is not getting a fair shake in the world Socialist system, Russia is not getting a fair shake in the Soviet Union. Russia contributes a disproportionate share of fuel, energy, minerals, timberland, and water resources to the Soviet Union, according to a recent report in *Sovetskaya Rossiya:* "Russia accounts for nearly two-thirds of the U.S.S.R.'s national product." But the Soviet economy is not geared to the needs of Russia's population. Russia "ranks last among the union republics in terms of the proportion of expenditures on social needs, and eighth in terms of housing provisions."

"Economic independence" is the preferred answer to the Soviet Union's trade imbalances with its Socialist dependencies and to Russia's problems inside the Soviet Union.

Why not? As the autonomous republics develop national identifications and demands, why should anyone expect that the Russians will not do so?

The Baltics are not the only republics who were independent nations. So was Russia. And a democratic national Russian movement has emerged in time tò win elections in Moscow and Leningrad.

This is very good news.

In the Soviet Union nationalism and democracy can go hand in hand. Both have been suppressed in the multinational internal empire. But Alexander Solzhenitsyn, Vladimir Bukovsky, and generations of Russian dissidents have rightly pointed out that Russian culture has been suppressed along with that of the Ukraine and all other nationalities.

Today virtually all the people of the USSR support democratic self-determination for themselves and for Eastern Europe.

The age of empire has passed for the Soviet Union as for Western Europe. The sacrifice of national interest to remote colonies no longer makes sense.

Does Action against Iraq Herald a New Age for the United Nations?

September 2, 1990

As the first international event of the post–cold war era, the Persian Gulf crisis reflected the dramatic reorientation of Soviet foreign policy. I found it interesting to reflect on what would have happened in the United Nations had this crisis occurred two years earlier.

A good deal has been written in the past week about how the United Nations has changed. The string of resolutions condemning Iraq's invasion and annexation of Kuwait, imposing sanctions and authorizing their enforcement, was evidence enough that the world organization does not work as it used to.

Also in the past week, although it received less attention, the permanent members of the UN Security Council reached a long-overdue agreement on a Cambodian settlement.

The consensus of the United Nations' five permanent members (the United States, the United Kingdom, China, the Soviet Union, and France) on these important issues demonstrates not only that the United Nations may prove more useful in the future but also that the world has changed and is changing with the continuing transformation of the Soviet government and its global role.

Suppose Iraq had invaded Kuwait two years ago—as Saddam Hussein undoubtedly wishes he had. The Security Council could not conceivably have passed a resolution condemning the invasion or calling for Iraq's withdrawal, much less imposing sanctions. In all likelihood, no resolution would even have been proposed, because members of the Security Council take a dim view of "idle gestures" that waste the body's time.

Had a resolution been proposed, the Soviet Union would have immediately associated itself with "the Kuwaiti revolution" that "fulfills age-old aspirations of two peoples wrested apart by colonial powers." (This was Iraq's own rationale.)

Iraq could have been 100 percent certain of the Soviet bloc's support inside the United Nations, and of support from the nonaligned movement, whose membership overlaps that of the Soviet bloc. Meanwhile, the Arab bloc would have been neutralized by internal division.

A long procession of speakers would have denounced the resolution as a machination of imperialist and Zionist powers and would have denounced Kuwait itself as little more than a corrupt remnant of the colonial era. Had it come to a vote, Iraq would have won a clear victory—with China and the Soviet Union, and Cuba, Yemen, and other members of the nonaligned bloc voting with Iraq, France abstaining, and the United States and perhaps the United Kingdom voting alone or nearly alone to condemn the invasion.

That is the way the United Nations worked for approximately two decades. That is why the Security Council took no action on Libya's invasion of Chad in the early 1980s and has to this day neither called for the withdrawal of Syrian troops from Lebanon nor condemned a PLO attack on Israel. It is also why human rights abuses in Communist countries (including Ethiopia and Pol Pot's Cambodia) were never cited until the mid-1980s, and then only with the most painstaking advance maneuvering.

Ideology provided the blocs with rationales to justify almost any action. One reason Iraq could not have been condemned for an act of aggression (as it was on August 2, 1990) was that aggression committed by the Soviet Union and its allies was defined not as aggression but as liberation. An invasion such as the Soviet invasion of Afghanistan was described as an act of fraternal international solidarity.

Doublespeak reigned.

Now that is past. The Soviet Union has abandoned that perverse vocabulary, so that last week, speaking of Iraq's action, Soviet Deputy Foreign Minister Aleksandr Belonogov could say: "It has been clear to us from the very beginning that Iraqi actions were an aggression pure and simple. This determines the Soviet attitude to developments."

Now, Soviet officials mean by aggression what we mean by aggression and what the UN Charter means by aggression. And they are against it. Now, when Soviet officials speak of the legitimate leaders of Kuwait, they do not mean Saddam Hussein. And when they denounce Kuwait's "puppet regime," they do mean the government installed by Iraq. Instead of defending Iraq as a treaty ally, Nikolay Shishlin, political adviser to the Soviet leadership, tells us that "Iraq broke its 1972 friendship treaty with the Soviet Union when it invaded Kuwait."

Soviet vocabulary has been transformed. Today, Shishlin tells us, "The people regard [the invasion of Afghanistan] as a crime and a criminal act." Gorbachev's closest adviser, Alexander Yakovlev, speaks of "a moral law" and the "transformation of the Soviet Union into a free society" (August 20, Moscow Television).

Now, for the first time since the founding of the United Nations, Soviet officials read the UN Charter as it was written to be read. And, after just a bit of equivocating, the Soviet Union joins in a series of unprecedented resolutions wholly consistent with that charter. China, which never likes to cast a sole veto, joins in. And a new permanent-member consensus is born.

Can this consensus become the basis for settlement of the Persian Gulf crisis? It has already defined the issues, imposed sanctions, and legitimized force in implementing them. It has provided a framework that leaves little room for the secretary general or anyone else to maneuver.

But can it force Saddam Hussein's withdrawal from Kuwait? That remains to be seen.

It is rumored around the United Nations that Secretary General Perez de Cuellar's mission to Jordan was greatly encouraged by the Soviets, who are eager for a settlement that will permit them to maintain a special relationship with Iraq. Perhaps. But they no longer base that relationship on a perverse redefinition of the UN Charter.

Apparently the age of doublespeak has passed. If that is indeed the case, we will finally see how useful the United Nations can be.

Approximately a week after I wrote the preceding column, it came to my attention that the analysis of a Soviet historian, Aleksey Vasilyev, had appeared in Pravda *on August 23, 1990:*

> *Red, green, and Palestinian flags are flying above Kuwait. Some 300,000 Palestinian immigrants were given citizenship of the Kuwaiti People's Democratic Republic and staged a joyous demonstration welcoming the creation of the Iraq-Kuwait federation. In Moscow, a mob protesting against U.S. imperialist intervention in the Persian Gulf, in direct proximity to the USSR's southern borders, tried to burn down the U.S. Embassy. The Soviet government stated it would not*

permit a blockade against friendly Iraq and sent a naval squadron to the Persian Gulf. The United States accused the USSR of trying to spread Communist dominion to the Gulf zone through its client—Iraq—and of suffocating the West by cutting off oil supplies in the Gulf. . . . Is the author off his head? the reader asks. No. He was just using the old Soviet propaganda cliches to create a scenario of events that could have happened only a few years ago but now seems the product of a sick imagination.

It is indeed a new era.

PART TWO

Summitry: Men and Arms

INTRODUCTION TO PART TWO

Summitry: Men and Arms

For four decades the expansionist policies of the Soviet Union drove the foreign policy of the United States and shaped the foreign relations among nations. The response to those policies made the United States a superpower. American statesmen—who had problems without solutions—devised "arms control" negotiations to deal with an intractable conflict rooted in the nature of the Soviet government.

The following essays make clear that I am not enthusiastic about summitry or arms control as major instruments of foreign policy. Each is fine in its place—which is subordinated to, not substituted for, enough strength and clarity to protect our interests and values.

There is nothing wrong with meetings between heads of states. They can be useful as a means of facilitating communication and avoiding unnecessary misunderstandings and static. But modern summits have become media extravaganzas that focus on personal and interpersonal aspects of world politics—as if heads of states were kings and everything depended on whether they (or their wives) "liked" or "trusted" each other. Exotic settings for meetings—such as fishing in Wyoming—further dramatize the personal, man-to-man dimensions of relations that are essentially institutional.

Relations are doubtless more pleasant if two heads of state "like" one another. But it is not very important. They do not meet as individuals seeking compatible company; they meet as representatives of governments.

Governments are, and should be, moved not by likes and dislikes of rulers, but by political mandates, constitutional principles, and collective interests. Heads of state or ministers who forget this and

101

act on the basis of personal affinities or enthusiasms or intuitions quickly—and properly—find themselves in trouble with their Congress or voters, their Politburo or Central Committee. The constraints under which a U.S. president and a Soviet first secretary must work are very different—but both are constraining. And they should be, because leaders are neither infallible nor permanent and their affinities are not affairs of state. The fact that Harry Truman "liked" old Joe Stalin did not deter Stalin from imposing Soviet control wherever he could nor Truman from responding with a plan to "contain" Soviet expansion. The fact that Winston Churchill and Charles de Gaulle did not "like" each other did not prevent France and Britain from becoming staunch postwar allies. Personal affinities matter only at the margins of modern international relations. It is idle at best to pretend that it really matters if George Bush and Mikhail Gorbachev or Jim Baker and Eduard Shevardnadze "hit it off."

The tendency to personalize relations invites gross and potentially dangerous misunderstanding. Inexperienced leaders are almost always surprised that their adversaries turn out to be intelligent, forceful, often charming people (otherwise they would not have succeeded in winning power) who love their children, enjoy hunting and fishing, art and history, and wear shoes. Then they are surprised to learn that none of this helps much in resolving concrete differences.

Marxist scholar Karl Wittfogel called the surprise of discovering the humanity of opponents the "you-wear-shoes, we-wear-shoes" effect. Adolf Hitler charmed many diplomats. Heinrich Himmler liked children and dogs. Hermann Goering was an art lover. Joseph Stalin impressed Harry Truman. Fidel Castro has beguiled many visiting Westerners.

There is a complex relationship between the personal characteristics of rulers and the policies of their governments. It is the policies of rulers that count in foreign affairs. And policies appropriately reflect the structure of governments and politics that take national interest into account. Our policies too should take these into account, not be guided by a president's personal affections.

Americans have a proclivity for conceiving international relations as a relation between persons—man-to-man, heart-to-heart—rather than in terms of politics and political institutions. This habit of personalizing foreign affairs is supplemented by another tendency to believe that what cannot be dealt with interpersonally can be settled by a contract.

Hans Morgenthau, George Kennan, and others have noted the American tendency to legalism in the conduct of foreign affairs. This manifests itself in our efforts to solve tenacious political problems by negotiating a legal agreement. We have attempted to outlaw war by contract, to guarantee human rights by contract, to eliminate categories of weapons by contract. The Covenant of the League of Nations was one elaborate contract written by Americans. The Charter of the United Nations is another of which Americans were the principal architects. Arms control agreements are the most common contemporary example of a contractual approach to international affairs. Experience indicates that such contracts achieve their goals only when they serve the interests and reflect the power relations of the signatories.

The most disturbing aspects of the arms control approach to international affairs are not the problems of verification—difficult as they are—but the absence of penalties for noncompliance. What is the penalty for Soviet cheating at Krasnoyarsk? It is the United States that pays the penalty.

There is no supranational referee to enforce international contracts and no supranational police to force compliance, and if there were one, it would be politicized by interested parties, as the United Nations has been. Contracts are not needed to prevent nonaggressive nations from engaging in aggression, and they do not bind aggressors. No arms agreement is needed to protect us from the nuclear missiles of France and Britain, and no arms agreement alone can be relied on to protect us from potential adversaries. No arms agreement has succeeded in containing or even slowing an arms race—although one has occasionally diverted weapons development into another track.

The point is clear and intractable: neither understanding among rulers nor contracts between governments eliminate power and its uses as a factor in relations among nations. We are stuck with power and politics and the permanent need to protect our interests and values. We cannot refashion relations among nations to fit utopian models. We can only operate more or less skillfully and successfully in the world as it is.

Getting Acquainted
November 4, 1985

There were intense interest and giddy expectations and much hyperbole in Ronald Reagan's first meeting with Mikhail Gorbachev—inside the government and outside it. Mike Deaver had cultivated the notion that Ronald Reagan could become "the peace president." Rumors were rife that Nancy Reagan ardently wanted a softer line inside the administration and that George Shultz was ascendant and Caspar Weinberger in eclipse.

The media, perceiving the summit as the greatest event of the decade, said the silliest things. Many commentators treated Reagan's meeting the Soviet leader as a breakthrough in and of itself. They forgot that Reagan had repeatedly proposed a meeting during the UN General Assemblies with whichever Soviet leader was in power but had been turned down by Soviet leaders too ill or too weak to travel.

It is almost summit time. Our national optimism is running at riptide. We Americans love negotiations. We expect they will end well. We believe in personal diplomacy, in interpersonal understanding, compromise, binding agreements, disarmament.

Ronald Reagan, a quintessential American, shares these tastes and proclivities. So do we all.

So, as the summit approaches, he and we want to believe that "meaningful progress" can be achieved, because we want it and because it is reasonable and right.

Maybe it will all work out. A new Soviet team and a new generation are in charge of the Kremlin. Generations sometimes differ in their goals and values. This one just might differ from its predecessors. The new leaders might be more interested in internal economic development than in external expansion, for example.

But if there is progress, it will be because the Soviet goals have changed, not because greater interpersonal understanding has been achieved. And we really ought to be clear about that.

Problems between the United States and the Soviets are not interpersonal problems. They were not caused by a falling out between Truman and Stalin, nor Kennedy and Khrushchev, nor Johnson and Kosygin, nor Nixon and Brezhnev. The Afghan invasion was not due to a quarrel between Carter and Brezhnev, and as hard as it may be for certain liberals to believe, the continuing difficulties of the past five years were no more caused by Ronald Reagan than by

François Mitterrand or Margaret Thatcher.

What is not caused by a misunderstanding between rulers cannot be cured by understanding, nor by personal affinity, nor by a diplomatic marriage counselor.

Problems between the Soviet Union and the United States were caused by a clash of goals—a clash between the desire of the United States and the West for a world of independent nations on the one hand and, on the other, the Soviet desire for a world organized on Leninist principles and subordinated to the USSR. The Baltic states, Poland, Czechoslovakia, and South Vietnam were not the victims of a misunderstanding that can be cleared up by frank talk. The suffering of Afghanistan is not psychological.

This is one of the reasons that no summit meeting between Soviet and American leaders has brought significant improvement in Soviet-U.S. relations—and a few seem to have sparked dangerous occurrences.

Nikita Khrushchev's poor impression of John Kennedy preceded and encouraged his construction of the Berlin Wall and the decision to install nuclear missiles in Cuba—each of which in turn provoked a head-on confrontation between the United States and Soviet governments. Successive American presidents have assured Soviet rulers that the United States has peaceful intentions, imagining perhaps that the Soviets built their military machine because they felt insecure and behaved aggressively because they felt threatened.

None of the postwar summits has resulted in an agreement that produced the desired results: neither Yalta, nor the Kennedy-Khrushchev agreement, nor the limited test ban treaty, nor the threshold test ban treaty, nor the biological and chemical weapons convention, nor the ABM Treaty, nor SALT II, nor the Helsinki Accords. These agreements failed to achieve their goals because they were violated by the Soviet Union—most recently by the deployment of SS-25s and the continuing denial of rights to dissidents.

Now Ronald Reagan and George Shultz will try their charm and skill where their predecessors have failed. They will assure Gorbachev of our peaceful intentions, and they will make concessions. It is not certain that they will fail.

What would it mean to succeed? When will we know? Signing an arms control agreement that provides real reductions in nuclear weapons would constitute a success, providing that the reductions actually took place and providing it was not bought at the price of permanent vulnerability. Securing Soviet agreement to promote regional peace as outlined by the president at the United Nations would constitute a major success and would deliver the peoples in question from war and conquest—providing it were implemented.

What would constitute failure? Why, obviously, an agreement that left the United States and the democracies less secure for the present or the future, or an agreement that is violated by the parties to it would constitute failure.

Perhaps it would be better if there were meetings, but no formal agreement. François Mitterrand lowered the risk and reduced the tension in his Paris meetings with Gorbachev by insisting there be no joint communique, but instead a shared press conference at which he and Gorbachev each commented on the conversations and answered questions.

Both leaders and both governments described the Gorbachev visit as successful. No formal commitments were made; no one's word and no one's integrity were on the line. The door was left open wide for future meetings. No wonder a good time was had by all.

Who Knows What Gorbachev Wants?

November 17, 1985

Americans knew little and hoped much about Gorbachev. There was a powerful national tendency to replace ignorance with fantasy and to attribute to the new Soviet leader the qualities and motives we wished he had. I regard wishful thinking as especially dangerous in world politics, and Americans as especially prone to it.

In fact, however, the wishful thinkers turned out to be more nearly right than I, even though there were no good grounds to think so during the first year of Gorbachev's tenure. Not only did it take us time to get acquainted, but also it took Gorbachev himself time to develop a new approach.

The idea of summit-level conversations between Ronald Reagan and Mikhail Gorbachev became a media event long before they were scheduled. "Will they?" "Won't they?" our commentators asked like anxious lovers. All this hype has been curious to observe.

I believe there are good reasons for an American president to meet and talk with a Soviet leader (or any other important head of state). Face-to-face meetings sometimes help to demystify relationships and to facilitate communication at high levels.

But there are also good reasons for not treating the upcoming meeting as an earth-shaking event. After all, every American president since World War II has met with his Soviet counterpart and nothing much came of these meetings. Why then the extraordinary excitement about this summit?

Our near obsession with the Reagan-Gorbachev conversations reflects, I think, a highly personalized and deeply flawed conception of international politics in which clashing civilizations and great states are seen to be embodied in two leaders—much as two men stand for the forces of law or lawlessness, good and evil, in traditional Western movies.

But the stars at summits must not shoot it out at high noon. They must instead, we all hope, sit down, talk it over, and settle their problems with new "understanding." The Great American Dream Machine is busy cranking out scenarios that make this outcome—resolution through understanding—seem plausible.

These scenarios feature an altogether likeable Gorbachev and his beautiful wife. Though the product of an impressive bureaucratic regime that stifles freedom and makes war, "our" Gorbachev knows there is a better way to live. Therefore, we are told, he "longs" for a return to détente. He is said to be "pro-European" and "pro-Japan" and "searching" for a way to improve Soviet relations with the United States.

Our Gorbachev "needs" to negotiate an end to the arms race because his priority is a better life for the Soviet people and development of the Soviet economy. "What Gorbachev wants to do at home requires that he freeze arms expenditures," a leading U.S. expert tells us. The expert does not tell us how he knows what Gorbachev wants or why, if his goals are domestic, Gorbachev is counting on freezing the arms race to achieve them—especially since strategic weapons are not nearly as expensive as conventional armies or the costs of empire.

Not only does our Gorbachev want to negotiate deep arms cuts but also many commentators suspect he probably would like to relax internal repression, release dissidents, and permit Jewish emigration but is "prevented" from doing so by his Politburo colleagues. Our Gorbachev has a special need to prove to those colleagues that he is as tough as they expect him to be.

Here we have come upon the all-purpose explanation.

Gorbachev's "need to prove he is tough" can explain anything. It can explain why, in spite of his presumed desire for improved relations, the Soviets surrounded the U.S. Embassy in Afghanistan and attempted to intimidate American personnel. It can explain why they drugged a Ukrainian sailor to prevent his defection. It can explain why they gave prominent media coverage to the allegations of a returned KGB double or triple agent. It can explain why they heavily censored the interview with Reagan that they had agreed to publish. It can explain why they stepped up military aid for Angola and Nicaragua and otherwise acted to strengthen the bonds of empire.

The fact, of course, is that we do not know and cannot know what Gorbachev "wants" and "needs." We do not know whether his personal position is vulnerable. We do not know whether or how his views of the world differ from those of Andrei Gromyko, who dominated Soviet foreign policy for so long. We do not know what he would do if he could, or could if he would.

We do know that the Soviet Union under Gorbachev has, thus far, proved tough and inflexible in international negotiations. In Paris, Gorbachev's chief proposals were found unacceptable by the French government. After proposing renewed fraternal relations with China, the Soviets refused to accommodate Chinese demands to reduce their forces on the Sino-Soviet border or to cease supporting the Vietnamese military occupation of Cambodia or to withdraw from Afghanistan.

So far under Gorbachev, the Soviets have cut no deals except with client states. The ties that bind Eastern Europe to the Soviet Union have been reinforced, and military assistance to third world clients has been increased.

Whoever Gorbachev is and whatever—in his heart of hearts—he wants, Reagan will be facing a Soviet leader who has so far made no move to ease repression at home or reliance on force abroad. He has not released Antoly Shcharansky or Andrei Sakharov or any other well-known dissident, nor permitted Jewish emigration, nor slowed the Soviet drive to conquer Afghanistan.

And while Gorbachev has made interesting proposals for intermediate arms cuts, these have been coupled with continuing deception concerning Soviet activity on antiballistic missile defense and intransigent demands that the United States not follow the lead of the Soviets in developing an ABM system.

Since Americans will find it difficult, if not downright impossible, to believe the Soviet Union has really produced a fourth repressive ruler in as many years, we will probably hear a lot in coming days about how basically uncomfortable Gorbachev is "proving" to his Politburo colleagues that he is as tough as they would like him to be. This will explain all the disappointments and leave the "real" Gorbachev untarnished by negative behavior or negative outcome—ready for another turn as a participant in a future dream.

Russian Power
January 5, 1986

Despite the dramatic changes in Soviet behavior, it remains true that the Soviet Union has more missiles and better elements of a missile defense system than the United States. And it remains true that the Soviets are outspending the United States on weapon research and development— right now.

The most important development in international relations in 1985 (as in the forty years since World War II) was the growing vulnerability of the United States. For the first time in American history an adversary has the ability to destroy our country—and us—in a matter of minutes. The Soviet advantage in nuclear missiles is real and still growing. Our capacity for deterrence is minimal and still declining.

American vulnerability is so new and so inconsistent with our history and our expectations that we find it nearly impossible to believe, to remember, or to cope with.

The facts concerning the military balance of power are clear. For two decades the United States and the West have watched as the Soviet Union's relentless arms buildup progressively transformed what they called the "correlation of forces." Twenty years ago we— the United States and the West—were stronger. Today the Soviets have more missiles, a better missile defense, and more conventional forces than we.

To overcome Western advantages in technology, plants, and capital, Soviet leaders borrowed, traded, spied, stole, and built the needed facilities. To slow Western advance, they negotiated arms control agreements. To evade the prohibitions of those agreements, they developed new mobile missiles and new means to avoid verification measures. All the while they built and deployed new and better weapons—often in clear violation of arms control agreements.

What difference does it make? What is strategic superiority good for in a world where both the United States and the USSR possess the power to destroy each other? That is the question with which Americans and the West have dismissed the growing Soviet military strength.

The answer is that growing Soviet power matters when it becomes overwhelming. The growth of Soviet military power matters when the Soviets have enough missiles of enough accuracy to knock out our missiles. It matters when they can ensure our destruction and we can neither destroy their missiles nor protect ourselves.

The theory of mutually assured destruction (MAD), on which we have relied to maintain nuclear peace, requires that both parties be able to destroy each other and that neither be able to defend itself. That is, it requires rough parity of offensive and defensive capabilities. But now the Soviet advantage in missiles threatens our retaliatory capacity, and their phased array radars put them well ahead in antiballistic missile defense.

The United States and Europe are already vulnerable to attack by the Soviet Union. How much more vulnerable do we dare to become to a power that daily demonstrates its will and skill in the use of deadly force?

In Afghanistan we can observe the Soviets' will to power over non-Soviet people. In Afghanistan we can observe the use of brute force to conquer a people who pose no threat whatever to Soviet security.

From the tragedy of Afghanistan the United States and the West can learn terrible lessons about Soviet attitudes toward the use of force. These attitudes of Soviet leaders can be observed each day in the behavior of more than 100,000 troops who bomb, gas, burn, and shoot Afghan civilians and *mujahedin*.

From Afghanistan we can learn about Soviet attitudes toward war. The war against the Afghan people has lasted for six years. It has been conducted by four Soviet leaders—Brezhnev, Andropov, Chernenko, and Gorbachev. The end of that terrible war is not in sight. But Afghanistan is not the Soviets' Vietnam as some wishful Westerners suggest. There is no pressure in the Soviet Union to end that war because Soviet citizens have no means to bring pressure to bear on their government.

From Afghanistan we can learn the fate of countries vulnerable to superior Soviet force. And we can learn about their terms for peace. Mikhail Gorbachev has indicated to the UN representatives the nature of an acceptable "political solution" to the problem of Afghanistan. All that is required is a "guarantee" by the United States that there will be no resistance to a Communist government of the Soviets' choice.

Surrender or be destroyed: those are the alternatives offered to people unable to defend themselves in Afghanistan, Nicaragua, Angola, Ethiopia, Mozambique, Cambodia, and elsewhere where superior Soviet force confronts a targeted people. Could it happen here? Dare we run the risk?

Some progress has been made in restoring American strength, but each year the Soviet advantage increases. Now we know and the

Soviet Union knows that the Strategic Defense Initiative (or Star Wars) offers the opportunity to reverse these deadly trends; 1986 can be the year that America is delivered from the threat of nuclear checkmate.

So, happy New Year.

High Hopes and Hard Experiences—SALT II

April 6, 1986

First, you settle on a bottom line. Then you make further concessions to achieve an agreement. Finally, you accept terms of agreement that give a little more than anyone regarded as prudent. Then you discover they have violated some provision previously regarded as essential. What do you do?

If you swallow the violation, you accept terms you rejected throughout the negotiation. If you scrap the agreement, you are accused of throwing out the baby with the bath water. It is called a double bind. I believe all arms treaties should contain clear provisions on the consequences of noncompliance.

Once upon a time—when he was a candidate rather than a president—Ronald Reagan found it easy to reach conclusions about the SALT II Treaty. Candidate Reagan pronounced it "fatally flawed" and "unequal," incapable of restraining the growth of Soviet strategic capabilities.

But, like most Americans, Ronald Reagan longs to slow the arms race with the Soviet Union—if he cannot end it entirely. Therefore, desiring to maintain a good climate and believing that some limits are better than none, President Reagan decided that the U.S. government should honor the SALT II Treaty on an interim basis while he tried to negotiate something better.

Five years later there is nothing better on the horizon, the evidence of treaty violations by the Soviets has accumulated, and the cost of "interim restraint" is rising sharply.

Now the president faces a treaty deadline and must make a crucial decision. To continue in compliance with SALT II limits, the United States must dismantle two Poseidon submarines when the new Trident submarine begins sea trials on May 20.

The president must decide what to do about the Poseidons and,

111

more broadly, what to do about the SALT II agreement. Since the agreement, negotiated by the Carter administration, was never ratified by the Senate, compliance is a matter of executive policy—not of law.

It is up to Ronald Reagan. He and his principal advisers are currently deliberating the pros and cons of continuing compliance, abandoning the treaty, or possibly setting a course that would systematically link U.S. and Soviet compliance, thus taking account of Soviet violations.

Those who advocate continued compliance emphasize the military disadvantages to the United States of abandoning the agreement. The chairman of the House Armed Services Committee, Les Aspin, has emphasized that ending the present restraints on production of new weapons systems would give the Soviets an advantage because they have greater capacity than the United States to produce strategic weapons systems and missiles with larger payloads.

Opponents of continued compliance counter that the United States pays too high a price for these limited and uncertain constraints. Abiding by SALT II, they say, will inhibit modernization of U.S. military forces (including Midgetman testing and development), prevent the United States from retaining needed weapons systems, raise American defense costs in this year of Gramm-Rudman, and diminish our already reduced margin of security.

Both sides acknowledge that the political consequences of a decision on SALT II are at least as important as its military effects. Supporters worry that U.S. failure to comply would damage prospects for future arms control negotiations and offend our allies—who are enthusiastic about all U.S.-Soviet arms agreements that will not affect British and French arms or decouple American and European defense.

Even the supporters of SALT II agree that some account must be taken of Soviet violations. Certainly, the president is not free to ignore them. His report to Congress on Soviet noncompliance with arms control agreements (December 1985) described deployment of the SS-25 missile as a "clear and irreversible violation" and noted that the Soviet policy of deliberate concealment was contrary to both the letter and the spirit of SALT II.

The latest Department of Defense report, "Soviet Military Power," cites several additional SALT violations and makes it clear they are part of a broader pattern of selective Soviet noncompliance with existing arms control agreements.

So far, the United States has charged the Soviets with important violations of SALT I and II, the ABM Treaty, the Threshold Test Ban

Treaty, the Biological and Toxin Weapons Convention, and the Geneva Protocol.

Because the Reagan administration has chosen to make Soviet violations a matter of public record, the decision on SALT II must be made in the light of that record.

Will Ronald Reagan commit the United States to compliance with an agreement the Soviets violate? Or will he decide that Soviet noncompliance has effectively—if informally—already vitiated the agreement?

Reaffirming the SALT II Treaty in the face of violations would send a clear signal that the United States is ready to settle for less than we say we will. Such a message is hardly conducive to negotiating new meaningful, verifiable arms control agreements.

What would be the domestic political fallout of renouncing U.S. compliance with a flawed treaty that the Soviets are violating? Polls conducted in the last six months indicate that a majority of Americans want our government to negotiate arms control agreements but do not believe we should honor agreements that are being violated by the Soviet Union.

The president's realism and common sense should lead him to the same conclusion.

Soviet Provocations

September 22, 1986

Remembering Nicholas Daniloff is a useful reminder of how harsh Soviet policies were as recently as the winter of 1986, how much Ronald Reagan was willing to swallow, and also how much U.S.-Soviet relations have improved.

By all indications, Ronald Reagan is facing his toughest confrontation ever with the Soviet Union at the same time that preparations for the long-sought summit have reached a critical stage. If *New York Times* reporter Leslie Gelb is right, Reagan is in real trouble. "For the first time in his White House years," Gelb writes, "Mr. Reagan is almost totally dependent on Moscow to get him off the hook." One hopes the president's future does not depend on Gorbachev's help, as Gelb thinks, for evidence accumulates that Soviet leaders are adopting an unusually unyielding stance in their dealings with the United States.

First came the Soviet cancellation of the Shultz-Shevardnadze meeting after the United States bombed Libya. Then came the wheat deal that wasn't, even after U.S. subsidies were offered and increased. Next came the arrest of Nicholas Daniloff. There was also a quiet announcement from the Soviet Union's ambassador to the United Nations that his country did not intend to reduce the size of its UN mission, as ordered by the U.S. government. All this occurs in a context of continuing Soviet arms control violations and arms shipments to Nicaragua, Angola, Afghanistan, and elsewhere. Soft Soviet words accompanying these hard actions have made it easier not to notice the pattern that has developed.

Thus, from Moscow, Soviet Foreign Ministry spokesman Gennadi Gerasimov has assured us, "The Soviet Union does not want this trivial and secondary incident to interfere with the development of relations between the United States and the Soviet Union."

The "trivial" incident was, of course, the arrest of Daniloff on spy charges. During the same news conference, Gerasimov noted his agreement with the U.S. government that the cases of Daniloff and Gennadi Zakharov are "completely different": Daniloff is a Moscow-based CIA agent, he said, while Soviet scientist Zakharov, charged with spying by the United States, was "framed" by the Americans and is the victim of "an act of provocation."

Are the Soviets kidding—accusing the United States of *precisely* what we charged them with? No, they are dead serious. In fact, it is not unusual for Soviet spokesmen to charge others with exactly the offense of which they are guilty. It happens often in the United Nations where, for example, the United States is regularly charged with interfering in the internal affairs of Afghanistan, while 120,000 Soviet occupation troops ravage that land.

But before we forget entirely who did what to whom in the matters of Daniloff and Zakharov, we should be clear about what it is the Soviets are asking of us. They are not only violating the rights of an American citizen, denying American journalists the right to seek and print information about the Soviet system, and lying about it but also are demanding that we give Soviet spies immunity from prosecution under American laws. They are saying, "If you seek to submit our spies to your laws, we will indict and imprison (or execute) an American in our jurisdiction." When they try to put their agents outside our laws, they seek to deny us the right of protecting ourselves against Soviet espionage. In the course of commenting on Daniloff ("We really do hope this is a temporary phase," the Soviets said), the chief Soviet delegate to the United Nations, Alexander M.

Belonogov, posed a new challenge, stating that his country considers the U.S. government's order to reduce the size of its UN mission by October 1, 1986, "as absolutely illegal and running contrary to the agreement between the U.N. and the U.S. government when our organization was established." He added, "We still think that there is time for the U.S. government to change its mind."

The order to which Belonogov referred was issued in March. It called on the Soviet Union to reduce its staff at its UN mission from 243 to 170 by April 1, 1988 (with parallel reductions in the staffs of the missions of the Ukraine and Byelorussia, which are treated as independent member states at the United Nations). When Belonogov made it clear that the Soviet Union was making no plans to carry out the first phase of these reductions, our government responded by designating 25 persons in the Soviet mission who should leave the country first.

It is well known that the Soviet mission to the United Nations houses a number of KGB agents, as does the UN Secretariat. Although the Soviet representative pretends the United States has no right, as host country, to limit the number of employees in its UN mission, the U.S. government insists that the host-country agreement gives us the right to protect our national security and to demand that all nations have missions of "reasonable" size. (The total Soviet "diplomatic" corps at the United Nations is far larger than that of any other country—some 275 as compared with approximately 130 Americans, for example.)

There are two categories of Soviet employees at the United Nations: the 275 attached to the Soviet, Byelorussian, and Ukrainian diplomatic missions and the approximately 600 Soviets employed by the UN Secretariat. The former enjoy diplomatic immunity. The latter do not. Most KGB agents are attached to the diplomatic mission for just that reason. The Zakharov case is the most recent illustration of how the Soviet Union uses its nationals in the UN Secretariat to recruit agents and carry out industrial and military espionage in clear violation of the UN Charter.

Not all Soviet employees in the UN Secretariat engage in espionage, of course. But according to former Under Secretary General Arkady N. Shevchenko, the highest-ranking Soviet official of the United Nations before his defection, and to our own observations, most Soviets who work in the Secretariat report to the KGB, and all Soviet UN officials are expected to do work for the Soviet mission.

The Soviet government exercises tight discipline over its nationals who work in the Secretariat. They are required to live in a Soviet housing complex, their passports are retained by their government, and they must attend regular political meetings. Moreover, the Soviet government pays Soviet employees in the Secretariat and pockets the difference between that and their UN pay—a practice that nets the USSR something over $20 million per year in hard currency.

The Soviet government maintains this tight discipline in the Secretariat by the skillful use of a practice called "secondment." Where most citizens of other countries work directly for the UN Secretariat as international civil servants, 100 percent of Soviets remain the employees of their own government, lent or "seconded" to the Secretariat on the basis of "fixed term" contracts, which are revocable by Moscow.

The United States has made several new efforts recently to defend itself from these Soviet practices. It has adopted the Roth Amendment, which applies to Soviets in the UN Secretariat the same travel restrictions that are imposed on Soviet diplomats, and the Sundquist Amendment, which requires the United States to withhold its share of the salaries of UN employees whose governments require a "kickback." The Sundquist Amendment ensures that we will not help pay the salaries of Soviets who spy against us.

The Soviet Union finds all these efforts of self-defense objectionable. Perhaps for that reason they are raising the price of a summit meeting. Or perhaps they are merely trying to teach us what dealing with them will be like in an era of Soviet military supremacy.

Gorbachev at Reykjavik—The High Roller in the Haunted House

October 19, 1986

Mikhail Gorbachev proved at Reykjavik that he is a cool, high-stakes poker player who can make serious mistakes. His miscalculations are most likely to flow from overconfidence.

Neither Gorbachev nor such counselors as Georgi Arbatov and Alexander Yakovlev hid their contempt for Ronald Reagan. They noticed his weakness, but they had not noticed that Ronald Reagan was almost always underestimated by his opponents—right down to the time they were definitively defeated.

At Reykjavik, Gorbachev overplayed his hand. Reagan demonstrated that while his desire to eliminate nuclear weapons, which had protected Europe for decades, was real and deeply serious, he would not sacrifice security in pursuit of it.

Even though it solved no problems, the summit that was not a summit answered some important questions.

The supreme seriousness that Soviet, as well as American, leaders attached to the Strategic Defense Initiative (SDI) should settle any lingering doubts about its feasibility. Media pundits may continue to describe SDI as "a defense that may never work," but at Reykjavik, Mikhail Gorbachev made it clear to the world that he and his Soviet colleagues think otherwise. They believe it will work—and they care terribly about stopping its development by the United States.

Reykjavik should also have satisfied any residual uncertainties about Ronald Reagan's interest in achieving arms control agreements. In Iceland, the president proposed deep cuts in strategic and intermediate missiles, and a ten-year delay in deploying a missile defense system. Dramatic agreements on intermediate and strategic weapons apparently would have been announced on the spot had Gorbachev not surprised the assembled company by making all agreements contingent on U.S. abandonment of its proposed missile defense. It was Gorbachev's "all or nothing," "take it or leave it" stance—not Reagan's reported inflexibility—that prevented the completion of multiple agreements.

Events at Reykjavik also demonstrated that the conservatives' fear that Reagan would "give away the store" was as misplaced as liberal concern that he would be unwilling to give away anything. Reagan's conservative core constituency is chronically worried about the influence of George Shultz, Nancy Reagan, Mike Deaver, et al. and concerned about the implications of the president's hunger to enter history as a peacemaker. The Daniloff deal heightened their anxiety. But even under the pressure of coming elections, this president, who is regularly underestimated by friends and foes, proved quite capable of negotiating with flexibility and also of walking away from a deal he judged damaging to national security.

For each question the Reykjavik meeting answered, however, it raised others.

Why did the Soviets want this meeting? Why, in a clear break with past understandings, did Gorbachev link all agreements to SDI? Is preventing U.S. development and deployment of a missile defense the Soviets' only interest in arms control? It may be. In that first grim communication, a dismal-looking George Shultz said: "As we came more and more to the final stages, it became more and more clear

117

that the Soviet Union's objective was effectively to kill off the SDI program."

Are reductions in strategic and intermediate-range missiles simply lures to persuade Reagan to forgo a missile defense? We should know soon. If the Soviets are interested in missile reductions, they will leave their proposals on the table.

"Why," as the president asked, "is the Soviet Union so adamant that America remain forever vulnerable to Soviet rocket attack?" We know why Ronald Reagan seeks to defend the United States against incoming missiles. He is made profoundly uncomfortable by our vulnerability to attack and destruction and has no confidence in a purely offensive strategy.

Why do the Soviets want so badly to stop U.S. development of missile defense? There are really only two possibilities. Either they think it would give us an advantage or that it will deprive them of one. But of what advantage, as the president keeps asking, would an American missile defense deprive the Soviet Union? Only of the opportunity to engage in nuclear blackmail.

Here we come to the most difficult question of all. Why do the Soviets want nuclear superiority? How would they use it?

As we consider these questions and Soviet behavior at Reykjavik, it is useful to recall that in recent years Soviet leaders have made great efforts to dissuade and intimidate NATO countries from enhancing their capacity for self-defense. Their efforts were evident in their campaigns against the neutron bomb, the deployment of Pershing and cruise missiles, the funding for Nicaraguan contras, and now SDI. In each case, a Western effort at self-defense has been treated as an obstacle to constructive East-West relations.

What will be the consequences of the stalemate at Reykjavik? Will our allies judge Ronald Reagan harshly for the failure to reach a settlement? In the end, our allies must make their own decisions about the level of risk to their independence and freedom they are willing to take. And we must make ours.

At Reykjavik, Reagan declined to trust our future to the good faith of a nation that occupies Afghanistan, denies self-determination to Eastern Europe, and deprives its own citizens of basic rights.

Will the American people judge President Reagan harshly because he refused to sign an agreement that would render us "forever vulnerable"? Of course not.

Will the stalemate at Reykjavik stymie prospects for arms control agreements for the rest of Ronald Reagan's term? Soviet behavior this week at the Geneva arms talks and in Moscow would suggest otherwise. It is more likely that future negotiations may actually benefit from this mutual testing of limits.

Unseemly Seductions I

April 20, 1987

How carefully the Soviets seduced Marine guards and penetrated the U.S. Embassy in Moscow! How bold and unapologetic the Soviet spokesmen were about the whole affair! How careless the State Department and Marines were of U.S. security there, permitting penetration of the new U.S. Embassy as well!

It is not yet clear when the trials of Marine Sgt. Clayton Lonetree and Cpl. Arnold Bracy will begin, or whether one of them will be offered immunity in exchange for testimony, or how many people will eventually be implicated in the still-spreading embassy scandal.

Investigation continues of the Marine guards in Moscow and into lax State Department attitudes and practices. Recriminations are still spreading. "The Marines have been difficult all the time," said Arthur Hartman, who served as U.S. ambassador to Moscow during the alleged espionage. Unnamed Marine spokesmen are complaining of indifferent, incompetent State Department management. And Soviet spokesmen invite us to laugh it all off. "I thought the fear was of reds *under* every bed," said Soviet Foreign Ministry spokesman Gennadi Gerasimov.

Meanwhile, investigative reporters of our adversarial media seem less interested than they might be in these problems, despite the presence of all the ingredients of a big-time scandal—national security, sex, spies, bureacratic bungling and far more money than in the Iran-contra case. So far, the Moscow scandals lack the *political* sex appeal required to keep an issue in the media's focus for long.

Before the whole multilayered affair is swept off the news pages, it is useful to reflect on who is responsible for this colossal failure of security and loyalty in Moscow and possibly elsewhere.

My answer to "Who's to blame?" includes the following:

First, the Marine Corps is to blame for sending young men of doubtful strength of character to Moscow and failing to provide adequate supervision and discipline.

Doubtless, the temptations in Moscow are extraordinary, the women beautiful, the entrapment exquisitely planned and executed, the State Department jealous of its rights. Still, the Marine Corps should obviously have been more discerning and more vigilant. Who can doubt it?

Second, the Department of State—including the former ambassador, his deputy, the chief of security, and various intervening layers of diplomatic officers—is to blame for claiming the right to manage security in embassies and failing to fulfill the attendant obligations. The State Department claims control of these matters on the grounds that its officers best understand foreign environments and the requirements of functioning in them. Presumably, this includes a reasonably accurate assessment of the kind and amount of resources the KGB devotes to infiltrating U.S. embassies.

The Marine case is only the most recent and dramatic evidence of the State Department's inadequate concern with providing minimum security for U.S. operations in Moscow (and various other posts). Employing Soviet nationals, including known KGB agents, inside the embassy is another example of the State Department's pattern of unconcern with security. Accepting a major Soviet role in constructing the new U.S. Embassy in Moscow is yet another indicator of passive attitudes toward Soviet penetration. The low-key reaction to Soviet bugging of U.S. typewriters in the Moscow embassy is yet another example—one which contrasts sharply with the French response.

As Marine commanders clearly underestimated the importance of discipline and discreet behavior by Marine guards on and off duty, State Department officers have come too easily to tolerate widespread Soviet and Soviet-bloc spying as an inevitable fact of life in international affairs. This is why scores of known Soviet and Soviet-bloc spies have been tolerated in and around the United Nations in New York. It is why State resisted imposing travel restrictions on Soviet and Soviet-bloc diplomatic personnel associated with the United Nations.

Third, we the people—and our schools—must share the blame for young Americans whose education did not give them a full understanding of the value of democratic institutions, the obligations of democratic citizenship, and the vast moral difference between free and unfree societies. The same issue of *The Washington Post* that featured Marine spying reported a "consensus" of school superintendents meeting in the nation's capital on the need for greater stress on democratic values and civic education. "The consensus is that schools should impart civic virtue and take clear positions on right and wrong behavior and personal morality," said California Superintendent of Schools William Honig. "We have not done a good job in the last 15 years in teaching values."

The fact that everyone shares in the blame for eroding standards of loyalty, however, does not mean we are all equally at fault.

The responsibility for admitting KGB agents into secure areas of the U.S. Embassy lies finally with those who did just that. Inadequate discipline, supervision, and vigilance constitute one kind of failing. They neither excuse nor explain the betrayal of one's country to a potential adversary.

Socializing or fraternizing with Soviet women is one kind of infraction—more dangerous perhaps than is readily understood. But giving KGB agents access to American communications and codes is quite another.

It is terribly important that we not join Soviet spokesmen who invite us to laugh off betrayal. Conspiring to betray one's country and collaborating with its most powerful, most dangerous potential adversary is not to be dismissed as one more proof that boys will be boys.

Unseemly Seductions II
April 13, 1987

It still shocks me to remember that George Shultz was willing to pursue arms talks in Moscow when the United States was without a building in which secure discussions could take place.

Shultz is a man with a strong sense of dignity. Yet he was willing to set up in Moscow in a Winnebago—because all U.S. quarters had been bugged. There must have been some other way to communicate to the Soviet government that the Reagan administration was really deeply interested in improving relations.

I always thought it was a mistake to make progress on arms talks the centerpiece, touchstone, and yardstick of improving relations.

It is bad enough to have members of Congress writing each other notes on a magic slate. It is surrealistic that the U.S. secretary of state should travel to Moscow on schedule, in the wake of a major espionage scandal, and operate from a Winnebago while pursuing critical discussions on major arms reductions.

Governments are sometimes reluctant to make instances of espionage public because they believe that once spying is revealed, it will be necessary to react to it—and the timing may not be convenient. George Shultz suffers from no such compunctions. The whole world knows the Soviet government has seduced our soldiers and bugged our quarters, our typewriters, our scramblers, our bubble, and our new embassy. The world knows that Soviet negotiators out-negotiated their U.S. counterparts about where our respective embassies should be located, how they should be constructed, and by whom.

Let me be clear. I support U.S.-Soviet discussions on intermediate-range nuclear missiles in Europe, and I see no objection to the United States and the Soviet Union removing their missiles from Europe, providing the deal does not jeopardize our allies' security and can be verified.

But it seems to me extraordinary that the United States should be—and should appear to be—so eager for discussions that we are ready to accept any site and any circumstances.

It was bad enough when we accepted Reykjavik in the wake of Nicholas Daniloff's framing. We have already delinked arms talks from the continuing Soviet invasion of Afghanistan. We have delinked arms talks from Soviet emigration policy and human rights practices. Neither delinking was unreasonable, since mutually verifiable arms reductions are a good in themselves.

Is it reasonable, however, to undertake critical talks at this time in a place where it has just been demonstrated that we are subject to total surveillance? Is it appropriate to accept for our representatives the lack of privacy imposed on subjects in a totalitarian state? How can the State Department even seem serious about security if our top officials so quickly accept and adapt to these conditions?

Arms control agreements do not require a high level of mutual trust, since meticulous verification procedures should be built into the agreements. But they require a common goal, a degree of mutual commitment to the terms of the agreement, and a disposition to deal fairly. It is very important that we make it clear—at this time and under this provocation—that we do not accept cheating as a normal part of the process of dealing with one another on this important matter and that decent quarters are a requirement for the discussion of serious issues.

We should insist on moving the talks to some neutral site, where our officials could speak to one another without eavesdropping. Soviet leaders will agree to such a request if they are interested in pursuing the talks. (If they are not, we will not get an acceptable agreement in any case.) Surely, we could not accept as a precondition for the talks that they be conducted from our "captured" embassy in Moscow.

Unfortunately, the Soviet penetration of the U.S. Embassy in Moscow is not an isolated case. The expulsion of Soviet agents from France has taken place simultaneously with the revelations concerning U.S. Marine guards. Both events follow the expulsion last year of identified KGB agents at the Soviet UN mission in New York. *The Wall Street Journal* reminded us that the most recent episode is part of a persistent pattern of Soviet efforts to penetrate the U.S. Embassy in Moscow and a persistent pattern of inadequate American responses.

Now that the current Moscow scandal has again raised the issue, we should also consider some other very strange and unequal agreements and practices tolerated in the name of diplomatic immunity.

It is true, as the Democratic senator from Vermont, Patrick Leahy, noted last week, "Their embassy is sitting on Mt. Alto here in Washington and has antennas going to the Pentagon, the White House, the Treasury, the CIA and everything else. Our new embassy is in a swamp. It is surrounded by buildings controlled by the KGB." In Washington, the Soviets occupy many times the space allotted to the United States in Moscow.

But even worse is the fact that the new Soviet embassy in Washington is only one of a number of Eastern bloc embassies and consuls in this country whose "diplomatic" activities include systematic electronic spying. Neither diplomatic privileges nor the traditions of an open society require tolerating institutionalized espionage. The president's announcement that Soviet officials will not be permitted to move into their new Washington embassy "until a simultaneous move by both countries is possible" helps, but it doesn't help enough.

Thirty years have passed since George Kennan suggested we might "reasonably and justly" look forward to a Soviet government that would be "reasonable, tolerant, communicative and forthright in its relations with other states and peoples." This is what we all hope Mikhail Gorbachev and the new generation of Soviet leaders will be. But accepting ignominious conditions for negotiations neither encourages the development of more forthright Soviet behavior nor accords with our national dignity and interests.

An Arms Deal We Should Refuse
May 3, 1987

To repeat, I think the Americans in both parties were too eager to conclude an arms agreement with the Soviets during the second Reagan administration.

The INF Treaty eliminated Soviet vulnerability from Western Europe. It did not eliminate Western Europe's vulnerability from the Soviets' great standing armies. NATO has no such equivalent attack force, no offensive doctrine or training.

It eliminated the only genuine deterrent against a Soviet attack on Western Europe, short of full-scale global nuclear war. And it was negotiated without adequate advance consultation with any NATO allies.

"What goes around, comes around"—now it is Richard Nixon's and Henry Kissinger's turn to worry about whether Ronald Reagan is too eager to strike a deal with the Soviet Union and Reagan's turn to be suspected of seeking détente at any price.

It is not clear why Americans are so extraordinarily attracted to arms control agreements. Past agreements have neither slowed the development and deployment of increasingly destructive weapons, nor reduced military budgets, nor ushered in an era of good feeling, nor made the world safer for anyone. Nonetheless, the conviction persists that signing an arms agreement is tantamount to taking a giant step toward peace.

It is a step that Reagan—like his predecessors—very much wants to take. That, presumably, is the reason he has permitted arms control negotiations to become the focus of his foreign policy.

Better than almost anyone, Nixon understands how this could happen. Nixon, after all, knows firsthand how much more appealing it is to be admired as a peacemaker than reviled as a cold warrior. And what he knows worries him.

So he and his former secretary of state, fearing that Reagan is about to conclude a dangerous deal with the Soviet Union, wrote an open letter to the president to explain the dangers to us all (see *The Washington Post*, April 26, 1987).

"Every president has an understandable desire to assure his place in history as a peacemaker. But he must always remember that however he may be hailed in today's headlines, the judgment of tomorrow's history would severely condemn a false peace," they wrote.

The deal offered by the Soviet Union may sound like an offer we cannot refuse, they counseled Reagan, but before you take it, *think*: think about whose power will be increased and whose power will be diminished.

In discussing what the Soviets stand to gain by removing intermediate-range missiles, Nixon and Kissinger engage in some unusually straight talk about the importance and the limits of the NATO Alliance and about what constitutes a credible deterrent to an attack on Europe.

The most important function of American intermediate-range missiles in Europe, they argue, is not to offset Soviet SS-20s, but to make it possible to protect Europe against a conventional Soviet attack without launching a full-scale nuclear war between the United States and the Soviet Union. The Pershings and cruise missiles "closed a gap in deterrence caused by the apocalyptic nature of strategic nuclear war." Because the overwhelming Soviet advantage in conventional forces would persist, removing the missiles would make Europe safe for conventional war and would "create the most profound crisis of the NATO Alliance in its 40-year history."

They have a point.

Denuclearizing Europe and weakening the ties that bind NATO with the United States have been the two major objectives of Soviet policy for more than a decade. One "peace initiative" after another has targeted the nuclear deterrent protecting Europe: antinuclear campaigns (like that which found a home in Britain's Labor party), massive peace marches designed to prevent deployment of Pershing and cruise missiles, "no first use" campaigns designed to secure from NATO a pledge not to use nuclear weapons against conventional invasion, and, of course, the arms control agreement on the table today. All these campaigns have the aim of denuclearizing Europe and increasing the power of Soviet conventional forces.

Nixon and Kissinger argue that two changes are required to make the proposed treaty consistent with European and American security: it should eliminate *all* intermediate-range missiles—not all but a hundred—and it should tie the elimination of short-range missiles to a substantial reduction of Soviet conventional forces.

I think they are right. The proposed treaty leaves our allies more vulnerable to Soviet conventional forces and chemical weapons and leaves the Soviet Union less vulnerable than with Pershings in place.

Is that the Soviet goal? Mikhail Gorbachev has sworn he will not play politics with nuclear weapons. He told the twenty-seventh Congress of the Communist party in February 1986, for example, that "to transform mass destruction weapons into objects of political machination is at the very least immoral and politically irresponsible."

But if Gorbachev wants a less dangerous world, there are more straightforward ways to work toward its achievement. The danger to our European allies lies not in this or that category of weapon but in the cumulative power of the Soviet Union's great armies and arsenals—and in that government's demonstrated proclivity for using force to achieve its objectives. When Soviet leaders are more interested in internal development than in military power, they will reduce their great armies and cease their restless striving after power around the world. Meanwhile, Afghanistan remains a vivid example of what can happen to a nation whose peace depends on Soviet restraint in the use of superior force.

I do not believe that Ronald Reagan will forget the lessons he has spent a lifetime teaching. Nor do I believe he will exchange tangible strategic deterrents for the psychic gratification of being called a peacemaker.

This Treaty Won't Change the World

December 7, 1987

The trick in the coming days will be neither to overestimate nor to underestimate the importance of the INF Treaty—its benefits and dangers. It will not be easy.

Mikhail Gorbachev's presence, the summit, and the signing ceremony offer a nearly irresistible temptation to the media and everyone else to treat the completion of the treaty as an event of colossal importance for U.S.-Soviet relations, the arms race, and the world balance of power.

Celebration, claims, and counterclaims will make it difficult to remember that the INF Treaty deals with only one type of nuclear weapon, a type, moreover, that is not deployed against the United States. It will be difficult to remember that it does not denuclearize the European theater, nor have any significant impact on the overall balance of military forces in that arena.

What, then, does it do? Removal of U.S. and Soviet intermediate-range missiles will leave Western Europe marginally more vulnerable, the Soviet Union marginally less vulnerable, and the NATO Alliance marginally weaker.

When Soviet missiles have been removed, Western European cities will no longer be vulnerable to destruction by the Soviet Union in a matter of minutes. But they will still be utterly vulnerable to the Soviets' overwhelming superiority of conventional forces. In contrast, when the United States removes its Pershing and cruise missiles from Europe, Soviet cities will no longer be vulnerable to any threat from Europe.

Although the treaty seems like a very good trade—weapon for weapon—it leaves Western Europe with fewer options for self-defense and the Soviet Union with less to defend against.

In any case, weapons are only one aspect of a nation's power, as Clausewitz, Sun Tsu, Lenin, Mao, and other supreme tacticians of power have understood. The strength of nations also depends on their will and skill, on their purpose and clarity. The strength of an alliance depends on the commitment and unity of its members.

NATO is a defensive alliance among democracies. A defensive alliance makes sense only if there is a meaningful threat and can only be sustained if that threat is widely perceived. More and more, sophisticated Western Europeans already doubt the reality of the Soviet threat and the reliability of the American commitment to Europe's defense. The INF Treaty reinforces both these tendencies.

Removal of the Soviet SS-20 missiles would eliminate the most dramatic symbol of a direct threat to Europe and therefore would also eliminate a powerful incentive for European commitment to NATO.

The manner in which the United States has conducted its arms negotiations has further disturbed the structure of confidence on which the alliance rests. Europeans are still shocked by Reykjavik. They find it difficult to believe that top U.S. officials would hold those freewheeling discussions with the Soviet leader without any prior allied consultation. And although U.S. officials deny it, there is a widespread feeling in Europe that subsequent to Reykjavik the United States has not consulted early enough, often enough, or at high enough levels with the European allies on matters of direct immediate relevance to European security.

It does not follow from the above that the INF Treaty should be rejected by the Senate. The damage to allied relations has already been done. Public political adaptations have been made—in West Germany, Britain, Italy, and elsewhere. Indeed, a U.S. refusal of the treaty now would be taken as more evidence of disarray in the American government and would leave many Europeans feeling that it was America's fault that Soviet missiles remained targeted on their countries.

Our government, however, is already far along in conversations toward yet another arms agreement. Surely it can consult first with our European allies in the process of these new negotiations. We cannot solve the treaty's problem by rejecting it at this stage. But we can seek to minimize its damage.

Like the damage, the benefits of the treaty are also largely political. Its completion constitutes a precedent for cooperation and creates a more constructive climate for U.S.-Soviet relations. This may be useful in the future, especially if we can learn from this experience.

Like all other weapons agreements, its value depends entirely on mutual compliance with its terms. So far, the great difficulty about U.S.-Soviet arms agreements has not been in negotiating their terms, nor even the terms of verification, but in securing compliance. From Yalta forward through Kennedy-Khrushchev, SALTs I and II, the ABM Treaty, and so forth, compliance has been the problem.

This and all future U.S. agreements with the Soviet Union should provide for monitoring compliance and automatically terminating the pact in the case of noncompliance. No such provision is included in the current treaty. Perhaps the Senate can take care of this oversight.

Deal Making, Soviet Style
October 3, 1988

The greatest shortcoming of the U.S. effort to contain power with legal contracts is that such contracts contain no protection or penalties for noncompliance.

Yet noncompliance is a regular aspect of deals with the Soviet Union. The construction of the Krasnoyarsk radar installation in clear violation of the ABM Treaty is one example. The fact that Gorbachev lived with the violation, lied about it, and sought to reap advantage from it is the most disturbing thing I know about the Gorbachev regime. It helps that the Soviets eventually confessed their noncompliance, but it took much too long.

Question: When is a deal not a deal?

Answer: When the Soviets think they can renegotiate the price.

Americans thought they had a deal with the Soviet Union regarding Afghanistan. It was called the Geneva Accords. The Soviets would withdraw half their troops by August 15, 1988, and complete the withdrawal by February 15, 1989.

But last week Soviet Foreign Minister Eduard Shevardnadze said in his speech before the United Nations General Assembly that the Soviet Union had "not yet begun the second stage" of withdrawal and indicated the pullout might depend on a halt in the flow of arms to Afghan resistance fighters, the *mujahedin*.

"There have been violations of the agreements," he said as he proposed a meeting of the Security Council's five permanent members to deal with "compliance."

The Soviets have been accusing Pakistan of violating the pledge of "noninterference" in Afghanistan by permitting supplies to the rebels to flow through Pakistan. The United States has been accusing the Soviet Union of violating Pakistan's airspace by repeated air strikes against *mujahedin* bases in Pakistan.

The United States thought it had an "understanding" with the Soviets about military supplies to the *mujahedin*. Although all parties have pledged "noninterference," the Soviets had made it clear they reserved the right to provide assistance to the Marxist government its armies had installed in Kabul, and the United States reserved the right to resupply the guerrillas.

Shevardnadze's speech amounts to a demand to renegotiate the agreement. The new price of Soviet withdrawal would transform the original deal and would be tantamount to international recognition of a Soviet "right" to ensure survival of the Kabul government (exactly the "right" claimed by the Brezhnev Doctrine). It would relieve the Soviets of any obligation to withdraw if there is continued assistance to the *mujahedin*.

Shevardnadze's demand makes even clearer the Soviet Union's desire to achieve by diplomacy the conquest of Afghanistan it was unable to win by force.

The Geneva Accords are not the only deal Shevardnadze reopened in his UN speech. He also spelled out before the General Assembly a Soviet proposal to complete the Krasnoyarsk radar installation and turn it into an international space research center. With breathtaking chutzpah, he challenged the Americans to transfer radar installations in Greenland and Great Britain to the newly created international center, even though the Krasnoyarsk radar station—by its location alone—is a clear violation of the ABM Treaty and American radars in Greenland and Great Britain are permitted under that agreement.

129

Thus the Soviet foreign minister has proposed to supersede the painstakingly negotiated ABM Treaty with a new agreement in which an important element of a Soviet missile shield would be completed on Soviet soil, while two important American components of an early-warning system would pass to international control.

With the ABM Treaty, the Soviets successfully stopped the development of a U.S. missile defense system. Having reaped the benefits of that deal, they now propose to renegotiate terms regarding the radar installations.

These Soviet tactics do not necessarily mean that the United States should not negotiate agreements with the Soviet Union. They mean that the United States should understand that for the Soviets a deal is not forever. A deal is valid only as long as nothing better is on the horizon.

The Shevardnadze speech contains an especially important warning for Ronald Reagan and American negotiators now working on a southern Africa agreement.

As in Afghanistan, State Department representatives are pursuing negotiations at tables where there are no representatives of indigenous resistance groups. As the *mujahedin* were not present in Geneva, Jonas Savimbi's UNITA forces are not present at the talks on southern Africa—talks held under U.S. auspices among South Africa, Cuba, and Angola's ruling Marxist government, the MPLA.

Savimbi is worried, and with good reason, that a cosmetic solution may be found that will leave the MPLA fighting with Soviet and Cuban support against UNITA, which stands alone, protected only by ambiguous assurances. On September 19, Savimbi wrote to Ronald Reagan of his worries.

Do not leave us to the tender mercies of local Communists and their foreign friends, Savimbi implored the American president. Two issues, he said, are of the greatest importance.

First is "the need to make clear to all parties that the United States will not stop providing necessary assistance to UNITA until the Soviets, the Cubans, the Eastern bloc countries . . . cease providing military supplies to the MPLA." And second is the need for a "government of national reconciliation" that would call for free elections in Angola by the date that UN forces are introduced in Namibia to monitor the withdrawal of South African troops and oversee the Namibian elections.

Jonas Savimbi, the *mujahedin*, and an American defense are what Ronald Reagan is all about. Presumably in his last months he will not abandon the goals he has served for a lifetime. He will not sacrifice his friends and his principles to a deal that can be renegotiated at someone else's convenience.

And Now, "Proximity Talks"

May 4, 1986

An early manifestation of the Gorbachev style was a new emphasis on negotiations as an instrument of international affairs, not just for arms agreements but as the preferred means of achieving political ends generally. Now peoples and movements that had resisted forcible subjection to a Marxist-Leninist government were to have their fate settled by negotiations.

The terms and frameworks of the negotiations became themselves the object of negotiation. The object clearly was to win by political and diplomatic means the control that it had not proved possible to establish militarily. That's improvement.

Still, I believed (and believe) the U.S. government was too eager for agreement to be a very effective negotiator on behalf of indigenous resistance movements and that the mujahedin *should have had a place at the table when Afghanistan's future was being settled.*

It is time to take a hard look at those "peace processes" called proximity talks regarding Afghanistan and the Contadora process regarding Nicaragua. At stake in both is the U.S. policy of aiding freedom fighters who oppose their countries' Marxist governments, a policy known as the Reagan Doctrine.

We should be clear about the circumstances of the discussions and realistic about the chances they will lead to a resolution favorable to freedom and U.S. interests.

These separate talks have reached crucial stages and may arrive at climaxes next week. Participants in both meetings believe peace may be at hand.

In neither process is the United States a participant, but in both cases the United States has offered assurances of its cooperation. The proposed settlements would have far-reaching consequences and would place heavy demands on the United States for guarantees and implementation.

We must ask how a "negotiated" settlement can be reached if

131

those who struggle against their country's subjugation and incorporation in the Soviet empire are excluded from the talks. Resistance groups—the *mujahedin* in Afghanistan and the contras in Nicaragua—are not directly represented in either of the discussions.

President Reagan has proposed to the UN General Assembly that the Marxist governments of the two nations (as well as Angola, Cambodia, and Ethiopia) should discuss with resistance groups the verified elimination of foreign troops, an end to the flow of outside arms, and internal reconciliation, with democracy and human rights for all.

So far, however, the Marxist governments in these countries have refused to deal with "bandit leaders."

On the theory that some negotiations are better than no negotiations, proximity talks were organized under UN auspices to bring together representatives of the Democratic Republic of Afghanistan (a Soviet client state that is neither democratic nor a republic and only marginally Afghan) and Pakistan, which refuses to recognize the DRA. In Latin America, an expanded Contadora process brings together the five Central American states and nine South American nations in an "all-Latin" process.

All sources agree that the proximity talks on Afghanistan have already produced tentative agreement on the safe return of 4 million Afghan refugees, on the neutrality of Afghanistan, and on the principle of noninterference in internal affairs.

"Only one issue remains," a UN spokesman announced in December, "the question of Soviet troop withdrawal." That, however, is not the way the Soviets see it.

The Soviet view of the problems of Afghanistan and Nicaragua is simple and straightforward. The difficulty, they say, is caused by those who resist conquest, and all that is required is that resistance should cease. They add that it will cease if all external assistance is eliminated and that it is up to the United States to eliminate it.

Soviet spokesmen reiterated this principle on behalf of their Afghan clients in Moscow last week when they also noted that the talks had reached a "particularly important stage."

Pakistan and the United States have insisted on a timetable for Soviet troop withdrawal. The Soviets have insisted that an American "guarantee" precede a timetable. American negotiators have offered a guarantee, with provisions that have not been made public.

The coming talks on Afghanistan, starting Tuesday in Geneva, come at a time when Pakistan is feeling heavy pressure. The Soviets have stepped up the war against the *mujahedin*. Relations have been strengthened among Afghanistan, India, and the Soviet Union, arousing reasonable Pakistani fears of encirclement and provoking ethnic rivalries.

Internal political pressures on the government of Pakistan have increased, and the economic burden of the refugee population weighs heavily. So does uncertainty about the U.S. commitment to Pakistan.

It seems unlikely that a settlement consistent with U.S. principles will emerge from the Geneva talks.

The Contadora nations will try once more next week to win agreement on comprehensive, verifiable, simultaneous implementation of the Contadora objectives.

Here, too, the agreement seeks to secure withdrawal of foreign troops, an end to the importation of arms, and an end to all external support for insurgents.

And here, too, the United States has hastened to give the requested assurances. U.S. Ambassador Philip Habib wrote to three Democratic congressmen last week that, though we are not a party to the negotiations and not legally bound by them, "we will as a matter of policy support and abide by it [an agreement]" providing, of course, that Nicaragua also fulfills its promises.

Both sets of assurances pose questions and raise doubts. The Afghan agreement makes no mention of the right to self-determination. The Habib letter omitted a mention of democratization as a Contadora objective, but the State Department acted quickly to repair the omission.

We are left with major questions. Does any authoritative official in the U.S. government believe that Nicaragua will cut its ties to the Soviet bloc, permit opposition, and hold free elections? Or that Soviet troops will withdraw from Afghanistan?

If not, what are these charades about? With them we confuse our friends without persuading our adversaries. Isn't it about time to level with the American people about the kind of problems and adversaries we really face in the world?

Legalism, Again:
The American Approach to Foreign Affairs
May 26, 1986

Americans trust negotiated solutions to international disputes because we believe a deal is a deal. We assume that other people are basically like us, sharing our values and objectives.

Our national penchant for the contractual approach to international affairs sometimes makes us careless about the record of those with whom we deal.

Governments, like people, try hard to reconcile events with their beliefs about how the world works. The Vietnamese government, for example, fit the Chernobyl accident into its conviction that everything is better in the Soviet Union than in America by solemnly broadcasting on May 6 that "there have been about 20,000 such accidents at U.S. nuclear factories since 1979, including 5,000 in 1983 alone, 247 of which were serious."

"The Reagan administration," the English-language broadcast concluded, "does not care a thing for the victims."

We Americans also work out imaginative, if perhaps less laughable, ways to make our problems fit our preconceptions. The preconception that exercises the greatest influence on the conduct of American foreign policy is that negotiating an agreement among nations is the same as solving a problem among them. Such distinguished students of foreign affairs as Hans Morgenthau and George Kennan have written that Americans bring to foreign policy an assumption that the most terrible struggles for power among nations can be contained by legal agreements. We put our faith in charters, treaties, and contracts—great and small. In this century we have repeatedly and unsuccessfully attempted to outlaw war by means of the Kellogg-Briand Pact, the League of Nations, and the United Nations Charter.

This same tendency toward legalism is manifest in our preoccupation with arms control negotiations as a means to contain conflict and in our confidence that it is possible to negotiate agreements that will restore peace and protect essential rights in such places as Afghanistan, Nicaragua, and Angola.

Indeed, a good many Americans—especially liberals—see decent agreements decently arrived at as a good in themselves—on the assumption that the *process* of negotiation itself brings countries closer

134

together. Some see U.S. commitments to such agreements as absolute and unconditionally binding, rather than as contractual obligations requiring reciprocal compliance.

This view of U.S. commitments leads some to argue that the United States should accept the comprehensive jurisdiction of the International Court of Justice, even though only four small nations in the world do so, or that the United States is obliged to pay all assessed dues to the United Nations, regardless of the failure of many other nations to do so. The same view of American commitments is present in the belief that Americans should continue to abide by the ABM Treaty, even though the Soviet Union's phased array radar violates its commitment not to deploy an antimissile defense. Some believe the United States should honor the limits of the SALT II Treaty even though the USSR has deployed two missiles in clear violation of that treaty.

Such people also argue that the United States should abide by the Kennedy-Khrushchev agreement, even though the Soviets and Cubans have violated all its provisions. Such people are also ready to see the United States assume new obligations to help maintain peace in Nicaragua and Afghanistan without dwelling on unpleasant questions about whether the Nicaraguan, Afghan, or Soviet governments are likely to fulfill their obligations under new treaties.

In the strange semantics of contemporary political discussion, it is seen as "liberal" to advocate negotiating an agreement and "conservative" to worry much about its implementation.

Yet all the experience of the postwar years proves that, in dealing with Communist states, compliance poses the principal problem. The greatest difficulties that afflict a Contadora treaty (or an agreement on Afghanistan, INF, or START) are not, as often perceived, the specifics of verification or timing. The greatest difficulty is compliance. Compliance cannot be negotiated.

Yalta remains the prime example of an agreement negotiated in good faith—at least by Roosevelt and Churchill—and violated by another of its parties, the Soviet Union. Neither Britain nor the United States intended to sell out Eastern Europe. To the contrary, they sought and received commitments that the Poles and other Eastern Europeans would choose rulers through free elections. But the presence of the Soviet army proved more important than a diplomatic agreement in determining the future of Eastern Europe.

Roosevelt has been described as angry and agitated during the last week of his life after receiving reports of Soviet violations. "We can't do business with Stalin," he said. "He's broken all the promises made at Yalta."

135

Churchill, too, was dismayed. "I've been thinking about how I was on Poland," he wrote, "and how we fought for Poland at Yalta and reached agreement, and how those agreements were broken in succeeding months."

It is not really fair to blame the British and the Americans for what happened to Poland, though prospective victims saw even then that diplomacy was facilitating the Soviet conquest of Eastern Europe. But it is fair to note that one could see at Yalta the American proclivity for negotiating agreements that had no realistic chance of being implemented.

Today a debate rages over whether the United States should encourage agreement on the Contadora treaty concerning Central America and guarantee its results. The debate once again pits the State Department, with its enthusiasm for an agreement of some sort, against the field. It is entirely possible that State will win, because of our deep-grained national proclivity to believe an agreement is the same as a solution.

At the United Nations, Ronald Reagan seemed to take a more skeptical stand. He promised that "America's support for struggling democratic resistance forces must not and shall not cease" until there was "definitive progress" in the resolution of regional conflict. Definitive progress will have occurred when democratization occurs in Nicaragua.

But if the United States, in its zeal for a settlement, chooses to dismantle the contras before the Ortegas dismantle their Sandinista dictatorship, the freedom of Nicaragua, the peace of the hemisphere, and the security of the United States will suffer greatly.

Malta Can't Be Yalta
November 29, 1989

President Bush's advisers promised that the December 1989 Malta meeting between the U.S. and Soviet leaders had no agenda and would be just a getting-acquainted session. They also promised there would be no surprises—as there were at Reykjavik.

This time the weather provided the drama. There were no major surprises, although there were more substantive discussions than antic-ipated. At the final press conference, Gorbachev said that he and Bush

agreed that "characteristics of the Cold War should be abandoned. . . .
The arms race, mistrust, psychological and ideological struggle, all these
things should be of the past."
    It looks more and more as though he really meant it.

Despite a certain amount of confused commentary, it has been clear from the beginning that Malta cannot be Yalta—or even Reykjavik. There are too many important differences between the participants and the circumstances.

Yalta was a meeting of victorious allied leaders near the end of a terrible war. Malta is a meeting of rival leaders at the end of more than forty years of competition, hostility, and peace. Cold war is different from real war. Rivals are different from allies.

At Yalta, Britain, the United States, and the Soviet Union had the power and the inclination to determine the fate of Eastern Europe. The United States emerged from World War II with unquestioned military and economic superiority. The Soviet Union emerged with the most powerful military forces in Europe. The British had demonstrated indomitable will. The other countries of Europe were in no condition to resist the decisions of the superpowers.

The leaders meeting at Malta cannot impose a settlement in Europe, even if they so desired, which George Bush, at least, most assuredly does not. The military power of the Soviet Union in Europe is still great, but the dramatic demonstrations of the past weeks cast doubt on the reliability of Eastern European forces. Why should anyone assume the Poles, Hungarians, East Germans, and Czechs in the armed forces have different views from those in the civilian population? Moreover, Gorbachev's policies have encouraged independence in Eastern Europe. There is no reason to suppose he would suddenly reverse those policies even though they shorten the Soviet Union's reach.

The military and economic power of the United States is also relatively less than in 1945 because other countries have made dramatic progress. Now U.S. economic superiority is challenged on all sides.

Today's Eastern Europeans have lost their fear, and this, too, diminishes the power of the Soviet Union and of the indigenous Communist parties. Today's Western Europeans have long since regained buoyant confidence and prosperity and are busily engaged in restructuring the continent according to their own designs.

The absence of a Western European leader at Malta further diminishes the representativeness and potential influence in Europe

137

of whatever agreements are reached.

So does the nearly universal perception that the cold war is over. The United States and the Soviet Union are military superpowers. Their influence declines as the likelihood of military conflict recedes. This is one of the important reasons that Malta cannot even be Reykjavik.

At Reykjavik, fear of nuclear war was much greater than it is today. So was the hope in the Reagan administration that a personal understanding could somehow lead to a breakthrough in superpower relations. Since Reykjavik there has been time to hear the allies' concerns, time to reflect on the consequences of denuclearization, time to consider the dangers of ill-considered "breakthroughs" in U.S.-Soviet relations.

There has also been time for American and European policy makers to learn more about dealing with Mikhail Gorbachev. At Yalta, the United States had had little experience in dealing with the Soviet Union except in wartime. This is one reason illusions turned quickly to misunderstandings. Joseph Stalin did not understand how eager FDR was to please him. FDR did not understand how eager Joseph Stalin was to impose a Communist system on as many countries as he could. Winston Churchill did not understand that for FDR British colonialism was as repugnant and potentially threatening as Soviet expansion. Neither Churchill nor Roosevelt understood that Stalin would break the promises made at Yalta as soon as it seemed feasible.

George Bush brings much better understanding of his Soviet counterpart to Malta. There has been time to observe Gorbachev's bold moves toward granting greater freedom to the people of the Soviet Union and Eastern Europe and also to observe less optimistic developments. Time to learn that the withdrawal of Soviet troops from Afghanistan was accompanied by stepped-up military assistance to the client government. That dramatic Soviet offers of arms reductions were accompanied by stepped up Soviet work on the highest of the high-tech weapons. That confessions of misrepresentation about the Krasnoyarsk radar were accompanied by countinuing misrepresentation concerning arms shipments to Central America.

By the time George Bush and Mikhail Gorbachev meet at Malta, Americans and others have had broad experience with Mikhail Gorbachev's bold policies. They have found therein much to admire and much to hope for yet still no grounds for a relationship built on mutual trust. Malta cannot be Yalta because the post-World War II era is finally behind us. It is a whole new world.

PART THREE

The United States and Its Allies

Introduction to Part Three

The United States and Its Allies

The Berlin Wall symbolized the division of Europe. Now the wall is down. Borders are open or nearly open between East and West Europe. New reform governments with some non-Communist participants have been installed in Czechoslovakia and East Germany, as well as Poland and Hungary.

George Bush is speaking—a bit prematurely—of Mikhail Gorbachev as a collaborator in the freedom movement. The structure of international affairs has undergone a political earthquake. Aftershocks are continuing. The carefully laid plans for integration of the twelve nations of the European Community have been shaken by the freedom movement in the East.

Will the twelve turn away Eastern countries hungry for contact with the West? Can the European Community absorb a united Germany? What of NATO and the Warsaw Pact and the relation of the United States to it all?

A "common European home" stretching from the Atlantic to the Urals has been a major objective of Mikhail Gorbachev. Now other European leaders are speaking of a common European policy. Will NATO survive the growing sense that there is no Soviet threat? Politics sometimes works like judo: weakness properly used can be made to function as a strength. Can Gorbachev achieve by the frank admission of Soviet weakness what he could not get by intimidation?

The structures through which international affairs have been conducted for the past forty years have been shaken to their very foundations. Now comes the time of rebuilding.

Turning the Tables on Allies

February 23, 1986

The idea of removing all American intermediate-range missiles from Europe was profoundly disturbing to our allies—most of whom had complained loudly about the Reagan administration's lack of interest in negotiating arms reductions.

Ronald Reagan was well known for his anticommunism. Leaders of several allied governments, adopting an anti–anti-Communist position, patronized and "regretted" Ronald Reagan's lack of interest in arms talks—right down to the time he began to talk as though he just might buy the zero option.

Mikhail Gorbachev's proposal to remove U.S. and Soviet missiles from Europe has already provoked some unfamiliar reactions among America's allies. Usually our allies position themselves as the "peace party" and hope aloud that the United States will be more forthcoming. This time our allies seem worried that the United States might be too forthcoming. To forestall any such possibility, strong negative reactions to virtually all aspects of the latest Soviet proposal are being expressed.

The British have made public statements about the "unacceptability" of nuclear reductions not accompanied by reductions in the Soviet Union's conventional forces.

The Germans have reminded everyone about how important it is not to decouple European and American defense.

The French have pronounced the proposal unsatisfactory and declared they would not be bound by any such agreement.

Even the Japanese have complained that the proposal is discriminatory because it would remove missiles from Europe while leaving them in Asia.

What has produced such an unaccustomed response? Why are our allies so publicly affirmative about the value of America's nuclear missiles to their security? What has so stirred them?

First, they have been impressed with the packaging of the latest proposal. It offers—or seems to offer—Ronald Reagan two things he badly wants. It offers negotiations without preconditions, specifically without the precondition that he abandon the Strategic Defense Initiative as a price for negotiating deep cuts in nuclear missiles, and it couches the offer in the language of Reagan's own "zero option," proposing a "zero option" for Europe as a "first step" to a "nuclear-free" world.

The allies had expected that the new proposal would flounder on the Reagan administration's refusal to abandon SDI. Instead, Gorbachev abandoned this precondition, leaving the allies to worry that Ronald Reagan would find the new offer too attractive.

Second, the British and French are concerned because they regard the planned modernization of their nuclear arsenals as a principal target of the Soviet proposal. The Soviet proposal calls for total elimination of Soviet SS-20s and American Pershing and cruise missiles, but it adds two supplementary demands: that Paris and London "freeze" their nuclear forces at current levels, and that the United States cancel its commitment to sell Britain Trident II missiles needed before retirement of Britain's aging Polaris submarines.

Europeans rely heavily on nuclear weapons to offset the Soviet advantage in conventional forces. They therefore see any diminution or possible withdrawal of America's nuclear force as threatening. The possibility of U.S. nuclear withdrawal from Europe underscores for them the importance of an independent British and French nuclear deterrent to offset the proximity and superiority of Soviet conventional forces.

Their comments on the recent proposal have emphasized that nuclear arms reduction will not affect the threat posed by conventional forces. Thus, a British foreign office official rejected utterly "a de-nuclear world, or even a world with substantial nuclear reductions, that is not accompanied by changes in Soviet conventional strength." And French Foreign Minister Roland Dumas asserted, "We cannot accept that the problem of conventional weapons should be given lower priority than nuclear negotiations."

The very thought of an American withdrawal seems to suggest the need for greater self-reliance. One French commentator quoted Andre Malraux's assertion that since de Gaulle, "the French people have the courage to defend themselves." And a top adviser to President François Mitterrand told Le Point, "Even if the SS-20s were to be entirely removed, we could not accept either current force levels, nor a freeze, nor a reduction in our deterrence." What do these European reactions mean for the future and for the American position in upcoming arms negotiations?

Obviously the U.S. commitment to NATO and the defense of Western Europe does not depend on the presence of American nuclear missiles in Europe. It depends on our treaty obligations, which are in turn underpinned by a sense of shared civilization. We know that, but apparently our NATO partners have persistent fears.

An agreement to eliminate U.S. and Soviet missiles (which have been deployed in Europe only since 1980) would not violate America's legal or moral commitments to our European allies. It just might stimulate Western European countries to assume a greater responsibility for their own defense. That, of course, would be a good in itself. The nations of Western Europe are populous, strong, technologically advanced, and, in principle, quite capable of self-defense against a Soviet threat. So is Japan.

The United States should do nothing to discourage tendencies to greater military self-reliance among our allies. We want and need allies who are strong. Obviously, too, the United States should not seek to do what we in any case could not do: commit Britain and France to abandoning modernization of their nuclear arsenals. That is their decision.

But we can enjoy our European friends' sudden realism about a potential Soviet threat and also about the American contribution to their security. It is refreshing to have them worry that the United States may be too eager for arms reductions.

Now it is our turn to be the "peace party" in the Western alliance.

Spooking the Allies at Reykjavik
October 27, 1986

Our European allies, whom I greatly value, developed a bad habit of relying on U.S. protection while publicly suggesting that the United States was more than a little paranoid for safeguarding our capacity to protect them and us. Too often, they presented themselves as peacemakers and suggested that Americans—especially Ronald Reagan—were insufficiently interested in denuclearization and demilitarization.

Reykjavik put an end to that particular brand of diplomatic hypocrisy.

Though arms control enthusiasts are reluctant to admit it, America's principal allies are making it clear that they did not enjoy the "high-stakes poker game" at Reykjavik as much as the participants apparently did. Their concern is less that the sweeping agreements fell through than that some of them were considered at all.

High officials in Bonn, Paris, and London and at the meeting of

NATO defense ministers in Scotland have both privately and publicly communicated that our closest friends are not ready to abandon nuclear weapons as the centerpiece of NATO defense, are not ready to see all American intermediate missiles withdrawn from Europe, and are not ready to forgo their own nuclear deterrence, and are not ready to have American negotiators make decisions for the entire alliance.

In addition, some have expressed particular concern with the haste and lack of consultation that characterized the American performance at Reykjavik. Though allied leaders obviously do not desire to embarrass the U.S. government, nor discourage its interest in negotiating arms control agreements, they have concluded it is necessary to be clear about their disagreement with some positions taken by the United States in Iceland.

This is why British Prime Minister Margaret Thatcher and French President François Mitterrand issued a joint statement from London reaffirming the importance of nuclear weapons to NATO strategy. That strategy has always featured a heavy reliance on nuclear arms to offset Soviet superiority in conventional forces. Neither the accumulation of nuclear weapons, the improvement of their accuracy, the rise of antinuclear sentiment in opposition parties, nor the arrival in power of a new Soviet leadership has changed the view of the allied governments.

While American leaders have come to view nuclear weapons as a problem and seek their elimination, Europeans still see them as a vital part of the solution to the problem of a possible Soviet military move against Western Europe.

NATO ministers meeting at Gleneagles, Scotland, told American delegates again and again that deep cuts in strategic nuclear forces would be desirable only if they are accompanied by controls to balance conventional forces and to eliminate chemical weapons— areas where the Soviet Union and the Warsaw Pact countries enjoy a significant advantage over NATO members.

Britain's Defense Minister George Younger reiterated that his government would be "extremely concerned" at any agreement that dealt only with strategic ballistic missiles.

Europeans are also worried by the thought of our withdrawing all U.S. missiles from Europe. French Foreign Minister Jean-Bernard Raimond told the French Parliament that a total withdrawal would be "terrible." Such decoupling of the United States from a European nuclear defense would "reduce the security of Europe," Raimond asserted.

In Washington, German Chancellor Helmut Kohl expressed his

concern that withdrawal of U.S. intermediate missiles would leave Germany more vulnerable to short-range weapons. In this area the Soviets enjoy a seven-to-one advantage. A 50 percent reduction, however, might be all right, German officials indicated. But they added that greater reductions "could be a danger for Western Europe."

European reservations about the substance of the proposals have been accompanied by outright criticism of the U.S. failure to consult with its allies as thoroughly as they thought appropriate.

West German Gen. Hans-Joachim Mack, NATO deputy supreme allied commander in Europe, complained publicly that the alliance had not been adequately briefed or consulted about American proposals that involved a sweeping revision of the basic principles of NATO strategy.

Criticism from allies grew still sharper after U.S. Secretary of State George Shultz informed them that British and French nuclear arsenals should be included in envisioned cuts exceeding 50 percent. A German official summed up his feelings with the comment that talks at Reykjavik "were broken off at the right time."

The French, as usual, were less diplomatic. "This is not serious," a French official asserted concerning the Reykjavik proposals. "My reflection on all of this is that you should not allow two men to negotiate on a Saturday night in a haunted house."

Treaty and Consequences
October 12, 1987

In foreign affairs the leg bone really is connected to the shin bone, the shin bone to the foot bone, the foot bone to the toe bones; and what happens to the leg is felt by the toes.

I did not believe that the administration took enough account of the effects on allies of the INF Treaty nor that it gave adequate weight to the effects on the alliance of U.S. decisions on matters of enormous importance to allied security.

The U.S. habit of assuming leadership of the alliance grew progressively inappropriate as European NATO members grew stronger and richer. I believe that the satisfactions of this type of leadership were and are greater for U.S. officials than for most Americans, the majority of whom have been eager to relinquish dubious and expensive burdens of such leadership.

The terms of a treaty are one thing; its consequences are quite another. Reagan administration policy makers are still reeling from the unanticipated effects of the "Wright-Reagan" peace proposal on Central America's presidents. I predict they will be still more chagrined at the unexpected consequences of the INF negotiations on Europe and on NATO.

Taken by itself, the impending treaty looks like a good deal. It requires the Soviets to destroy more intermediate-range missiles than we do—because they have more. In the abstract it seems to move Europe's strategic position back to where it was before the Soviet Union targeted SS-20s against Western European capitals, thus stimulating NATO's decision to deploy American Pershings and cruise missiles.

But weapons systems do not exist in the abstract. They exist in particular political and cultural circumstances. As Pasteur said once of disease, "The germ is nothing, the environment is everything."

The beliefs, doubts, and fears of our European allies give the INF Treaty an impact remote from the intentions of our negotiators.

Coloring Europe's interpretation of the treaty are two widespread beliefs: that U.S. negotiations were driven by domestic political factors rather than strategic concerns and that Mikhail Gorbachev, to the contrary, was driven by strategic goals rather than domestic political pressures.

Our European allies follow our politics more closely than we follow theirs. They have heard about Nancy Reagan's dream of having her husband enter history as a peacemaker. They know about Ronald Reagan's abhorrence of nuclear weapons and about the Iran-contra hearings and the erosion of presidential power. They know polls show broad American support for an arms accord. They believe that Ronald Reagan plans to recoup his faltering political fortunes with an arms treaty and that in this he is urged on by George Bush.

"What an election gift Gorbachev can make to the Republicans in general and to Bush in particular if he visits Washington before the end of the year," observed *Le Point* magazine. In the European view, helping the Republicans achieve their political ends helps Gorbachev achieve *his* strategic goals.

A French official wrote in *Politique Etrangere*: "Never have the Soviets advertised so openly the objectives the West has always attributed to them: denuclearization of Europe, de-linkage of Europe

147

and the United States, and creation of a new all-European 'security system.' "

In this view, Gorbachev laid a "remarkable diplomatic trap" into which the United States willingly fell. The French weekly *L'Express* saw the "Gorbachev effect" at work on both sides of the Atlantic—sowing doubts about the reality of the Soviet threat and exacerbating the psychological distance between the United States and Europe, all the while raising hope and intensifying anxieties about the German role in Europe.

The impending INF accord has heightened Europe's concerns about its security, and, as Richard Perle makes clear, that is an anticipated and welcome side-effect of the proposal. But certain other effects on Europe were surely neither expected nor desired.

Ronald Reagan surely did not intend to strengthen the argument of antinuclear unilateralists in Great Britain and West Germany, but his focus on nuclear weapons as a unique source of danger did just that.

It seems unlikely that Reagan or George Shultz intended to strengthen those advocating a denuclearized, neutral, unified Germany as a first step to a denuclearized, neutral Europe. But, as Marxists like to say, it is surely no accident that in the same month when general agreement on the INF accord was reached, Mikhail Gorbachev permitted the leader of Communist Germany to pay his first visit to Bonn, reminding everyone that it is within the Soviets' power to arrange the closer relations that all Germans once again seem to desire.

It seems unlikely that Reagan or Shultz intended to speed the disintegration of NATO or the development of a new framework for European defense. But the combination of Reykjavik and INF talks shook sober Europeans' confidence in American judgment and especially in the reliability of the United States as the leader of the Western Alliance. They were stunned that basic elements of NATO strategy were put on the table at Reykjavik, regarded as negotiable, and nearly negotiated away—all without consultation of European allies.

Finally, I do not believe that Ronald Reagan or George Shultz intended to render Europe more vulnerable, nor the Soviet Union less vulnerable, nor the Atlantic Alliance weaker. But that is what the proposed agreement does. Because the Pershing IIs and cruise missiles are what the Soviets fear most, they have become the centerpiece in deterring Soviet moves against Europe and a symbol of U.S. commitment to the defense of Europe. Their removal has a symbolic as well as a military significance.

The INF accord has not even been concluded, but the fallout

from these particular intermediate-range missiles has already altered the climate of Western Europe.

Limited Partners in Europe
April 28, 1986

Most Americans found it shocking when the French refused the U.S. request to overfly France en route to bombing terrorist installations in Libya. The only European ally to give consistent support to antiterrorist moves was Mrs. Thatcher's Britain. For one reason or another, the others have tended to give priority to maintaining good relations with terrorist states.

The failure of cooperation at crucial moments is an irritating but finally salutary reminder that while Americans have idealized NATO, our allies regard the purpose of the alliance as limited to defense of Western Europe.

Many Americans seem worried about, even resentful toward, the European response to the U.S. bombing of Libya. It has even led some to ask if we will be able to sustain our relations with our allies.

These Americans would be less worried, I believe, if they came to terms with the limits of our alliances and recalled that we have had differences before.

If we fail to understand and accept these limits, we may endanger our alliances by expecting too much. Obviously we should respect our friends and at the same time understand that it is as legitimate for the United States to protect Americans and defend American interests as it is for France, Britain, Germany, or any country to protect its citizens and defend its interests.

What surprised and dismayed many Americans was the early European response to the U.S. request for cooperation in dealing with the problem of Libyan terrorism.

Most Americans are probably not aware that in Strasbourg the European parliament, where centrist and conservative parties have a majority, voted to condemn the U.S. attack as a "threat to international peace." But most Americans did understand that France, citing "independence" and "prudence," denied U.S. planes permission to

149

overfly that country en route to Libya—and most Americans were stung by the French decision.

They probably do not know, or care, that the decision was consistent with previous French policies. France also refused the United States permission to overfly during the 1973 Middle East war. Gaullists see overflight as a threat to France's "national independence."

It is hard for Americans, a large majority of whom supported the strike against Libya, to understand why our allies and friends did not respond like members of a team—"one for all and all for one"—but instead responded like nations seeking to serve their own interests.

Events of the past two weeks have both illustrated and illuminated differences in how the United States and its NATO partners perceive their problems and their relations with each other. Some of these differences derive from traditions, some from situations.

European countries have a habit of dealing with problems such as terrorism secretly, silently, and alone. They think their way works better than our public threats and bombings. For some of our allies—especially Italy and Germany—the economic stakes of confronting Libya are high. They think, moreover, that the risks are greater.

When Qaddafi announced that after April 11 all the cities in southern Europe would be part of his zone of counterattack, the Paris newspaper *Le Monde* asserted that this was tantamount to treating Europeans as "hostages to execute in case of an American attack." Apparently many Europeans thought they could choose not to be hostages, forgetting that Qaddafi already felt free to operate in their cities—as demonstrated in the Rome and Vienna airport massacres, the German disco bombing, and the London shootout with the Libyan "People's Bureau."

The most important difference between U.S. and European reaction to the Libya problem is explained by Europeans' differing conceptions of the alliance. Contemporary Americans think of NATO as an alliance of democratic peoples who share a civilization and have agreed, as Harry Truman said, "to unite their efforts for collective defense." We tend to forget that NATO was conceived for a limited purpose—as a means of protecting the democracies of Western Europe against being overrun or subverted by the Soviet Union—and that NATO has demonstrated unity only when confronting a threat to European security.

We tend to forget that all NATO members, including us, have always claimed and exercised the right to pursue independent foreign policies with regard to all other matters. In 1954, for example, the United States joined with the Soviet Union in opposing British,

French, and Israeli military action against Egypt. In the 1950s and 1960s, the United States complicated French policy in Indochina and North Africa by making clear our anticolonial sympathies. In the 1960s, the Kennedy administration dealt with the Cuban missile crisis without consulting European allies, and, of course, NATO as such was involved in neither the Korean nor the Vietnam War.

That is the way it was, not the way we want it to be.

Now Americans have developed a greater desire for coordination of difficult policies with Europe. Or at least we have developed a greater concern about Europe's approval of our policies. These desires could be seen in the visits of Deputy Secretary of State John Whitehead and UN Ambassador Vernon Walters to the capitals of Europe as they sought collaboration in a response to terrorism. At the same time, European nations have developed stronger tendencies toward European unity and independence from the United States. These tendencies were manifest in the negative response of all European leaders except Britain's Margaret Thatcher to the American appeal for support in its response to Libya.

The initial European refusal not only bothered us, but also bothered a good many of our allies. In France former president Giscard d'Estaing and his influential political associates Jean Lecanuet and Simone Veil registered public disagreement with the decisions of the French government. Public opinion polls showed a solid majority of the French approved the American action in Libya.

Perhaps for this reason France, like other European governments, looked for ways to narrow the distance between Europe and the United States. They spoke publicly about problems caused by Qaddafi and Libya, and in several cases they proved their concern by expelling Libyan representatives. Certain less-public steps have also been taken, including closer coordination of intelligence.

And in the United Nations, Western allies—the United Kingdom, France, Denmark, and Australia—voted with the United States against a resolution that pictured Libya as a victim of U.S. violence, while other American allies and friends voted for the resolution.

Clearly our allies are not speaking with a single voice, and just as clearly we should not expect that of them. We must respect our allies, yet be willing to act with confidence to protect vital American interests. If we expect too much of alliances, we will too soon declare them a failure.

Limited Partners in Asia
December 9, 1986

European allies were not the only ones to disappoint Americans in the 1980s, and NATO was not the only alliance that was manifestly growing weaker with time. Neil Kinnock's antinuclear policy was deeply disturbing to the Reagan administration, whose key members thought any compromise on nuclear weapons with ANZUS would quickly spread to NATO and unravel allied defenses.

George Shultz was firm on the proposition that New Zealand must choose between its nuclear policy and the alliance. The rest is history.

While American attention is riveted on internal politics, the world keeps turning. New facts overcome old doctrines; new problems challenge old solutions.

Last year the U.S. security treaty with Australia and New Zealand (ANZUS) began to unravel after New Zealand's Labor government banned visits by any American ship that was not clearly identified as bearing no nuclear weapons. Now antinuclear ideas are spreading in the Pacific, in Europe, and in the United States. Doctrines that have sustained NATO for the past four decades are being called into doubt by more and more governments no longer sure that a good nuclear offense is the best defense, no longer certain that NATO is the alliance through which they can best be secure.

The visit of British Labor party leader Neil Kinnock to the United States last week symbolized some of the trends affecting our closest allies and most stable alliances. Kinnock's party is committed to a policy of unilateral nuclear disarmament and ending Britain's involvement with nuclear weapons. The party has promised, if elected, to dismantle Britain's independent nuclear forces and to remove from Britain U.S. nuclear missiles and bases.

Labor party leaders deny this constitutes a serious breach of their alliance commitments. Kinnock has said Labor favors Britain's continued membership in NATO, and he has promised to beef up Britain's conventional forces. American bases would be welcome, he says, providing they house no nuclear weapons. Britain would not threaten the Western Alliance, Labor party leaders say, and they predict that the United States would not retaliate against the forced removal of American nuclear forces. The United States, they insist, defends Europe for its own reasons.

American leaders of both parties, however, have made it clear that they see Labor's policies as incompatible with Britain's NATO obligations. Senators Claiborne Pell of Rhode Island and Paul Sarbanes of Maryland, ranking Democrats on the Senate Foreign Relations Committee, told Kinnock during a recent London visit that implementation of his policies would end the special defense relationship between Britain and the United States, force the United States to pull all its troops from Britain, and require Britain to withdraw its troops from West Germany, where they serve under an American nuclear umbrella. Democratic Representative Stephen Solarz of New York told the *London Observer,* "What Labor intends to do would bring the biggest crisis in the NATO alliance since the Soviets built their wall in Berlin. The removal of American nuclear missiles would inevitably lead to the removal of all American troops from Britain. Our soldiers require the protection of the nuclear umbrella."

Of course, the Labor party cannot put its ideas into practice unless it first wins national elections. That might happen. Polls show Labor neck and neck with Margaret Thatcher's Conservative party. Even if Labor does not win the next elections, it may do so within the decade. And even if Kinnock is unable to win the majority in the next British elections (likely to take place next year), the Labor challenge to NATO must be taken very seriously because Britain has a distinctive role in the alliance, and if Labor policies are implemented, they would likely prove contagious.

In West Germany, the Green party is doggedly antinuclear, and now the Social Democratic party has produced its own platform for a partly denuclearized Western Europe. The leaders of West Germany's principal opposition party have joined the East German Communist party—of all people—in proposing the creation of a 186-mile-wide nuclear-free zone straddling the border between East and West Germany.

Some critics like Kinnock reject nuclear deterrence as unbearably morally offensive. Others, like the government of France, reject a strategy of nuclear offense as a deterrent in favor of one that includes defensive nuclear weapons. France, which has no inclination toward unilateral disarmament, has developed an operational neutron bomb to defend against invading forces. French leaders have also proposed that Italy, Spain, and France form a group to explore the construction of a new alliance of Mediterranean countries to provide for its own security. Italian Prime Minister Bettino Craxi, citing the spirit of Reykjavik, has proposed that Europe's governments seek the removal of all Soviet and American missiles from Europe. "We would support it," he announced.

The United States has contributed to this ferment: proposing a switch from deterrence based on offensive weapons to missile defense, from MAD to SDI; considering at Reykjavik and in Geneva the withdrawal of U.S. missiles from Europe; and in considering, at least momentarily, the total elimination of nuclear missiles.

We should not be surprised at the groping for new approaches. The world has changed dramatically. Today we are vulnerable to economic competition and trade barriers; to intercontinental ballistic missiles, nuclear submarines, long-range bombers; and to Soviet military power projected from client states near our borders.

Our own defense needs have expanded at the same time we confront increasingly intense economic competition. It could be, as Lord Peter Carrington, secretary general of NATO, commented in Philadelphia last spring, that taking all American military commitments into account "once all the figures and percentages were added up, it might emerge that there was nothing left for the defense of the United States. That, of course, would be absurd."

Lord Carrington is right.

Neither we nor our friends should jump to conclusions. But surely as our allies rethink their policies and commitments, we should rethink ours.

End of an Era?
March 30, 1987

The arrangements and alliances growing out of World War II have been coming unraveled for several years. Too many of their underpinnings were being undermined by changes in the world. Realistic analysis of these changes and their consequences began first in Europe.

Have we, almost without noticing it, arrived at the end of the post–World War II era and entered a new, far more dangerous period in international relations? One of France's most seasoned foreign affairs specialists makes a convincing case.

According to former French Foreign Minister Jean-François Poncet, the post–World War II period had three main characteristics. First was the clear economic supremacy of the United States and its nuclear protection for allies. Second was a militarily powerful, but socially stagnant Soviet Union. Third was an emergent Europe whose leaders—such as Charles de Gaulle and Konrad Adenauer—played major roles on the international scene and whose independent nuclear forces helped maintain a military equilibrium based on deterrence.

Now, says Poncet, each of the elements on which this military balance rested has been altered. The United States and Europe have grown weaker, the Soviet Union more dynamic.

In his view, American economic power has been successfully challenged—especially by Japan and other Pacific rim nations. American leadership has been weakened by internal division and by a general erosion of governmental authority, of which Irangate is the most recent example. Europe has suffered a prolonged period of economic crisis and decline, has become progressively less influential on the international scene, and is unable today to control even its own destiny. Meanwhile, Mikhail Gorbachev's bold leadership has taken center stage.

Poncet is not the only French observer deeply disturbed by the changing balance. French Defense Minister André Giraud warned recently of a "European Munich." And French Foreign Minister Jean-Bernard Raimond warned last fall that the Soviet goal was first the denuclearization of Europe, then the destruction of the Western alliance.

The French government is no longer speaking so clearly of its deepest fears concerning pending U.S.-Soviet negotiations on removal of American and Soviet medium-range missiles from Europe, but the fear remains of a U.S.-Soviet negotiation on Europe at which Europeans are not even present.

Poncet's analysis moves our attention from the intricacies of arms control to more basic concerns.

Have American economic power and governmental authority so eroded that the United States has truly lost the ability to hold its own in the international sphere? Is the Soviet Union under Gorbachev really in control of the international agenda? Has the United States lost control of its own priorities to the new leadership of the Kremlin? Is this why the administration and Congress so often sound as though they believe arms are the source, not the symptom, of international conflict?

What of the proud and still powerful nations of Western Europe? Are they willing to have their security negotiated—over their heads—by the United States and the Soviet Union? Have they no items to place on the European security agenda? Are these democracies really ready to risk their security on an escalating game of "arms control chicken" in which each dares the other to risk more to prove his commitment to arms reductions?

Why is the United States ready, at this time of strains on the alliance, to make on its own decisions and commitments with potentially momentous consequences for NATO members? Why doesn't Ronald Reagan meet his good friends in the Western Alliance—in Washington or elsewhere—for serious discussions at the highest level about our mutual security? It would be important to all of us to know the considered views of Western leaders.

Soviet leaders think the Western world has entered a "transitional era" of "advancement from capitalism to communism." They see declining American and Western military strength and growth of the Socialist world system (that is, the Soviet Union's colonial empire) as proof not only of the "changed correlation of forces" but also of the irreversible movement of history.

It is never easy to know when one historical epoch ends and another begins. It is time, however, to think about it. Most Americans do not believe, and do not want to believe, we have entered a period of historical decline.

If Poncet's analysis is even half-true, it has compelling implications for an administration and Congress that continue to propose and accept trade policies that do not secure a fair deal for American products and foreign-aid programs that have only a remote relation to our national security.

Presumably, there will be serious discussion of these questions before November 1988.

Europe's Drift Away from the United States
May 25, 1987

Economic power was shifting away from the United States and toward Europe and the Pacific rim. But affections of our European allies were also shifting.

In the last half of the 1980s the harsh criticism of American motives and society had spread from the United States (where it was purveyed by the counterculture) to Europe. As the reality of a Soviet threat dimmed, more and more Europeans and Americans thought of the United States and the USSR as morally equivalent superpowers vying for world domination.

In Britain they call it "equilateralism." In West Germany they call it "equidistancing." But throughout the world, "US equals SU" means viewing the United States and the Soviet Union as equally unattractive. That attitude is spreading—among America's allies in Europe and elsewhere. It goes hand in hand with the rise of neutralism and is loosening the bonds that maintain our principal alliances.

Opinion polls conducted during the past year confirm the diminishing reputation of the United States and rising regard for the Soviet Union among key American friends. In an article in *Public Opinion* magazine (March/April 1987), "Why the British Don't Like Us Any More," British political scientist Ivor Crewe analyzed spreading disaffection with the United States in the United Kingdom. He reported that the British have come to see the United States as a "greater threat to world peace" than the Soviet Union by a margin of 37 to 33 percent. *The New York Times* reported a recent West German poll found that 49 percent of West Germans saw Mikhail Gorbachev as "really concerned about peace," as compared with 46 percent who believed the same of Ronald Reagan.

Such views are growing in all age groups but are especially marked among younger voters, who display a consistently poor opinion of American motives and policies. Among adults, increasing numbers in West Germany and Britain doubt the desirability of continuing the present close relationship with the United States. The number of Britons who believe their country should work less closely with the United States in foreign policy grew from 17 percent in 1974 to 32 percent in 1984 to 43 percent in 1986. In West Germany, attitudes were even less favorable toward the United States and more favorable toward the Soviet Union. A recent West German poll found that 58 percent of West Germans wanted Bonn to cooperate equally with America and Russia, as compared with only 31 percent who preferred the present practice of working more closely with the United States.

Ferdinand Mount of London's *Daily Telegraph* labels this "false equation" the "new treason of the clerks," and he notes that

> the line now is not so much to present Russia as a "new dawn in human history," but rather to equate West and East as inhabiting the same gray twilight, both muddling through by trial and error in the general direction of peace and reform, but with the Soviet Union leading the way, due to its blessed lack of monopoly capitalists and warmongering cliques.

Why do so many of our best friends feel so negative about continuing an alliance with us when it has so clearly helped to secure the longest period of peace that Europe has enjoyed in two centuries and has provided stability to the developed world? They know we are reliable allies. They know we are a democratic nation. But they do not think well of our conduct of foreign affairs.

Crewe explained that British doubt "concerns neither the capacity nor the will of the United States, but concerns its good judgment. We worry not about the warmth of its commitment to Britain, but about the coolness of its relations with the Soviet Union."

In late 1986, only 19 percent of Britons thought the United States had done everything reasonable to reach an arms agreement with the USSR. Seventy-five percent believed we should do more.

These subjective opinions have already become an objective factor in alliance relations and in the politics of allied nations. They are manifest in the strong neutralist tendencies of Britain's Labor party program in the current election and of West Germany's Social Democratic party, where large numbers doubt American commitment to fairness and a good society.

In these groups, the United States is widely viewed as a stronghold of Darwinian ethics and moral indifference—selfish, materialistic, racist. Only 6 percent of Britons under thirty-five believe the United States seeks to help the poor in less-developed countries. Lack of confidence in Ronald Reagan is part of the problem, but the same societies held a poor opinion of Jimmy Carter. Mikhail Gorbachev's global diplomacy is widely admired. Soviet credibility is growing as American credibility declines.

The terms in which our allies reproach us bear a strong resemblance to Soviet criticism of American society, and European observers friendly to the United States believe the Soviets' relentless criticism of American society has taken its toll. Among allies, as well as in *Pravda*, the United States is described as "a dangerous and aggressive player in international politics"; as "double-dealers that cannot be trusted"; as "hypocritical and duplicitous"; and, above all, as a "base self-seeking society in full moral decline."

Of course, these reproaches also resemble the charges American politicians hurl at one another in harsh domestic debates carried out before a worldwide audience. While senators participating in the current Iran-contra hearings may believe—as several said in opening statements—that these hearings are evidence of the strength of the system, foreign audiences think otherwise. They believe the charges of lawless government and abandoned allies.

Finally, it is important to remember that growing anti-Americanism is not (yet) triumphant. British voters will almost surely return Margaret Thatcher to power and reject the Labor party. Antinuclear, anti-American feeling has no base in France outside the French Communist party. West Germany's governing party, the CDU, is a staunch friend of the United States and of the alliance.

But even these good friends note our grandiose tendencies and our failure to consult, as before the Reykjavik negotiation. And they sometimes remind us that, as it is necessary to be a friend to have a friend, it is also necessary to behave like an ally to have allies.

More Alliance Problems
June 15, 1987

France's *Le Monde* reported from Venice that there was one point not in doubt at the summit meeting of the world's seven leading industrial democracies: "that Ronald Reagan was determined to sign an accord with the Soviet Union as soon as possible on the removal of nuclear missiles."

Although the allied leaders at the conference are apparently convinced of this, Reagan continues to encounter difficulty in persuading citizens of Western European nations that he is indeed committed to reaching an agreement with Mikhail Gorbachev.

Last week, as Reagan tried once more to reassure West German pacifists that his heart is with them—that he, too, seeks a world free from the threat of nuclear annihilation—reports leaked of a new poll of Europeans showing Gorbachev the clear winner in the 1987 "peace war."

The poll, sponsored by the U.S. Information Agency, showed that large margins of British, French, and West Germans give Gorbachev more credit than Ronald Reagan for progress toward an arms agreement. In Britain, 63 percent thought Gorbachev deserved the credit as compared with 13 percent who gave the credit to Reagan. In West Germany, it was 72 percent for Gorbachev to 9 percent for Reagan. In France, the Soviet leader was credited over the American leader by 45 percent to 16 percent.

Our European friends do not even give Reagan credit for initiating the proposals he did, in fact, initiate. For example, large majorities think Gorbachev first proposed the "zero option" for removal of intermediate-range nuclear missiles from Europe.

Europe's leaders know better. They understand that Ronald

Reagan is, as one said, "hellbent" on signing an agreement with Gorbachev.

What accounts for the great gap in perception between allied leaders and the European public? For one thing, leaders are better informed, often at firsthand.

The people are more susceptible to propaganda and stereotypes. Publics respond to deep-set impressions. As Walter Lippmann explained in his brilliant book *Public Opinion*, publics understand public figures through oversimplified stereotypes that resist change. Information that contradicts these stereotypes tends to be ignored, forgotten, or reinterpreted.

For much of the world, European as well as American, Ronald Reagan is seen as a John Wayne figure—a tall, strong, laconic defender of freedom.

During his first term, he played the part and won widespread kudos for a polished performance—with his speech to the British Parliament, his visit to the beach at Normandy. By promoting a strong dollar and a strong America; offering solidarity to the people of Poland; supporting the *mujahedin* in Afghanistan and the contras in Nicaragua; insisting on the reversibility of tyranny and the inevitability of freedom, Reagan made his mark. With the Reagan Doctrine, he projected a vision of the future that contradicted Marxist claims and affirmed that freedom works better than collectivism or force. Reagan seemed almost typecast for the role he played. No wonder he did it so well.

The president's new message does not fit the old role or the old Reagan. It involves too much contradiction with too many past positions. Reagan saw too many flaws in past arms control agreements and spoke too often about how and why they left the United States and its allies weaker and the Soviet Union stronger. He spoke too often about the Soviets' expansionist tendencies and the necessity for strength. The old message not only criticized specific arms agreements but also criticized the "arms control" approach to American and Western security.

The president and his advisers claim there is no contradiction between the old message and the new posture. But Western publics think otherwise. Some are dismayed by Reagan's new enthusiasm for sweeping arms agreements. Others are disbelieving. Almost no one is ready to applaud Ronald Reagan for signing an agreement that counters his teachings of a lifetime.

There is a moral in the Western publics' reluctance to credit Ronald Reagan with a major role in arms negotiations. It is that

Ronald Reagan cannot establish his place in history by signing an arms accord—no matter how dramatic.

Gorbachev and the Germanys
September 14, 1987

More and more, Germany was at the heart of concern about the new Europe. The French were worried. The Soviets were worried. The East German government worried about the role Germany would play in Europe and NATO.

The specter of a reunited Germany is again haunting Europe, called up by the visit last week of East German Communist leader Erich Honecker to Bonn, where he has been treated with pomp, ceremony, and great hospitality by Chancellor Helmut Kohl and the West German government. In Europe this is regarded as an extremely important event.

More than six years passed between the day that former West German Chancellor Helmut Schmidt extended the invitation and the day that Erich Honecker, the man who built the Berlin Wall and has governed Communist Germany with an iron hand, set foot in the Federal Republic. Several times visits were scheduled only to be canceled at the behest of the Soviet Union. That alone gave the meeting a significance beyond itself. Since it could take place only with the blessing of the Soviet Union, it now obviously has that blessing. Today Mikhail Gorbachev judges that greater intra-German contact coincides with the interest of the Kremlin.

The visit is one more proof of Gorbachev's determination "to play a role in the great European family." The Soviets' own "dynamic dialogue" with the Federal Republic got under way earlier this summer when West German President Richard von Weizsacker visited Moscow. At that time Gorbachev also stated—with a clarity some called threatening—his views about the limits of rapprochement between East and West Germany: "The existence of two German states is a fact. Any other analysis would have very serious consequences."

For Honecker and his entourage the visit means the Federal Republic has finally accepted the existence and the legitimacy of the

161

Communist state. They do not seem to understand that Helmut Kohl and his West German colleagues do not see it that way. To them, Honecker's visit is one more step in their determined campaign to break down the barriers between East and West Germany. As Kohl said in his opening statement, "The people of Germany know there exist two states which have to deal practically with many issues . . . but the idea of the unity of the nation is as awake as ever, and the will to keep it is still there."

At the top of the list of "practical issues" with which the two Germanys must deal is the Communist state's desire for economic assistance and West Germany's desire to promote freer passage between peoples.

With credits, technology, and favorable terms of trade, Bonn buys greater freedom for their fellow Germans—to visit, to travel, to immigrate. This year a million East Germans under retirement age will be permitted to visit the West (those past retirement age already enjoy greater freedom of movement). But travel is still tightly controlled. This year Kohl hopes to buy a change in East Germany's policy of shooting to kill anyone attempting to flee over the Berlin Wall. It is not clear he will succeed.

No one—least of all the East German government—knows how many of its citizens might seek to leave if the penalties were less drastic. Demonstrations beside the wall this summer were but one reminder among many that East Germans badly want greater freedom to travel.

When they travel they see for themselves what Honecker's dismal deals reflect: that the West is able to provide its citizens with greater economic well-being and more freedom. Permitting more East Germans to see for themselves is the risk that Honecker—and Gorbachev—run with the new policy of "dynamic dialogue" with Western Europe.

There is also a risk for Western Europe and for the United States in the new rapprochement. Former French Foreign Minister Jean-François Poncet spelled it out in a commentary in *Le Figaro*. Poncet believes that

> the denuclearization of Europe, to which Washington is imprudently ready to agree, will be accompanied by an eventual reduction in American forces stationed in Europe. It could lead the Federal Republic to seek in the East the guarantees of its security which the West will no longer seem able to offer.

A neutral Germany is already the dream of West Germany's Greens and of an influential part of the Social Democratic party. It is the nightmare of the French and other Western Europeans who understand the removal of nuclear weapons will leave them far more vulnerable to the Soviets' huge advantage in conventional forces and who understand the importance of a strong West Germany to the defense of Western Europe.

A neutral West Germany is not yet a probability in Poncet's view, but he and others think it "sufficiently plausible to stimulate France and West Germany to construct together a new European foundation of which the Atlantic Alliance has clearer and clearer need." Helmut Kohl has already spoken in favor of just such a Franco-German collaboration in building a European defense of Western Europe.

One hopes the U.S. government will have the realism and foresight to encourage development of a European defense capacity that will enable the prosperous and competent Western European states to defend themselves while they wait for Eastern Europeans to see for themselves the benefits of freedom.

The Transformation of Europe
May 14, 1989

By 1989 the accumulating changes—in the Soviet Union, Western Europe, Asia, and the Pacific—were giving birth to new thinking in Europe, not only about integration of the European Community but also about the relations between the EC and Eastern Europe.

In Europe, change and talk of change are everywhere. The approach of 1992 and the new Europe, the democratization of Hungary, Poland's new freedom, the rise of nationalist and democratic movements in the Soviet Union, Helmut Kohl's difficult and unexpected demands for the removal of short-range nuclear missiles, the British Labor party's return from the political desert of unilateral disarmament—these and other transformations dominate the conversations of Europe's political class. There is an atmosphere of excitement and expectation.

The new Europe emerging from its long gestation will be as different as a butterfly is from a crawling caterpillar. No one is certain about the size or the shape of the new Europe or exactly how it will function, but its evolution is already having an impact on the politics

163

of member states and on the imagination of Europeans.

The opportunity to win (or preserve) political prominence through the institutions of the new Europe is attracting creative, ambitious political figures who are already busily trying to expand the scope and power of the new domain. The prospect of membership in this huge, rich market is exciting and stimulating in countries that have reluctantly learned since World War II to regard themselves as something less than powers of the first rank.

"If there can be a market of 300 million [people], why not a market of 600 million?" said a rising star in the French political firmament.

Why not? Austrian Chancellor Franz Vranitzky says his country is nearly ready to make a formal application for membership in the EC. Why should not the countries of the East—as they retrieve their national independence—be part of the new Europe?

The Soviet grip on Eastern Europe has already loosened enough that Hungary has been granted observer status in the European parliament at Strasbourg. The economies of Eastern Europe are open enough that there is competition for their markets and growing Western participation in their industrial development.

The rapid democratization of Hungary's politics, the less dramatic but real political reforms enacted in Poland, and the progressive openings of *glasnost* in the Soviet Union have raised hopes and stimulated democratic and nationalist movements throughout Eastern Europe. The most exciting political struggles today are inside the Communist countries of Eastern Europe, where reformers vie with Stalinists or Brezhnevists for control of the future.

In Western Europe, discussion also focuses on Gorbachev's economic and social failures and on his diplomatic successes. Western Europeans worry aloud that Gorbachev's reforms are still reversible but fear that his diplomatic victories might be permanent.

There is a widespread view that the goals of Soviet foreign policy are to separate West Germany from the new Europe and the new Europe from the United States, leaving West Germany and Europe unprotected.

Anxiety about the West German role in the new Europe was, of course, heightened by Chancellor Helmut Kohl's demand that the United States negotiate the removal of short-range nuclear weapons from German soil.

But this proposed denuclearization is only one facet of resurgent concern about a resurgent Germany. The depolarization of East-West relations recreates the possibility of a Central Europe, and there is no question about who is the dominant power in Central Europe.

West German economic power is viewed as awesome. West German economic penetration of Eastern Europe has already enhanced it. Western Europeans, and some Eastern Europeans, scare themselves with images of a powerful, reunified, neutral Germany dominating Central, and perhaps Eastern, Europe.

Manifestly, Europe is in flux. And that means U.S. foreign policy in the region is in flux. West German reluctance to accept nuclear weapons threatens NATO's "forward strategy," the centerpiece of which is the defense of Germany. The United States could not conceivably maintain large numbers of exposed, outnumbered U.S. troops in Germany without nuclear protection.

Of course, a reformed democratic Soviet Union would dismantle its huge conventional and unconventional forces and would constitute a threat to no one. But the Soviet Union is not so reformed, and it has not yet begun serious reductions in military forces and military budgets.

Confronting all this change, what should the United States do?

First, we should remember that maintaining American troops in Europe is a burden and not a privilege. In fact, it is not clear that today's rich, technologically advanced Europe requires the kind and amount of protection the United States has provided since World War II. A united Europe can surely provide a greatly strengthened European "pillar," as they call it, for the defense of its own independence.

It is a hopeful time. I believe Americans should enjoy rather than fear the changes under way in Eastern and Western Europe. We cannot control these processes, and we do not need to try. We should instead spend our time boning up on what it is like to live in a world with multiple power centers and multiple competitors—for that is what tomorrow will be.

A United Germany?

November 13, 1989

Concern over the role of a unified Germany grew as East Germans poured into the West and, with a little help from Mikhail Gorbachev, brought down the wall and two successive governments.

After more than forty years of not worrying much about German power, Western Europe's political class is now preoccupied with the question of how a reunified Germany will "fit" in the Europe of the future.

I say *will* rather than *would* because almost everyone seems to assume that reunification is inevitable in the not-too-distant future. Many believe that reunification will be an early consequence of the crisis of authority now under way in East Germany—a crisis that last week prompted East Germany to open its borders to the West.

Western leaders worry about the resurgence of German power in Europe but do not really want to say so. Instead, they are hurrying to make it clear that they don't mind.

Last week, George Bush and François Mitterrand went on record in support of reunification. Germany's allies feel the need to make clear their support for reunification because all were involved in the original occupation and division of Germany after World War II.

That first division was designed to prevent the resurgence of the "German threat" in the years after the war. The second division of Germany—symbolized by the Berlin Wall—reflected the determination of Joseph Stalin to consolidate an Eastern European empire and staunch the hemorrhage of people and resources to the West.

From 1961, when the wall was built, until May of 1989, when the government of Hungary opened its border with Austria, the people of Eastern Europe have been sealed inside the fortified borders of their respective "people's republics." Until East Germans began to rush through the hole in Hungary's borders, no one knew how the people of East Germany felt about their government or anything else. Specifically, no one knew how they felt about the harsh regime of Erich Honecker.

It was supposed that, if East Germans were satisfied with their Marxist-style "people's republic" and their eastward-looking foreign policy, there was no reason to expect a reunited Germany in the foreseeable future.

All that changed when the people of East Germany perceived that they had an alternative. When Honecker's policy of repression did not staunch the flow west, he and his policies were replaced. New leaders, new concessions, new demands, and the continuing flow of East Germans to West Germany have now not only created a crisis of authority and legitimacy for the East German regime, but also reminded others that East Germany had no history or prior existence as a country—but was only that part of Germany occupied by the Soviet Union after the war.

Recent events made it clear, moreover, that East Germany had not become a country that could survive liberalization. If it is reformed, it will self-destruct.

Informed European observers doubt that Mikhail Gorbachev would use the kind and amount of force necessary to preserve East Germany. What, then, would he do? Many observers believe he would bargain for reunification on the best terms available.

A neutral, unified Germany would be a giant step toward the kind of neutral Europe Gorbachev has dreamed of. A neutral Germany could not be a member of NATO, and NATO could not survive without Germany. Therefore, a neutral Germany would require dismantling the structures of the Western Alliance.

Would the government of West Germany accept neutralization in return for reunification? It would mean betting its security and independence on Soviet benevolence. How many German leaders and parties would take such a risk? No one knows for certain.

Perhaps the Soviet Union could not extract so high a price.

A fallback position still attractive to Gorbachev is thought to be a "confederation" of European members of NATO and the Warsaw Pact, presumably excluding the Soviet Union. Such a hypothetical confederation, it is thought, could preserve and transform both alliances. Obviously, this arrangement would mean an end to the U.S. role in Europe and would raise the prospect of the "Finlandization" of the entire continent.

Another, less radical scenario looks toward the integration of a unified Germany in a strong, integrated Europe.

Much depends on how the Soviet Union emerges from its own reform processes.

One thing, however, is apparent. The dramatic events now under way in East Germany could easily transform the character of Europe.

Worrying about Germany
February 19, 1990

I believe those who worry about a resurgent, unified Germany are living in the past. Much has changed for Germans since they were a threat to the world. West Germans have had long experience with democratic institutions, and East Germans have suffered their absence. Both seem intent on exploiting the economic possibilities allowed by German unification and the European single market. Both have suffered the devastating impact of defeat, division, occupation, and humiliation.

I argue in the following column that neither Germans nor any other people pose an inherent genetic threat to others. Certain ideologies are inherently threatening. Fortunately, these are under assault the world over and, in Europe, are fully discredited.

A strong unified Germany firmly tied to the West should not threaten its neighbors. But a unified neutral Germany detached from the democracies would be far more troublesome—except that the way events are developing, there may be no East-West conflict about which to be neutral.

The die is cast, the commitment made. Britain, France, the United States, and the Soviet Union have agreed on the creation of a new Germany and to a process by which it will occur. Still, on the morning after, Europe is feeling ambivalent about the whole matter.

Although Western governments long ago endorsed reunification of the two Germanys and recent pools show that more West Europeans support than oppose reunification, misgivings abound, and second thoughts multiply as the reality looms.

Although it finally signed onto reunification in principle and to the process by which it will occur, the Soviet Union remains the most outspoken of the four powers about its concerns.

"Small boys, when they play soldiers here, still play Russians against Germans, not Russians against Americans," a Soviet political scientist said in explaining Soviet reluctance about German unity.

Substantial minorities of adults in Poland, France, Britain, and the Benelux countries, among others, share this reluctance to see the reconstruction of a powerful Germany in the heart of Europe. Poland has demanded a major role in the reunification process on the grounds that prior suffering gives it a special interest.

Germans are acutely aware of the concerns of their neighbors. They have heard the bad jokes about how their neighbors like Germany so much they want two of them, about how the purpose of NATO is to keep the Russians out, the Americans in, and the Germans down. They know they are still widely feared. West Germans in particular have made repeated efforts to reassure their neighbors. They are still working on the problem.

"We Germans are aware of the historical dimensions of this [reunification] process," West German Foreign Minister Hans-Dietrich Genscher told Mikhail Gorbachev in Moscow. "We are aware of all the suffering inflicted on other nations in the name of Germany," he said. "We do not have territorial claims against any of our neighbors," he added, seeking especially to reassure Poland. But the fear remains.

Perhaps because the United States never suffered physical destruction or defeat from the Germans, or perhaps because it is an
ocean away, Americans are less worried than Europeans about a
resurgent Germany, although they are fully sensitive to the power of
the German economy and especially the deutsche mark.

There is another reason Americans do not worry as much about
a resurgent Germany. To be deeply concerned about "the German
problem," you must believe there is something inherent that predis-
poses the German people to expansion and aggression and that this
tendency is stronger than the experiences of war, defeat, occupation,
division, and forty years of democratic politics. Americans have a
habit of believing experience is more powerful than inheritance in
shaping social behavior.

I do not believe there is a permanent predisposition to conquest
in the German psyche, but I do believe there is a predisposition to
aggression and war in totalitarian politics and that this made the
Germans of the Nazi period a special menace to Jews, Gypsies,
Jehovah's Witnesses, and all Germans who opposed Hitler's vision
and commands.

We know from the brief, violent history of Hitler's rule that the
Nazis first made war on German society, then made war on the
world. They moved quickly from the quest for total control within
one country to quest for control beyond its borders. The Nazi political
machine was responsible for the deaths of tens of millions of people
inside and outside Germany.

It is right to fear the destructive dynamic that drives such politics.
But it does not follow that we must fear Germans. Nor does the
Soviet record prove we should forever fear Russians. Instead, we
should fear totalitarianism.

Both Nazi Germany and the Soviet Union adopted policies that
involved huge bureaucracies and mass murders. To collect and ship
Jews and operate the death camps of the Final Solution required the
active participation of tens of thousands of Germans—just as it
required great bureaucracies of Soviet citizens to staff the secret
police, the interrogations, prisons, executions, and slave labor camps
of Stalin's gulag.

It does not follow, however, that the national character of Russians or Germans drove this destruction. It was rather the quest of
dictators for total control. Totalitarian politics is dangerous because it
strips individuals of rights and societies of protection and leaves them
exposed to the state's claim of total power.

The lesson of this century is not that Germans or Russians are
intrinsically dangerous to the world, but that small bands of violent

169

men who claim special powers over the rest of us should be restrained at all costs.

Gorbachev and Kohl: Mutual Aid

July 9, 1990

In mid-1990 the shape of the new Europe was not yet clear. Would NATO survive the end of the cold war, and in what form? Would Mikhail Gorbachev (and François Mitterrand) succeed in building a new, all-European community based on the Conference on Security and Cooperation in Europe? How much assistance would Gorbachev receive from Western Europe, through which institutions, and to what effect? Would he achieve Stalin's goal of a neutral Germany? And would the United States remain an active participant in European affairs?

What had become clear was the skill of both Gorbachev and Helmut Kohl as politicians and diplomats.

From the time he was appointed general secretary, Mikhail Gorbachev has had three principal goals vis-à-vis the West: to prevent the resurgence of a German threat in the heart of Europe, to break the Soviet Union out of its technological and economic isolation, and to eliminate a major U.S. presence in Europe.

If Gorbachev stays in power, he has a good chance of achieving all three in this season of change and reconfiguration in Europe.

For such success—if he achieves it—he will be beholden not only to his own undoubted ability but, above all, to the extraordinary diplomatic skill and activity of German Chancellor Helmut Kohl and his foreign minister, Hans-Dietrich Genscher. For their trouble, they will also have achieved a united, sovereign Germany and left the Soviets, the French, and the Americans each feeling that the country whose interest most closely coincides with their own is Germany.

It promises to be a stunning achievement for both Gorbachev and Kohl.

Soviet officials have made no secret—ever—of their fear of resurgent German power. Of the World War II allies, they have most strongly and consistently resisted moves toward German reunification.

What a surprise then to hear Soviet Foreign Minister Eduard

Shevardnadze say—as he did a few months ago—that the security of Europe is better served by the reunification of Germany than by its division, *providing* that it take place in the context of an appropriate pan-European settlement.

The European settlement that Gorbachev has had in mind, even before the appearance of his book *Perestroika*, is one that would "overcome" the division of Europe into blocs and hostile alliances, would integrate the Soviet Union and the East into a common European family, would give the Soviets' hard-pressed economy access to Western technology and financial assistance, and, of course, would almost as a byproduct eliminate a significant U.S. role in Europe.

It is not wholly clear at what point Gorbachev realized, as Shevardnadze put it, that "it is necessry to utilize in depth the potential of a German-Soviet economic cooperation." By the time the Soviets understood the Germans could help solve their economic problems, the Germans had already understood there would be no reunification without Soviet support. A marriage of convenience was quickly negotiated, which promises to help both partners achieve their hearts' desires.

Kohl and Genscher made themselves representatives of increased Soviet inclusion in international arenas. In addition, Bonn offered financial assistance highly favorable to Moscow. It guaranteed $3 billion credit for the USSR and agreed that East Germany will pay approximately 1.25 billion deutsche marks ($750 million) toward the cost of supporting 360,000 Soviet troops and their families in East Germany the last six months of 1990, providing Moscow hard currency at a highly subsidized rate.

Now Kohl, with French President François Mitterrand, has sponsored a proposal for massive Western aid ($15 billion) in the EC and the G7, and he is working on proposals to make NATO less objectionable to the Soviet Union and on the construction of the Soviets' favorite pan-European institution, the Conference on Security and Cooperation in Europe. On July 15 Kohl will travel to Moscow to report to Gorbachev on progress so far and to appeal for the Soviets to drop opposition to German membership in NATO—which the United States and Western Europeans want as their price for supporting German reunification and which the Germans themselves presumably desire.

But the Soviets' price is likely to be high, and some of its terms may be ultimately incompatible with meaningful German membership in a meaningful NATO. The last Shevardnadze proposal left Soviet troops in Germany for five years, mainly at German expense.

171

To assist Gorbachev in Europe, Kohl has needed and gotten French support. Mitterrand has been a willing and active participant in the Gorbachev-Kohl policy. His own quasi-Gaullist vision of a stable Europe without the blocs coincides with Gorbachev's in some crucial ways. They also share a barely articulated desire to reduce the role of the United States and NATO in Europe and to enhance the CSCE. This is the reason Mitterrand is just now opposing American efforts to transform and broaden NATO's mission and is working to prevent NATO from taking a position on the structure of the CSCE.

Like Gorbachev, Mitterrand looks toward a Europe for the Europeans.

The desired American contribution to the Gorbachev-Kohl design is now clear: it is for economic aid and a "flexible" policy toward NATO. Where the Bush administration will come out is not yet clear. My own sense is that a meaningful long-term role for NATO will not survive the current reconfiguration of Europe—if present trends in the Soviet Union continue—and that Bush cannot join Kohl and Mitterrand in a major financial aid program—even if he should desire to do so—not when the Soviets are still spending nearly 20 percent of their GNP on a military budget, sending at least $5 billion a year to Cuba and more to Angola, Afghanistan, Mozambique, et al.; not when Bush proposed to raise American taxes; not when Japan flatly refused to join an aid consortium.

But the no's of Japan and the United States will not matter that much to the emergence of the new Europe, which is once again absorbed with itself and is creating its own complex correlations of power.

A Safer World?
May 28, 1990

Because it is impossible to predict the future with accuracy, it is also impossible to prepare for it. The U.S. stake in the world will remain large, but the nature of that world remains uncertain. None of the important developments after World Wars I and II were predicted. Neither will be events after the cold war.

Is the cold war over? Not if Mikhail Gorbachev and his colleagues are having second thoughts about withdrawing Soviet troops from Europe.

Is the world becoming safer? Not if the United States accepts constraints on advanced weapons while dangerous Soviet intercontinental ballistic weapons remain unrestricted. Has democracy triumphed? Not yet. Not in the Soviet Union or China or almost anywhere in Asia outside of Japan. Not in the Middle East or Africa. While democracy spreads in Latin America, fundamentalism spreads in Moslem nations.

Reason has not yet replaced force in Kashmir or Lebanon, Gaza, Iraq, or Lithuania. George Bush cannot write enough notes to comfort all the families of all the victims of violence—in Nepal, Malaysia, Afghanistan, Jordan, Beirut, and Nazareth. James Baker cannot cut enough deals to eliminate all the proliferating weapons of mass destruction.

It is not true that the case for democracy has vanquished all opposing philosophies, only that it has vanquished European Marxism. We have not arrived at the Heavenly City of eighteenth-century philosophers or the Crystal Palace of nineteenth-century prophets.

The fact is that no one knows what will happen next. The great movements of the twentieth century have come as a surprise. Communism, fascism, Nazism, Islamic fundamentalism—each was an unexpected development. Each seemed unlikely even as it fastened a fanatical grip on an unwary society. Lenin and his Bolsheviks were as implausible a band of conspirators as ever moved into a volatile political situation. They were as implausible as Hitler and the freakish freebooters who met with him in Bavaria and Berlin, as implausible as the Ayatollah Khomeini and his frenzied followers, as implausible as the Chinese Red Guard or Pol Pot's baby-faced killers.

Ours is a century of violent revolutions, each more unexpected than the last. It is a century of utopian dreams and megalomaniacal revolutionaries who, as rulers, move their subjects about like so many pawns on a gigantic chessboard—into cities, out of cities; from reeducation onto farms, from farms into reeducation.

Always the world is surprised. We are surprised that "trends" should change so rapidly, surprised that a man with a band of followers can have such an impact, surprised that grand schemes to collectivize, villagify, and nationalize can produce so much murder and mayhem.

We are surprised by war and surprised by peace; surprised by economic growth (as in the Asian miracle) and surprised by economic failure (as under socialism). We were surprised by Stalin's ruthless conquest and by Gorbachev's abandonment of those conquests.

In truth we have not discerned the "laws" of historical development, probably because there are none. Individual leaders have a greater impact on history than we prefer to think, because individuals are so unpredictable. It is disconcerting, for example, to think that the theoretical speculation of a small band of exiles may shape the future of the world.

Much of what has happened since World War II has come as a surprise. And much that lies ahead will also surprise us. We did not foresee the resurgence of German and Japanese economic power, nor do we know the consequences for them or us of Japan's highly leveraged security market and wide-ranging acquisitions. No one anticipated the rapid liquidation of the Soviet Union's European empire. Nor did we foresee the Soviet government's sudden halt of its withdrawal from Eastern Europe. We do not know how long Mikhail Gorbachev will retain power or what his policies will be while he remains.

We are more involved with one another than ever, but that does not mean that we like each other better. Some Japanese dream of saying no to America. Some French will not say yes to NATO or to a special role for the United States in Europe. The size and shape of the European community are less certain than Brussels pretends. Difficulties in breaking East Germany out of the Warsaw Pact expand that unknown. Uncertainty hangs as heavy as London fog over the future, obscuring it.

It is a good time now, in advance of the American-Soviet summit, for the U.S. government to step back and think again about a sweeping arms deal that does not affect the presence of Soviet troops and tanks in Europe or the continued production of ICBMs with a well-understood first-strike capability.

It is time for the Bush administration to reiterate Ronald Reagan's message at Reykjavik: a deal? Yes, but not at the price of enhanced American vulnerability in a still very uncertain world.

PART FOUR

The Last Colonial Empire

Introduction to Part Four

The Last Colonial Empire

After World War II, as the British, French, Dutch, and Belgians were more or less reluctantly giving up their overseas empires, the Soviet Union got serious about acquiring one.

Expansion had been a major feature of the foreign policy of Russia throughout its modern history, and although Lenin had called the multinational czarist empire a "prisonhouse of peoples," after a moment of hesitation he resumed the policy of expansion. Adlai Stevenson, as U.S. ambassador to the United Nations, summarized in 1961 the conquests and incorporation that established the boundaries of the USSR as of that time. His description reminds us of the origins of the contemporary separatist movement:

> An independent Ukrainian Republic was recognized by the Bolsheviks in 1917, but in 1917 they established a rival Republic in Kharkov. In July 1923, with the help of the Red army, a Ukrainian Soviet Socialist Republic was established and incorporated into the USSR. In 1920, the independent Republic of Azerbaijan was invaded by the Red army and a Soviet Socialist Republic was proclaimed. In the same year, the Khanate of Khiva was invaded by the Red army and a puppet Soviet People's Republic of Khorezm was established. With the conquest of Khiva, the approaches of its neighbor, the Emirate of Bokhara, were opened to the Soviet forces which invaded it in September 1920. In 1918, Armenia declared its independence from Russia. . . . In 1920, the Soviet army invaded, and Armenian independence, so long awaited, was snuffed out. In 1921, the Red army came to the aid of Communists rebelling against the independent state of Georgia and installed a Soviet regime.
>
> This process inexorably continued. Characteristically, the Soviets took advantage of the turmoil and upheaval of the Second World War to continue the process of colonial subju-

177

gation at the expense of its neighbors. The Soviets' territorial aggrandizement included the Karelian province and other parts of Finland and the Eastern provinces of Poland, the Romanian provinces of Bessarabia and Bukovina, the independent States of Estonia, Latvia, and Lithuania, the Koenigsberg area, slices of Czechoslovakia, South Sakhalin, the Kurile Islands, and Tanna Tuva.

When the Soviet Union emerged from World War II, it was the dominant military power in Europe. Joseph Stalin moved to exploit this correlation of forces by sucking in the independent nations of Eastern Europe, imposing a Soviet style of political, economic, and social organization and challenging the governments of Greece, Turkey, France, and Italy. After the U.S. and Western European response ended Soviet expansion in Europe, the Soviets began to develop a new style overseas, based not on direct rule but on a new formula that combined propaganda, force, organization, and economics. These governments in the new Soviet Union came to power by force and feature close political, military, and economic ties to the Soviet Union.

The process of overseas expansion and development of a "world Socialist system" began with Cuba and South Vietnam and accelerated during the 1970s after the fall of Saigon. From time to time it encountered obstacles and setbacks as in Venezuela, Bolivia, Latin America's Southern Cone, El Salvador, and Grenada. Nevertheless, by 1980 it constituted the only global empire in the late twentieth century.

That force has been the essential element in this world Socialist system could be clearly observed in the Soviet crushing of Hungary's 1956 revolt and Czechoslovakia's 1968 effort to take control of its own affairs and in Soviet-sponsored civil wars in Angola, Ethiopia, Mozambique, Morocco, El Salvador, and Nicaragua.

Still, force was never the only instrument of Soviet expansion or Soviet governance. Instead, successive Soviet governments have seen force as Clausewitz recommended: as politics by other means. Diplomacy is also politics by other means. The Soviet campaign to expand its reach obliterated distinctions between war and peace, diplomacy and politics, and internal and international struggles.

In the five years after the fall of Saigon, a dozen countries were sucked into the Soviet orbit. In each of these countries, a government tied to the Soviet Union came to power through an effective combination of politics and force—with weapons and often advisers as well, supplied by the Soviet Union or the Soviet bloc. Each country was integrated into the world Socialist economic and military systems, symbolized by the basing rights each offered to the Soviet Union. Each was provided a Praetorian Guard to guard it against second thoughts. In half a dozen of these countries—Afghanistan, Mozambique, Angola, Ethiopia, Nicaragua, and Cambodia (whose circumstances were somewhat different)—resistance to the new Marxist governments and insurgencies developed.

What has been called the "struggle between the superpowers" has been the often intermittent, sometimes skillful, sometimes half-hearted, sometimes incompetent efforts of the United States to assist those resisting incorporation into the Socialist system. What was called the Reagan Doctrine was the conviction of Ronald Reagan and much of his administration that it was legitimate for the United States to provide assistance—including military assistance—to peoples seeking to reestablish or to preserve their independence against incorporation by force into the world Socialist system.

This aid became the subject of one of the bitterest, most sustained, partisan conflicts in American politics. The following section deals with some key aspects of this struggle inside and outside the United States.

Afghanistan . . .

Soviet Logic on Afghanistan
December 9, 1985

The Soviet invasion of Afghanistan in December 1979 marked the end of the period of rapid Soviet expansion after the fall of Saigon. The brutality and cynicism of the invasion shocked the world—and stirred the Carter administration to respond with aid to the mujahedin, *a policy continued and expanded under Ronald Reagan.*

Although the Soviets claimed they had responded to a call for help from a fraternal Socialist ally, one of their first acts on invading Afghanistan was to murder the president, who had offended Brezhnev with a very tentative move toward nonalignment. An extremely brutal war against the Afghan people continued for nearly a decade, driving approximately a third of the total population into exile in Pakistan and Iran, devastating the land, sovietizing the culture, but never finally conquering its people.

The invasion of Afghanistan was one of the very few events for which the General Assembly of the United Nations criticized the Soviet Union—although never by name and, until the appointment of Felix Ermacora as special rapporteur, never straightforwardly describing its true brutality. Ermacora had the courage to tell the truth, for which he suffered harsh attacks from the Soviets and their allies.

Even after Mikhail Gorbachev had withdrawn Soviet troops, Soviet spokesmen continued the fiction that they had responded to outside "interference" in Afghanistan. Finally, in an extraordinary mea culpa *in the winter of 1989 Foreign Minister Eduard Shevardnadze admitted that the invasion had violated civilized norms.*

The agony of Afghanistan continues unabated. According to a report prepared for the United Nations Commission on Human Rights by a special rapporteur, Felix Ermacora, and submitted last week to the General Assembly, the torment includes mutilation, torture, rape, imprisonment without trial, conscription and deportation of children, booby-trapped toys, soap, and snuffboxes, forced rural evacuations, destruction of crops, and starvation. These Soviet atrocities are routinely wreaked on the Afghan people in an effort to subdue opposition and destroy their traditional society.

Even before receiving Ermacora's report, the General Assembly, by a vote of 122 to 12 (19 abstaining), called for the immediate withdrawal of "foreign" (read Soviet) troops from Afghanistan as a necessary step to ending the suffering of the Afghan people.

If the list of atrocities seems astounding to us, the arguments put forth by the Soviets for the invasion seem even more astounding. With approximately 120,000 occupation troops in Afghanistan, the Soviets consider the UN discussions, debates, and vote an outrage. The Byelorussian delegate, speaking for the Soviet Union, made this point clear again and again:

> The continuing provocative fuss surrounding the so-called Afghanistan question constitutes inadmissible interference in the internal affairs of Afghanistan and represents a blatant violation of the United Nations Charter.
>
> The malicious imposition of discussion of this question against the just and determined protests of the Democratic Republic of Afghanistan . . . is extremely dangerous and harmful to the cause of peace because it distracts us from the search for a political solution to a situation that has been created by the forces of imperialism and reaction.

The Soviets' position on Afghanistan is clear enough: They had, they said, a right to invade Afghanistan without interference. The move into Afghanistan, declared Yuri Andropov, "was a lofty act of loyalty to the principle of proletarian internationalism, which was necessary to defend the interests of our motherland."

In the Soviet view, the solution to the suffering of Afghanistan is also clear. Those who caused the war must end it. The United States, the French, the Chinese must stop supporting the Afghan resistance. Then there will be peace. The UN negotiators have long reported that Soviet withdrawal from Afghanistan depends on "guarantees" that support for the Afghan resistance movement will end. Refusal to guarantee "nonintervention" in Afghanistan is, in the Soviet view, the major obstacle to peace.

Soviet invasion, occupation, repression are not obstacles to peace. Resistance by others is the obstacle to peace. Once the "bandits and counterrevolutionary gangs" have been disarmed and peace restored, Soviet troops can depart.

This Soviet argument is not limited to Afghanistan. It is applied everywhere. Thus Soviet spokesmen insist Cuban troops in Angola do not constitute external interference. Those who aid UNITA are interfering. Sandinista repression in Nicaragua does not disrupt peace in that country. The contras disrupt peace. When their resistance ends, there will be peace.

We have heard this argument from Lenin's day forward: class war is not caused by Bolsheviks. It occurs when the bourgeoisie or the kulak or whoever resists conquest. In the Soviet catechism, questions and answers are simple and clear:

• When is external assistance illegitimate interference in the internal affairs of a nation? When it impedes consolidation or extension of power by a Communist group or government.
• When is external assistance legitimate? When it extends Soviet power.
• When is resistance aggression? When it is an obstacle to consolidation or extension of a Marxist group's power.
• When is resistance national liberation? When it extends the power of a Marxist group.
• When is liberation aggression? When, as in Grenada, it resists an irreversible revolution.
• When is aggression liberation? When it assists extension or consolidation of power by a Soviet associate.

A national liberation movement is a group such as the PLO, SWAPO, or the FMLN, supported by the Soviet Union and associated states in its struggle for power. Resistance movements that oppose government links to the Soviet Union are "hired assassins and ban-

181

dits who have lost their human aspect" (*Pravda*, November 17, 1985).

Thus, Soviet support for the FMLN serves the cause of peace and justice in El Salvador. But U.S. support for the contras causes war and havoc in Nicaragua. Soviet support for anyone advances peace, but "the hallmark of U.S. dollar mercenaries here in Afghanistan, as in El Salvador, Nicaragua and Lebanon, is one and the same . . . blood" (*Krasnaya Zvezda*, November 14, 1985).

Inevitably, Ronald Reagan's proposals made at the United Nations for resolving regional conflicts were rejected by the Soviets as "nothing else than an attempt at justifying the interference of the United States and the countries that depend on it in the internal affairs of Afghanistan, Angola, Nicaragua, Kampuchea and Ethiopia" (Tass, November 11, 1985).

Inevitably the Soviet alternative peace proposal for Afghanistan puts the burden of proof on the United States to provide "guarantees of nonintervention" to facilitate Soviet withdrawal.

It is really too absurd. A process that puts pressure on the U.S. government to provide guarantees of nonintervention in a country ravaged by 120,000 Soviet troops will not, cannot lead to internal reconciliation with respect to Afghan rights and national self-determination. Everyone should be clear about that.

New Thinking on Afghanistan
February 29, 1988

Public discussion in the Soviet Union of the invasion of Afghanistan marked a major and extremely important departure from previous policy. It was obviously peaceful. The Soviet investment in men, material, and reputation was huge. Withdrawing required acknowledging at least that the means, if not the ends, had been ill chosen. It is always difficult for governments to admit error.

I thought this enormously significant but worried that mistakes in U.S. policy might prevent the Afghan people from benefiting. I was worried that our government's longing for an agreement would lead to a policy of preemptive capitulation and was fearful that the United States would hand the Soviets a victory they had not been able to win. Perhaps my concern was unnecessary, since in May 1990 the United States and the Soviet Union entered serious discussions over free elections in

Afghanistan. Nevertheless, Communist Chief Najibullah remains in power in Kabul, well placed to influence (and maybe to control) the prospective elections, and Moscow seemed determined to preserve him in power.

Immediately after this column appeared, I received a call from the State Department offering assurances that George Shultz was in fact taking the position I said he should.

By now, nearly everyone has heard that the Soviets want to withdraw from Afghanistan. Secretary of State George Shultz has said he does not doubt it, although some remain skeptical. More important, however, the carefully worded pronouncements from Mikhail Gorbachev and other Soviet officials leave critical questions unanswered.

Will all Soviet troops depart? Do the Soviets intend to leave a permanent presence? How will the next government be chosen? Will refugees and their leaders be permitted to participate? How much Soviet aid will there be for the puppet government in Kabul?

What did *Pravda* say? "The Afghan problem has been used from year to year to block peace initiatives. . . . Hawks across the ocean say 'Afghanistan first, regional conflicts first.' Until they are settled, it is pointless to talk about the cardinal problems of war and peace or to embark seriously on nuclear disarmament."

An extremely interesting article in a recent issue of Moscow's *Literary Gazette* is said to constitute the recommended interpretation of the Afghan experience. Terming the current Afghan policy one of "national reconciliation" and "an expression of the new political thinking on the Afghans' side," the *Literary Gazette* recalls the euphoria in the Soviet Union when the April 1978 "revolution" in Kabul was announced. The writer remembers the pleasure at hearing "that we might find ourselves with a socialist neighbor on our border to the south," and later recalls "disaster . . . threatened the red flag over Kabul." There was outside interference—American, Chinese, British, and Pakistani guns appeared to threaten the regime. So, naturally, in response to the Afghan state's call for help, "We sent in the troops" to offset "the mighty presence from abroad."

The *Literary Gazette* recalls how, in the early happy days, everyone assumed "the victorious party [the People's Democratic party of Afghanistan] would be able to create an effective structure covering the whole country, the whole territory and all the social strata of the society, and stability would prevail."

It did not happen.

The PDPA "offended against tradition." It "turned into violence and repression." It fell into factionalism. Afghanistan turned out to be a "medieval melting pot." Everyone could see that some accommodation was required with traditional culture and Islam. The process of compromise began.

"State forums were introduced by mullahs' prayers," continued the *Literary Gazette*, "The flag ceased to be red and acquired a green Islamic stripe." The party proclaimed its pluralism. It proclaimed a "policy of national reconciliation" and "unprecedented compromise with enemies," and a readiness to "see them not as enemies but as patriots, colleagues in a future traditionally Islamic society."

Now, the *Literary Gazette* tells us, the original aim of the revolutionary government "has been renounced by the government itself." Everyone now has come to realize that the "experts were wrong in their assessment. Errors were made."

"The departure of our troops is not a defeat," the *Literary Gazette* explains, adding the soldiers will leave as "the vector of politics changes into reverse and the army follows that vector."

It will all happen "if the pens in Geneva sign the peace agreements." Gorbachev has decided to withdraw, but the decision, the Soviets explain, is not unconditional.

What must the pens in Geneva sign? The terms of the proposed agreement have not been made public, but reports have circulated for weeks. According to these reports, the Soviet Union—which now claims 90,000 troops in Afghanistan—will begin withdrawal by May 15 if the agreement is completed by March 15 and will complete withdrawal within ten months.

But, and it is a very large but, the United States must cease all assistance to the Afghan *mujahedin* as soon as the Soviet Union begins its troop withdrawal. The Pakistanis must dismantle the *mujahedin* base camps, and the existing Afghan government will remain in place. That this government calls itself a government of national reconciliation does not change the fact that it was installed by the Soviet Union and is maintained by Soviet troops.

Obviously, the withdrawal of Soviet troops from Afghanistan is intensely desirable. Eight long years of war have left 1.25 million Afghans dead, 4 million in exile, and the country devastated.

Afghan resistance leaders, however, fear they have already been betrayed by an American government that seems too eager for any agreement.

It is inconceivable that the administration of Ronald Reagan would accept a deal that leaves a residual Soviet presence in Afghanistan, a Communist government in Kabul aided by Moscow, while cutting off the flow of assistance to the Afghan resistance.

It could not be.

If there is to be an end to "outside interference" in Afghanistan it must be applied equally. Cutoff of aid must include a cutoff of Soviet assistance to the Kabul puppet government.

George Shultz should make it clear to the Soviets that it takes more than a change of name to make a government a "national reconciliation."

Afghanistan: Filling in the Blanks

April 4, 1988

Debate inside the United States and the United Nations over U.S. aid to the mujahedin continued throughout the negotiations on Soviet withdrawal. In fact, it continues to this day.

There have always been journalists and policy makers who believe that Afghanistan should be treated as part of the Soviets' legitimate sphere of influence and others (like me) who believe the Afghans have a right to self-determination and self-government.

In this debate professional diplomats at the United Nations and the Department of State have frequently sought not only to conduct negotiations in secrecy but to make agreements without consultation with the political and policy arms of government. That, I think, is not compatible with foreign policy in a democracy.

UN Deputy Secretary-General Diego Cordovez, whom *The Economist* described as "the world's most patient man," has tried for years to persuade parties to the conflict in Afghanistan that the problem created by the Soviet invasion could be solved by the withdrawal of Soviet troops.

It sounds plausible, so plausible that Cordovez persuaded some still-anonymous U.S. officials to agree in a still-classified secret memorandum that the United States would end assistance to the *mujahedin* when the Soviet Union provided a timetable for the departure of its soldiers and actually began withdrawal.

William Safire has provided the best account of this secret agreement—a pact arrived at so secretly in December 1985 that even the president was not informed (although another clause in the agreement made the United States a guarantor).

185

But secrets have a way of leaking, and before long the administration and Congress began to realize how many questions the agreement left open. The closer the Soviets came to beginning an actual withdrawal, the more pressing these questions became.

By the time the date of March 15 had been set to begin the "front-loaded" Soviet withdrawal, the administration and Congress had realized that under the agreement the Afghan government installed by Soviet occupation forces would be left in place and would continue to be supplied and protected by the Soviet Union under longstanding treaties between Afghanistan and Moscow.

Slowly, Washington remembered that the withdrawal of Soviet troops from Afghanistan was not the goal of the *mujahedin*—who had fought with such incredible heroism against Soviet occupation for eight long years. Their goal was self-determination for Afghanistan, which they and everyone else believe will result in a non-Communist Afghan government.

Absent a non-Communist government, the *mujahedin* will not stop fighting, and the Afghan refugees will not go home. Instead, they will continue to place nearly unbearable strains on the government of Pakistan—already hard-pressed by economic burdens, the sense of solidarity with fellow Moslems, demands by the Soviet Union, and pressures from a progressively menacing Indian government.

For reasons that are not wholly clear, the *mujahedin* are the Democrats' favorite freedom fighters, and in the Senate, Majority Leader Robert Byrd personally oversaw the passage of a resolution requiring withdrawal of all Soviet troops, return of the refugees, and a nonaligned Afghanistan.

The U.S. government, under pressure from Congress and from conscience, made what the Soviets have ever since denounced as a "new" demand for an end to Soviet aid to the Kabul government. Congress also insisted that U.S. termination of aid to the *mujahedin* should take place simultaneously with Soviet termination of aid to the Afghan regime.

Ever since, the United States has been accused of reneging on the agreement (which it did not do; it merely filled in blanks), and all manner of vile motives have been ascribed to the Americans and the Pakistanis.

Pakistanis have been accused of seeking to control Afghanistan by insisting on a government they could manipulate. A Soviet foreign ministry spokesman told Tass last week: "It is clear to all sober-minded people that the Pakistani approach represented by the attempt to link external aspects of the settlement with the establishment of a so-called interim government is nothing but overt interference in the internal affairs of the Afghans." (Presumably only the Soviets are permitted to take an interest in the composition of Afghanistan's government.)

The Soviets have also offered various explanations of U.S. behavior. *Pravda* published last week the reported views of an unnamed "American journalist": "It may seem absurd to you, but I am sure our "hawks" don't really want you to withdraw your troops from Afghanistan. . . . There is some logic to that way of thinking. The longer you stay in Afghanistan, the more chance we have to sling mud at you."

One journalist who regards U.S. demands for a nonaligned Afghanistan as "unrealistic" is Selig Harrison, who made his view clear in *The New York Times*. Harrison said the United States, in calling for the cutoff of Soviet aid to the Kabul government or in asking for a new Afghan regime, is asking Moscow "to acknowledge defeat." "Yet Moscow has not been defeated" and should not be placed in a position of "conceding defeat by abandoning its client," even though Harrison noted, "Moscow is disenchanted with the [client] Communists."

In Harrison's view, U.S. agreement to leave the client state in place would only be realistic and would reflect the fact that "Moscow has more of a stake in adjacent Afghanistan than Washington does." Harrison does not seem overly concerned about the Afghans' stake in their future government.

Now it is widely rumored that over the next several days Pakistan will sign another secret agreement, secretly arrived at. It is said the administration has approved the agreement and Byrd has been promised a look.

Meanwhile in Kabul, Afghan General-Secretary Najibullah is making plans for this month's election of the National Council of the Republic of Afghanistan—an election that will be held under the helpful eyes of Soviet troops.

The Real Reason the Soviets Left Afghanistan
February 20, 1989

1989 was the year the Soviets' talk of change was replaced by action. Withdrawal of Soviet troops from Afghanistan was dramatic action— the kind that had enormous significance both inside and outside the Soviet Union. It took political courage, even daring, for a Soviet leader to liquidate a military commitment in which so many lives had been invested.

It was dramatic evidence of Gorbachev's determination to deemphasize military action and also to change the Soviet image. It did not, however, mean an end to Soviet interest in controlling Afghanistan—as some American commentators concluded.

This essay gives Gorbachev less credit for leaving Afghanistan than I now think appropriate, especially since the Soviet government has admitted that the invasion of Afghanistan was a violation of civilized values, not a legitimate exercise of "internationalist duty."

The departure of Soviet troops from Afghanistan is a momentous and extremely interesting event, but explaining it is not nearly as easy as one might suppose.

First, it did not happen because the Soviets wanted to save money. The Soviet government sustains military budgets year after year that consume truly incredible portions of their gross national product. It has not reduced those budgets, nor has it attempted to reduce the high cost of empire, for example, by cutting its heavy subsidies to Cuba, Nicaragua, Vietnam, and Ethiopia.

Second, the decision to withdraw was not made because the war had grown unpopular in the Soviet Union. Although their own casualties were high, the Soviet people regularly suffer miseries, indignities, and frustrations and still lack the institutions through which to make their rulers responsive to public opinion.

Third, the withdrawal did not occur because Mikhail Gorbachev hates war or could not stand to wreak devastation on the Afghan people. Not only did efforts to conquer Afghanistan continue under Gorbachev, but the bombings, burnings, gassing, and starving intensified as he unleashed on the Afghan people the Soviet Union's most sophisticated weapons and forces.

Fourth, the Soviets did not decide to withdraw because of "pressures" from the United Nations. For eight years UN majorities appealed for withdrawal—to no effect. For nearly as long, the UN

Secretariat's mediation efforts yielded no fruit. The Soviets tried hard to achieve through UN negotiations what they could not win on the battlefield, and though the negotiations helped them save face and ease the orderly retreat, they cannot reasonably be said to have *caused* the withdrawal.

Fifth, the Soviet Union did not withdraw because Gorbachev regarded Afghanistan as insignificant or without implications for Soviet policy elsewhere. He is far too intelligent to imagine that inferences will not be drawn about Soviet reliability and invincibility concerning national liberation struggles elsewhere.

Gorbachev has too often explained Soviet intervention as a classical example of "internationalist duty" in a struggle between "progressive forces" and "imperialist circles." In his book *Perestroika*, Gorbachev explained the Soviet presence in Afghanistan exactly as Leonid Brezhnev had: when Afghan society began to make "progressive changes," "imperalist interferences" developed "from without."

"So in keeping with the Soviet-Afghan friendship treaty, its leaders asked the Soviet Union for help. They addressed us 11 times before we assented to introduce a limited military contingent into that country," Gorbachev said.

Withdrawal—in a situation where Soviet political allies have no reasonable chance of surviving—looks a lot like abandonment. It suggests there are limits to how far the Soviet Union will go to help a fraternal socialist ally and, like Grenada, demonstrates more "reversibility" than Marxists prefer to see in history's march toward the triumph of "progressive forces" everywhere.

Finally, the Soviets did not withdraw from Afghanistan only because of the incredible courage, skill, and determination of the Afghan people, nor because of the steadfast loyalty of Zia's Pakistan, nor because of the flow of arms to the *mujahedin* from China, Iran, Europe, and the United States. It did not happen because of the Stinger missiles, though these forced a dramatic change in Soviet strategy.

All these factors played a role, but cannot quite be said to have *forced* the Soviet military withdrawal.

The reason for the withdrawal, I believe, is that Gorbachev, playing for high stakes on a global board, concluded that sacrificing a pawn would improve his overall strategic position.

Europe interests Gorbachev much more than Afghanistan. "We are Europeans," he has said repeatedly. Building the "common European home" is his number one foreign policy priority, but doing it requires eliminating the idea of a "Soviet threat."

The living symbol of that threat was 120,000 Soviet troops laying waste to a small neighboring country.

It was therefore necessary to liquidate this obstacle to achieving larger Soviet goals, which may be variously described as the resolution of "regional conflicts"; the construction of a "common European home"; an end to the division of Europe; the dismantling of NATO; the creation of a defenseless Western Europe.

Gorbachev's decision to end the Afghan war was a step in his broader campaign to "put an end to lies about the Soviet Union's aggressiveness."

Good.

Now it is time for more steps—in Central and South America, in Africa—to put an end to the "myth" of Soviet aggressiveness.

It is said that Mikhail Gorbachev prefers to compete by political and diplomatic means. So, of course, do we.

Nor should we worry much about the Soviets' undoubted superiority in political skills and tenacity. In the absence of coercion, the advantages of freedom readily become manifest.

Angola . . .

Support the Contras in Angola
October 27, 1985

In 1975 the Soviet-backed MPLA group subverted planned elections and seized power in Angola. Civil war spread and has continued until today. While the U.S. Congress prohibited aid to the regime's opponents, the Soviet Union provided arms, and Fidel Castro sent some 50,000 Cubans to prop up the MPLA regime. But the forces of UNITA, headed by Jonas Savimbi, never stopped fighting. They came instead to control about one-third of Angola. And in the Reagan years, U.S. military support for Savimbi was undertaken. It was sometimes resisted and slowed—it was never stopped. Angola became an example of the Reagan Doctrine, help for forces against a government sustained by the Soviet bloc. The next two columns address the issue of aid for Savimbi as it developed inside the U.S. government.

There is nothing ambiguous and nothing casual about Ronald Reagan's support for people struggling against large odds to prevent their country's incorporation by force into the Soviet empire.

Twice in the past week he reiterated his commitment. "True peace must be based on more than just reducing the means of waging war," he asserted in his October 18 radio broadcast. "It is based on self-determination, respect for individual and human rights. . . . We want countries to stop trying to expand their power and control through armed intervention and subversion."

The president returned to these themes in his speech before the United Nations General Assembly Thursday. He urged that countries now torn by civil war—Afghanistan, Cambodia, Ethiopia, Angola, Nicaragua—seek internal reconciliation based on respect for one another and for human rights. But until such internal reconciliation is achieved, he said, and until foreign forces have departed and the flow of outside arms has ended, "America's moral and material support for struggling resistance forces must not and shall not cease."

How strange, then, that in the same week the president reaffirmed his commitment, Secretary of State George Shultz acted to head off a bill providing humanitarian assistance to Angola's resistance forces.

"I understand that Congressmen Pepper and Kemp have introduced legislation which would provide $27 million in nonlethal assistance to Dr. [Jonas] Savimbi's movement, UNITA, in Angola," the secretary of state wrote to Minority Leader Bob Michel (R-Ill.). "I ask that you . . . use your influence to discourage the proposed legislation.

"The legislation is ill-timed," Shultz continued, "and will not contribute to the settlement we seek."

Now, anyone familiar with the State Department knows that the secretary of state almost certainly did not write that page and a half single-spaced letter. Although such letters become policy when signed by ranking officials, they originate in the regional bureaus. Sometimes the policies originate there as well. In the case of southern Africa, it is widely understood that the architects of our policy are the ranking officers of the Africa Bureau. Shultz's letter is one more manifestation of that bureau's convoluted policy.

What kind of "settlement" requires withholding humanitarian assistance from UNITA's brave struggle against what Shultz himself calls "Soviet designs" in Africa?

The letter to Michel provides an answer of sorts, an answer which remains ambiguous. The State Department seeks a settlement that will secure the independence of Namibia and "in that context provides for the withdrawal of Cuban combat forces from Angola."

That means, as I understand it, that the State Department hopes to trade Cuban withdrawal from Angola for South Africa's withdrawal from Namibia.

One of the obstacles in the path of such a settlement is the weakness of Angola's Marxist government. Without the Cubans to prop it up, that government probably could not stand for long against UNITA, not even with the $2 billion of Soviet military equipment it recently acquired. Therefore, there is no chance the MPLA will agree to a Cuban troop withdrawal unless it is first strengthened—and UNITA weakened.

This is presumably the reason that the Africa Bureau discouraged an adminstration initiative during the first term to repeal the Clark Amendment, which prohibits U.S. assistance to any group opposing the government of Angola. And once Congress repealed it, State quickly announced there were no plans to assist UNITA. It is presumably the reason the State Department last month approved an Export-Import Bank credit of $130 million for Angola's Marxist government.

It is also presumably the reason the State Department sought to head off the Pepper-Kemp amendment.

But Shultz's letter to Representative Michel and another from Assistant Secretary William Ball to Sen. Steve Symms indicate that Namibia is not State's only preoccupation. "The Angolan war destablizes Southern Africa," wrote Ball to Symms. "The United States seeks to end this cycle of violence."

UNITA's recent defeat of a massive offensive by the MPLA under Soviet direction would seem to have demonstrated that even 35,000 Cubans, 3,500 East Germans, and several thousand assorted North Koreans, Bulgarians, Czechs, and Soviets cannot provide "stability" to Angola.

Savimbi keeps winning. Things have gotten so bad for Angola's Marxist regime that it has even asked the State Department to help in "containing the fighting."

Apparently the State Department way to stop the violence and contain the fighting is to make certain Savimbi's forces get no help from Congress. One hopes it will find other, better ideas. One hopes that in any case a majority of Congress will join Representatives Pepper, Kemp, and Michel (and President Reagan) in support of Angola's beleaguered contras.

Beyond Profit in Angola
September 15, 1986

Traditionally, Marxists attacked multinational corporations for support-
ing repressive "right-wing" regimes. But some of the biggest multina-
tionals have apologized for and supported a Communist regime in
Angola—as ready to "sell the rope" as Lenin had predicted.

It has become a familiar scene. The same House and Senate members
who have consistently opposed significant U.S. aid to resistance
fighters everywhere have now mounted a new effort to block American assistance in Angola's struggle against incorporation into the
Soviet system. They have rallied behind an amendment that would
effectively bar aid to Angola, an amendment that could come up for
a House vote as early as Tuesday.

The anti-freedom fighter bloc has mobilized to support Rep. Lee
Hamilton's (D-Ind.) amendment to the Intelligence Authorization Act
of 1987. The amendment provides that no forces fighting in Angola
could receive any covert assistance unless Congress first passes a
joint resolution "publicly specifying in detail all assistance and all
recipients." The stated purpose of this amendment is to provide for
public discussion and debate of aid to Jonas Savimbi's anti-Marxist
UNITA forces. The effective consequence—as most amendment supporters understand—would be to prevent any U.S. assistance to
Angolans fighting for their country's self-government and sovereignty.

"But this time there is a big difference from most previous
congressional struggles over aid to resistance fighters. This time it is
two *Democrats,* Reps. Claude Pepper and Dante Fascell, who are
leading the fight to block the people who would block assistance to
UNITA.

On September 8 Pepper and Fascell wrote to House colleagues
alerting them that the amendment would "erode our prospects to
bring freedom to Angola . . . provide valuable information to the
MPLA [Angola's pro-Soviet government] . . . increase the potential
political cost to nations and groups who are discreetly giving aid to
UNITA . . . and encourage the Soviet Union to further increase its
level of support."

This latest chapter in the struggle over U.S. policy in southern
Africa is, of course, part of a much larger issue with a much longer
history. The struggle in southern Africa is as complex as it is impor-

193

tant—to the people of the region and to us.

At stake in Angola is the national independence of the Angolan people versus that country's incorporation into the Soviet bloc. The outcome of that struggle will have serious consequences for the future of Namibia and the whole of southern Africa, including South Africa, where a struggle for democracy is also under way.

The United States is properly seeking a southern Africa made up of independent, self-governing nations. No other outcome is consistent with our principles and our interests.

People who oppose U.S. aid to UNITA argue first that we should not seek to overthrow an existing government (the MPLA), and second that to aid UNITA is to associate ourselves with the South African government—which provides military assistance to UNITA.

These arguments will not wash. The government of Angola is a de facto government imposed by the force of more than 40,000 Soviet military personnel and approximately $2 billion in Soviet military assistance. It was not chosen by the Angolan people, and it is unable to govern more than two-thirds of the country because the Angolan people do not support it. In this context it is disingenuous to speak in opposition to "outside interference" in Angola.

The argument that by aiding UNITA the United States would associate itself with South Africa's government is tantamount to claiming that to aid the Allies in World War II was to help Joseph Stalin.

It is true that the struggle in South Africa is related to that in Angola. Savimbi represents the armed forces supporting self-government by Angolans. Zulu Chief Gathsa Buthelezi and his allies represent unarmed forces supporting self-government and democracy in South Africa.

The United States should firmly ally itself with the supporters of self-government in both countries. Just as we should not support the racist government of South Africa, neither should we permit ourselves to be gulled into believing the struggle for self-determination, democracy, and human rights is served by helping Communist forces consolidate power. Yet that is what Angola's MPLA government and its friends would have us believe.

Those friends include an all-too-familiar coalition of certain corporate and banking interests willing to work with any government that will permit them to make a profit and some benighted "progressives" who still believe the people of the third world are not capable of effectively governing themselves.

Unfortunately some of the latter are found inside the U.S. Department of State, where various efforts are under way to assist the

Marxist governments of Angola and Mozambique by helping them upgrade their transportation systems and where plans are already afoot for Secretary of State George Shultz to visit the area in October and meet with regional leaders, probably including Oliver Tambo, leader of the African National Congress.

If these corporate interests, State Department bureaucrats, and congressional activists succeed in blocking aid to UNITA, the Reagan Doctrine would be undone in southern Africa.

The political and strategic stakes are very high in this rich region, where our principles and our interests are engaged. They are threatened by Hamilton's sleeper amendment.

Slandering Savimbi
July 3, 1988

Jonas Savimbi is an authentic African nationalist leader who learned guerrilla warfare from the Chinese and is by any standards one of the most impressive leaders in Africa. Linguist, philosopher, poet, and warrior, Savimbi is the principal target of the MPLA.

Savimbi was excluded from the southern Africa peace talks in 1989 because he threatened the agendas of the other participants. The Angolan regime and its Cuban and Soviet backers refused him a seat at the talks on the pretext that he was a lackey of South Africa and an obstacle to "peace." The U.S. government acquiesced because the State Department gave priority to a comprehensive settlement in the region and, doubtless, because it felt fully competent to represent UNITA's interests. Like the contras and the mujahedin, *Savimbi was deeply disturbed at the idea that he should not be able to participate in talks where his country's future is settled.*

Dr. Jonas Savimbi's visit to the United States this week was one of those rare events that illuminates the political landscape—revealing myths we should have abandoned and facts we would rather not know about the commitments of some American leaders.

Savimbi, head of Angola's resistance UNITA forces, is one of the most brilliant and durable leaders on the African continent. Yet he was the target of a well-orchestrated campaign during his U.S. visit that included expensive full-page ads in major newspapers and organized pickets in small southern towns. Repeatedly, American black political leaders joined in denoucing Savimbi.

Why?

It is easy to understand why the Marxist MPLA government of Angola sent its officials to lobby the U.S. government against Savimbi. He seriously threatens the MPLA's hold on power, even with its 57,000 Cuban, 2,500 Soviet, and 3,000 North Korean troops. When the number two man in Angola's Politburo, Pedro Castro van Dunem, called Savimbi a "big traitor," we knew where he was, so to speak, coming from and why.

Van Dunem wants an end to U.S. support for UNITA, U.S. recognition of Angola's Marxist government, and the extension of Soviet power in Africa, if for no other reason than that his own power depends on the Cuban presence, which in turn depends on the Soviet Union.

But this is not the case for American black leaders who protested the visit—leaders like congressional delegate Walter Fauntroy, Washington Mayor Marion Barry, and Southern Christian Leadership Conference leader Joseph Lowery, who joined Randall Robinson in intemperate denunciation of Savimbi. Barry, for example, said Savimbi should be treated "as the scourge of the earth that he is."

How could these men have become so deeply involved in the international politics of west Africa, yet understand them so little?

"Angola is not a Marxist state," said Robinson, though the MPLA boasts just the contrary. Is Robinson confused? Or is he trying to confuse others?

"Aid to Savimbi is aid to South Africa," he said, though that is clearly not the case. Aid to Savimbi is aid to an independent Angola.

The facts on Angola are too clear to be so misunderstood.

Angola's history as a modern nation began with the Alvor agreement, which provided independence from Portugal in 1975, a multiparty interim government and free elections of a constituent assembly.

The agreement fell apart when the MPLA—reinforced by Soviet arms and Cuban advisers—decided it was easier to seize power than compete for it in free elections. Confronted with tangible evidence of growing Soviet and Cuban involvement in Angola, Savimbi sought and secured aid from a dozen countries in Africa, the Middle East, and elsewhere—including South Africa.

As the number of Cuban troops multiplied, a myth was carefully cultivated that they came to Angola at the request of the government to help defend the country against South Africa. (This is the Angolan version of the myth that Sandinista repression was caused by the organization of the contras or that the Soviet invasion of Afghanistan was caused by the Soviet desire for a nonaligned government on its southern border, or the equally durable canard that the Israeli-Palestinian problem was caused by Israel's occupation of the West Bank and Gaza.

In each case the facts are readily available, but to some the myths are far more useful.

Cubans came to Angola not at the request of the government but to help one faction—the MPLA—overthrow that government. Since then, their numbers have increased and their role in Angola's civil war has grown. So has their voice in Angola's government. Meanwhile, the integration of Angola into the "Socialist world system" also progressed, while Angola's economy stagnated and Savimbi's support spread.

South Africa's stake in the Angolan conflict is dictated by geography and its intense interest in SWAPO's ongoing "war of national liberation" on the Namibian–South African border.

The U.S. role in the region is based on our global strategic interests and on our general desire to see a world of independent nations. In southern Africa, our goal is a Namibia independent of South Africa and an Angola independent of the Soviet-Cuban bloc.

Chester Crocker, the assistant secretary of state for Africa, has worked since 1981 on a strategy linking Cuban withdrawal from Angola to South African withdrawal from Namibia, but with little success.

Now the United States—with a little help from its friends—has succeeded in getting four-power talks under way involving itself, South Africa, Cuba, and the MPLA. Although he supports the talks, Savimbi is understandably frustrated that UNITA has not been included.

So far there has been a lot of talk about what to talk about, but no agreement even on that.

Presumably, most Americans would like to see a peaceful settlement, withdrawal of foreign troops from both Namibia and Angola, and an inclusive democratic government of Angola by Angolans, of Namibia by Namibians.

These goals are also those of Jonas Savimbi. It is therefore extremely difficult to understand why anyone who supports peace and self-determination for southern Africa should oppose Savimbi, whose nationalistic credentials are long and extremely impressive.

It is also difficult to understand how any serious person could believe that national independence or peace is promoted by ending U.S. aid to UNITA while Soviet arms pour in to support 57,000 Cuban

197

troops. Yet Michael Dukakis proposed just that. The U.S. policy "must be changed," he said. "The continuing military aid to UNITA fans the flames of regional conflict in southern Africa and should be halted."

The argument sounds familiar: we should end aid to the contras to promote peace in Nicaragua; end aid to the *mujahedin* to permit Soviet withdrawal from Afghanistan.

It is called appeasement, and it does not work.

Still Moscow's Satellites
June 18, 1990

It seems anomalous that Mikhail Gorbachev freed Eastern Europe from Soviet domination but continued to prop up brutal client regimes in the "outer empire." If the Kremlin could watch Poland, Czechoslovakia, and Hungary go free and East Germany disappear into West Germany, why did it continue to support less-important and less-viable regimes—in Cuba, Angola, Cambodia, and Ethiopia—at such ruinous cost?

Why, having liquidated its East European empire, does the Soviet Union continue to pour billions in scarce resources into unreformed, non-European Marxist governments that rely on old thinking and old tactics in their effort to maintain power?

If the Soviet government is no longer committed to the idea of an international class war destined to end with the triumph of Marxism, why in the world should it invest such disproportionate amounts of money and material in such unpromising places as Afghanistan, Ethiopia, Mozambique, Angola, and Cambodia—places where repressive one-party governments manage hopelessly inefficient economies under continuing siege by insurgent armies?

Why shouldn't the Soviets accept for these countries the same sort of settlement they accepted in Nicaragua and in Namibia: free elections under international supervision?

It makes no sense for a Soviet government willing to submit its own majority to the test of opposition and election to squander resources on such artifacts of a previous era as the one-party dictatorships of Afghanistan's Najibullah or Angola's Eduardo dos Santos.

Consider Angola. No government has any real interest in protecting the sinecure of Angola's ruling Marxist regime, the MPLA. It is, in any case, extremely unlikely that any amount of money or war materiel can finally maintain this government in power.

Former "colonials" call the sorry state of affairs in Angola the result of "Africanization." The MPLA blames civil war. Neither is correct.

It is not fair to describe as "Africanization" the process of continuing deterioration and decay to which the cities and economy of Angola have succumbed in the fifteen years since Portugal's abrupt departure from that country. Angola was overcome less by "Africanization" than by the very European disease of Marxism, with its policies of nationalization, central planning and control, its reliance on coercion, and its elimination of the market and associated incentives.

It is also not true, as MPLA apologists pretend, that civil war has caused the decay of Angola's economy and the disorganization of its society. The reverse is more nearly the case. Luanda is not a city under military attack. It is a city ravaged by incompetence, corruption, and waste.

Even with 60,000 troops and additional thousands of Soviet, Czech, North Korean, and East German advisers, and even with military assistance amounting to billions of dollars annually, the MPLA has been unable to defeat the challenge of Jonas Savimbi and his UNITA resistance. It is true that Savimbi's forces have also enjoyed assistance from various non-Communist governments in Africa, the Middle East, Europe, and Asia—including the United States and South Africa—but UNITA's aid has never approached the billions provided by the Soviets and the "world Socialist system."

The MPLA is simply outmatched.

UNITA has survived, even against the recent offensive at Mavinga, because its forces are well organized, highly motivated, and well led.

Of Jonas Savimbi himself, an African head of state said to me, "He is a classical hero who lives with his army in the bush and shares its hardships, who leads his men into battle and shares their risks. He is also the only African who has understood how to sustain a guerrilla war."

I do not know if Savimbi is the only contemporary African leader who possesses the skills required to sustain such combat. But it is clear that he has managed to inspire the kind of loyalty the MPLA has found it necessary to coerce and that he has had the imagination and political skill to win needed support from a wide variety of other governments.

199

Savimbi learned from the master of guerrilla war, Mao Tse-tung, how to strike where it hurts most and how to organize his own forces for a long-term struggle. He knows how to build a revolutionary army that provides food and clothing, schools and hospitals to its soldiers and their families.

He is also sophisticated enough to understand the irony in the fact that he practices socialism in Jamba while advocating a market economy for Angola. "We are an army at war," he shrugs, "not a normal society."

His overriding goal now is to end the war and become that normal society. Savimbi wants for Angola what Namibia achieved: free elections under UN supervision.

With Clausewitz, he understands that the principal target must be the will of his adversary. In fact, he thought he had already effected it.

"One might have thought that the MPLA's defeat at Mavinga would leave them ready to negotiate," he observed to me two weeks ago. "The fact that we seek negotiations in the wake of victory should persuade them that we seek peace and want to rebuild the country.

"Africa needs peace and democratic elections just as much as Europe does," Savimbi asserts. "The Angolan people have waited for fifteen years for democratic elections. It is not reasonable that they should have to wait longer."

What Angolans want is probably what Afghans, Cambodians, Mozambicans, Cubans, and Vietnamese want as well.

Why should the Soviet Union not cooperate in giving these unfortunate client states the same privileges it now accepts for Eastern Europe?

Nicaragua . . .

New Thinking on Nicaragua

Everyone understands that more than a decade ago the small poor countries of Central America were sucked into the great political and ideological contest of the age—and that ever since three tendencies have contended for control of governments and streets: Nicaragua, El Salvador, Guatemala, and Honduras became a battlefield in the ongoing contest between old politics and what Napoleon Duarte called the two revolutions: the democratic or bourgeois revolution based on periodic competitive elections and associated freedoms of speech, press, and assembly grounded in a rule of law and the Marxist-Leninist revolution that relied on one-party dictatorship to "guide" a Socialist state.

The two revolutions differed in goals, ideologies, allies, and adversaries.

In Nicaragua the Marxist revolution triumphed. The FSLN (Sandinistas) took power in Nicaragua in July 1979 as part of a broad anti-Somoza coalition. During its first two years in power, as the new regime received $118 million in U.S. economic aid, the FSLN squeezed out non-Marxist allies, constructed a Cuban-style state with an impressive Cuban-style army, and immediately began to aid guerrillas in El Salvador.

The Reagan administration responded with a two-track policy: support for Nicaraguan insurgents and diplomatic negotiations, both of which continued with diminishing success to the final days of the administration. The Latin Americans responded with the "Contadora process" in which four nearby Latin countries joined the five Central American countries in a search for a negotiated settlement. The U.S. supported the Contadora process until it was overtaken by the Arias plan.

Meanwhile, the Reagan administration sought to provide military support to Nicaraguan resistance forces against ferocious domestic political opposition. Extraordinary restrictions were imposed by the Boland Amendments on the administration's capacity to act. These restrictions set the scene for the ill-conceived and ill-fated efforts to get money through arms sales to Iran. In 1987 the 1986 appropriations were not renewed, largely because of Iran-contra, even though the contras were scoring victories throughout Nicaragua.

Facing seemingly insurmountable opposition to contra aid in Congress, the Reagan administration in August 1987 accepted the "Wright-Reagan" deal, which in turn led to Central American approval of the Arias plan. In subsequent months, the Sandinistas systematically violated the democratic commitments they had accepted under the Arias plan, and the contras also lost much of their remaining support in Congress.

In February 1989 the Central American presidents agreed to disarm and demobilize the contras in return for a Sandinista promise of open elections in February 1990. The following month President Bush announced a bipartisan accord with congressional Democrats, under which humanitarian aid would continue to flow to the contras until the February 1990 elections.

Violeta Chamorro's victory in that election surprised liberals who assumed the revolution was irreversible, conservatives who assumed that Ortega would not accept defeat, and the Sandinistas themselves, who mistook the people's conformity for support. Violeta Chamorro herself was nor surprised. She never doubted that she would win.

The following columns retrace the tortuous road that led to the Sandinistas' humiliation and defeat.

Many Threats, Little Bread

July 28, 1986

Long on confidence and short on skills, the Sandinistas wrecked the Nicaraguan economy with nationalization and comprehensive, centralized controls. The Nicaraguan people paid the price in empty shelves, unemployment, and a worthless economy.

The special delusions of a Socialist dictatorship are clear in Nicaragua. Whatever made the nine FSLN comandantes and their young colleagues imagine that they could manage the economy of a nation? In fact, they could not. Nicaragua has paid a high price for their delusion of omnicompetence. But many Nicaraguans knew it. They turned out in large numbers and handed a stunned Daniel Ortega a stinging defeat in the first real elections in a decade.

It was a big week for official Nicaragua. There was a three-day mourning period for Vietnamese Communist party leader Le Duan, who, Nicaraguan officials said, was "always on our side." The Soviet minister of communications was on hand to help inaugurate a new satellite communications station linking Nicaragua to Intersputnik, thus providing a direct link from Managua to Moscow. And of course, on July 19, as the Nicaraguan people slid ever deeper into poverty, there was a celebration at Esteli of the Sandinista government's seventh anniversary in power.

The celebration was a modest affair as compared with previous Sandinista anniversaries. The crowds bused in from Managua were small, and it was reported that they listened without much enthusiasm to President Daniel Ortega's familiar litany of charges, excuses, and threats. Foreign guests were fewer and less eminent than in past years. Where once there had been Fidel Castro, Maurice Bishop, and

Yasser Arafat, this year there were only the Soviet minister of communications, Czechoslovakia's minister of food, and the chief of Libya's People's Bureau of Liaison. But then, there was less to celebrate in Nicaragua than in past years, and more to fear.

In choosing Esteli as the site of its anniversary celebration, Nicaragua's government sought to recall the successful Sandinista stand there against the forces of Anastasio Somoza in 1978 and 1979 and to associate itself with the earlier "traditional, historic national struggle" of namesake Augusto Sandino in the same area.

The association with Sandino has been attenuated by the large and still growing Soviet bloc presence in Nicaragua, considering Sandino's strong aversion to Soviet-style "internationalism." As *La Prensa*'s publisher, Pedro Joaquin Chamorro, wrote before the journalist's murder: "Sandino should be exalted precisely as a contrast to the Communists who obey signals from Russia and China. . . . There was a great difference [between Sandino] and the Communist Fidel Castro, who, in his false battle for the independence of his country, has filled it with Russian rockets, soldiers, planes and even canned goods."

Today most Nicaraguans would be happy enough to get some Soviet canned goods. Rockets, soldiers, and planes are plentiful, but there is a terrible shortage of almost all foodstuffs, including the flour and cornmeal used to make tortillas. As feverish preparations for the anniversary celebration were under way in Esteli, in Managua the Minister of Internal Commerce announced its determination to fight the "commercialization" of bread by instituting new controls. The ministry, which had already clamped tight controls on the sale of milk, closed Managua's largest bakery, the Plaza España. It was one way to eliminate the long lines that formed each night around the bakery.

Scarce bread is only one of the problems facing Nicaragua's government. There has been a severe deterioration in the standard of living. Health problems have multiplied as a result of large population migrations, a disorganized public health service, and the emigration of health professionals. The Ministry of Health was forced to announce during the very week of the celebrations that recent floods and related problems had caused an "alarming increase" in diarrhea, meningitis, and several other diseases.

Ortega acknowledged in his anniversary speech that the corn and coffee harvests have not been good and that "there will not be much corn or beans to distribute." He added that soldiers would get priority. As usual, he blamed the United States for these problems and justified Sandinista government repression as a necessary re-

203

sponse to U.S. aggression. The campaign against the Catholic church, the exclusion of Bishop Pablo Antonio Vega and of Msgr. Bismarck Carballo, the closing of *La Prensa*, the further suppression of the internal opposition, and the State of Emergency decree were all described as necessary responses to U.S. aggression.

Of course Ortega did not mention that the FSLN first began repressing the opposition in 1980, at a time when the new government of Nicaragua was receiving generous economic assistance and encouragement from the United States. In fact, after seven years Nicaragua shows all the familiar characteristics of Communist rule: repression, militarization, economic stagnation, scarcity, Cubans, and other *"internacionalistas"* drawn from throughout the Soviet empire.

At Esteli Ortega affirmed that Nicaragua has entered a new, still harsher phase of repression. All necessary measures will be taken to "defend the revolution," he promised. Only speech and action that is "within the institutional framework" will be permitted. Those who oppose "the institutional framework" (that is, the one-party Communist state associated with the Soviet Union) are seen as allied with Nicaragua's American enemies. Thus Ortega accuses *La Prensa*, Bishop Vega, and Msgr. Carballo of treason. There is, he says, no room in Nicaragua for such people.

"Those thinking of a national unity that runs counter to the institutional framework or refusing to accept its principles should once and for all unmask themselves and join the contras," he said. "They should leave for Miami or camps in Honduras."

That's about as clear as it possibly could be: accept communism or get out.

This week is also a big week for official Nicaragua. Ortega will take his case against the United States to the United Nations, and the same Security Council that condemned the U.S. raid on Libya (after refusing for years to take any action against terrorism) will probably support Nicaragua's accusations—less because its members have a good opinion of Nicaragua than because the majority seems to doubt it is legitimate for a Latin people to resist Marxism or for any other nation to help them do so.

Ortega will be making his case in the Security Council at about the same time the U.S. Senate votes on final approval of aid for the contras. Some Democratic senators have been threatening a filibuster. In any case, the debate promises to be bitter.

Opponents of aid can be expected to concentrate on the contras' real and imagined shortcomings, because it has become harder and harder for an American elected official to defend the government of Nicaragua.

Nicaragua and Libya
May 11, 1986

Throughout Managua the Sandinistas erected billboards bearing the slogan "No se vende, ni se rinde"—do not sell out or surrender—referring of course to the yanqui, not to the Soviet bloc and associated terrorist groups. They welcomed into Nicaragua military advisers from the USSR, Cuba, East Germany, Libya, and the PLO, and East bloc specialists in repression help to direct the Sandinista security apparatus. Naturally, ordinary Nicaraguans resent these foreigners.

Sandinista support for terrorism in Colombia, Peru, and elsewhere was documented. It was one more reason to hope these violence-prone new-style military dictators would be driven from power.

Maybe knowing about Nicaragua's Libyan connection will help the U.S. Congress and others understand the nature of the Sandinista government and why developments in that country are important to the peace and security of the hemisphere. Governments, like people, can be known by their friends. The ties between rulers of those nations were reaffirmed last week when Nicaraguan President Daniel Ortega communicated with Libya's Muammar Qaddafi.

"My brother, given the brutal terrorist action launched by the U.S. government against the people of the Libyan Arab Jamahiriyah, I wish to send sentiments and solidarity from the FSLN National Directorate and the Nicaraguan people and government," he said.

It is not the first time leaders of Libya and Nicaragua have sworn eternal friendship. They have been working together for more than a decade. Years before they came to power—in July 1979—Sandinista leaders trained in PLO camps in Libya and Lebanon. Strong bonds were forged with the Middle Eastern terror network, and those bonds were reinforced when the Sandinistas seized the government of Nicaragua. Qaddafi then pledged political and financial aid and has made good on his promise.

"Our friendship with Libya is eternal," said Sandinista commander Tomas Borge on September 1, 1984.

Another member of the Nicaraguan junta, Sergio Ramirez, testified that "the solidarity of the Libyan people, of the Libyan government and comrade Muammar Qaddafi was always patently manifest. This solidarity has been made real, has been made effective, has been made more fraternal since the triumph of our revolution."

Sandinistas received a $100 million "loan" from Libya in the early years and last year signed a trade agreement that exchanges Libyan oil for Nicaraguan bananas and coffee. The world got a look at another dimension of the relationship in April 1983, when Brazilian authorities inspected four Libyan planes bound for Nicaragua and found that crates marked "medical supplies" contained eighty-four tons of military equipment—missiles, machine guns, bazookas, mortars, bombs, cannons and two unassembled fighter planes.

"Nicaragua is a wonderful thing," Qaddafi has emphasized. "They fight America on its own ground."

Most Americans have been reluctant to recognize the connections among terrorist groups, but those ties can no longer be denied. Neither can Sandinista links with Libya, the PLO, and Iran, links that place Nicaragua in a network of violence that murders and maims from the Bekaa to Bogotá.

We prefer to think that violence originates in each country out of strictly indigenous problems and reflects indigenous hostilities. We prefer to think civil wars result from popular discontent and social injustice. We do not at all like the notion of international bands training together, working together, wreaking violence and making revolution together. And yet, the reality of Nicaragua's training with the PLO and Libya can no more be denied than the reality of Libyan economic, financial, and military assistance for the Sandinistas.

Today resources from throughout the Soviet bloc aid in consolidating Sandinista power in Nicaragua and spreading violence in Central and South America. Managua has become the capital city of terrorism in the Western Hemisphere.

Germany's Bader-Meinhoff gang, Spain's Basque ETA, Colombia's M19, Peru's Sendero Luminoso, and El Salvador's FMLN meet with those of Libya and the PLO. Italian Premier Bettino Craxi has publicly complained of the presence of fugitive Italian terrorists in Managua.

Nicaragua's support for Colombia's principal guerrilla group, M19, has been documented in some detail. M19 has offices in Managua, its members are honored guests at Sandinista functions, and they travel on Nicaraguan passports.

When an M19 group attacked Colombia's supreme court last December, more than 100 were left dead. Many of the guns captured in that raid were linked to Libya, Vietnam, Cuba, and, of course, Nicaragua. Some of the rifles used in the raid had been sold by the Vietnamese to Libya and from there were shipped to Nicaragua and then to the Colombian guerrilla movement. Sandinista army rifles (M-16s and R-16s) were also found at the scene.

Sandinistas directed preparation for the attack, which was modeled on their 1978 seizure of the parliament building in Managua. An FSLN commando group traveling on Colombian passports arrived in that country a day before the bloody occupation and coordinated it. Other Nicaraguans handled communications. And Tomas Borge himself eulogized the slain Colombian guerrillas at a "people's mass."

The Libyan link was also clear. Leading participants (for example, Diana Morales, who inflicted the most casualties on the military) had been trained in Libya, Nicaragua, and Cuba.

These facts make the relevance of Nicaragua to U.S. security undeniable. Speaking after the American bombing of Libya, Borge commented, "Who has given the United States government the right to determine what is terrorism and what is not terrorism?" One might well ask instead: who has given the Nicaraguan government the right to spread violence in this hemisphere?

Congressmen and others who have been hoping for the best in Nicaragua are being confronted with new details of the Sandinista role in the international support system for violent politics.

The cost to Central America in loss of peace and freedom is already high. If the full consolidation of Sandinista power and the full incorporation of Nicaragua into the world Socialist system is permitted, U.S. congressmen will look back with nostalgia on a time when $100 million in American aid to the contras could have made a real difference.

Promises, Promises I
May 19, 1986

During the mid-1980s' search for a diplomatic settlement in Central America, few people remembered that the Sandinistas had already agreed to a settlement. In the last stage of the war against Somoza in June 1979, the Sandinistas promised the Organization of American States that they would allow multiparty competition, respect human rights and

207

civil liberties, and create a mixed economy. On the basis of the promise, the OAS recognized them as Nicaragua's rightful government.

The history of broken promises and dishonored commitments was sufficient grounds for skepticism about the reliability of subsequent agreements to which the FSLN became a party.

There is a widespread belief in Washington that Nicaragua will sign the Contadora treaty on June 6 at a meeting of foreign ministers of five Central American countries and eight associated South American nations. This belief persists even though some Nicaraguan junta leaders indicate the contrary. There is also widespread fear that Nicaragua will sign the agreement, never fulfill its terms, and nonetheless reap the benefits of compliance by its neighbors and the United States.

It is a reasonable fear based on the past behavior of the Sandinistas.

After all, in 1979 the Sandinistas promised democratic elections, free press and assembly, and rule of civil law. These commitments were made when Sandinista leaders needed help in ousting Somoza and winning power. Once in power, the junta leaders rejected talk of elections, claiming that Nicaraguans had already voted "with their blood and with the guns in their hands."

None of the promises made to the Organization of American States was kept. Instead, the Sandinista government gagged the press, denied the right of assembly, subjected businesses and trade unions to comprehensive controls, and suspended the rule of law. When elections were finally held in 1984, the government controlled the choice of candidates, the campaign, and the outcome.

What reason is there, then, to believe that the same leaders who made solemn written promises of democracy six years ago will honor them now if they sign the proposed treaty?

The treaty would commit its signatories to democratic freedoms and elections, the removal of foreign military and security personnel, an end to importation of foreign arms, and noninterference in the internal affairs of each other. The twenty-one Contadora objectives are wholly consistent with the goals of U.S. policy in the region.

But Nicaraguan President Daniel Ortega and the junta do not speak as though they are planning a democratic transition.

"We are not going to disarm the revolution," Ortega said last week. "Not one rifle will leave Nicaragua in any negotiations."

Junta member Sergio Ramirez Mercado said Nicaragua would be disposed to sign the Contadora treaty only if the United States pledged to respect its terms. Special envoy Ambassador Philip Habib has already informally indicated the United States would do so. In a letter to three Democratic congressmen, Habib asserted that the United States would support a treaty that provided for "comprehensive, verifiable and simultaneous implementation," adding "we would not feel politically bound to respect an agreement that Nicaragua was violating."

But would the United States move to demobilize and disband the contras while Nicaragua stalls and dissembles? One of the treaty's provisions, the one Nicaragua is most concerned with, would outlaw "irregular military forces" and dismantle their bases.

The Sandinistas might even cut off their flow of weapons and guerrillas to neighboring countries. It would be easy enough, however, to resume full-scale support a year or two later.

Such a swindle would not be the first one experienced by the United States. We have already made real concessions in exchange for promised goods that never materialized. At Yalta, Stalin promised free elections for Poland. North Vietnam promises a cease-fire and withdrawal of foreign troops from Laos and Cambodia. At Helsinki, the Soviets promised to respect human rights and permit emigration. Following the Cuban missile crisis, Nikita Khrushchev promised President Kennedy the Soviet Union would not install offensive weapons in Cuba and would not use that country to export revolution in the hemisphere. The Communist record of treaty compliance reminds one of Thomas Hobbes's dictum that "covenants without swords" are not to be relied on.

Obviously, the United States should not acquiesce in an agreement that will not be fulfilled. To acquiesce in tyranny for Nicaragua, turmoil for Central America, and enhanced risks for American national security is simply unthinkable.

Promises, Promises II

March 31, 1986

The contra issue will not die. The House Democrats tried to kill it but failed.

Now the Sandinista *comandantes* have turned the tide against themselves and once again embarrassed their supporters in Washington—not as before by going to Moscow, but by violating the Honduran border in unprecedented numbers, penetrating deep into Honduras while pursuing Nicaraguan freedom fighters.

They had the good fortune of doing it the day after a vote in the House turned down aid for the contras, but the bad fortune of having it reported just before the vote in the Senate.

It was an eye-opener for even the heavy lidded.

What others had seen clearly before was the mounting evidence of concern throughout Central America about the Sandinistas.

Public opinion polls conducted by the Gallup organization in Central America during the past two weeks establish that solid majorities of Costa Ricans and Hondurans believe it would be better for Nicaragua and for themselves if the contras won. Very few believe a Sandinista victory would be good for Nicaragua or for the region.

Those in the United States who oppose aid to the contras may think Nicaraguans support their government, but Nicaragua's neighbors—who are much closer to the scene—think otherwise.

The further erosion of Contadora as a viable alternative that will protect American or Central American interests was also seen. The notion that conversations among Central America's neighbors—all of whom had a direct stake in regional peace—would sort things out was worth a try, and try the original Contadora group did for three years.

Contadora today is less a diplomatic process than an incantation for a good many opponents of assistance to the contras. They hope that, if it is invoked often enough, it can be made to sound like a policy. Four facts have been lost sight of by those who most often invoke the name.

First, they forget that Nicaragua withdrew from Contadora negotiations and recently refused further cooperation for at least six crucial months, during which time they expect to consolidate power. Second, they ignore that the new "expanded" Contadora group includes Argentina, Brazil, Peru, and Uruguay, geographically remote members who have no direct stake in Central America's conflicts. They will not suffer the consequences of failure. Third, they take no note that the new Contadora group is profoundly distrusted by Nicaragua's Central American neighbors, who feel they are most concerned and least consulted about the region. And fourth, they fail to note that the past three years of Contadora negotiations have produced virtually nothing—which suggests that chances are dim for a negotiated settlement.

Further evidence of the Sandinistas' unwillingness to negotiate came in their rejection of a proposal from President Napoleon Duarte of El Salvador to create simultaneous negotiations between the government of El Salvador and its insurgents and the government of Nicaragua and its insurgents, the contras. None of this indicates to people in the region an active Sandinista interest in negotiation.

Nicaragua's neighbors see more reason to fear Nicaragua than to expect a political solution. More than three-fourths of both Costa Ricans and Hondurans regard Nicaragua as a military threat to their respective countries. They understand the Sandinista government's commitment to "revolutionary internationalism."

That commitment was made still clearer by the release last week of the recently translated internal Sandinista "document of 72 hours," which firmly aligns Nicaragua with world revolution.

To doubt the character and intention of Nicaragua's current government requires real ignorance or willful blindness. Indeed, that government has few open supporters in Congress today. Too many former sympathizers have learned too much about the *comandantes* and the region. Congressional opponents of the contras have become more realistic about the Sandinistas, but no more realistic about their meaning for American national security—in the Gulf, the Panama Canal, or off the Pacific coast.

It must be clear to all now that Sandinistas were willing to accept help from House Democrats but did not want to earn it with improved behavior.

Can We Now Trust the Sandinistas?

September 9, 1987

The long road to free, competitive elections in Nicaragua featured some embarrassing behavior by American lawmakers who urged forbearance in judging the Sandinistas' compliance with their democratic commitments. But would Oscar Arias be happy with something less than full democracy for his own country? Would Senators Christopher Dodd or Tom Harkin accept a "flexible" adherence to law by the Reagan administration?

Their attitude recalls the stinging comment of Mario Vargas Llosa concerning such double standards. Vargas Llosa wrote to Günther Grass:

> *When an American or European intellectual or liberal newspaper or institution advocates for Latin American countries political options or methods he would never countenance for*

211

his own society, he is betraying a fundamental doubt about the capacity of Latin American countries to achieve the liberty and respect for the rights of others that prevail in Western democracies. In most cases the problem is an unconscious prejudice and, in poet's sentiment, a sort of visceral racism which these persons who generally have unimpeachable liberal and democratic credentials would sharply disavow if they were suddenly made aware of it.

Finally, it took the work of many to persuade the Sandinistas to hold the elections promised in June 1979.

Is it possible that Nicaragua's Marxist military junta is willing to dismantle its dictatorship and submit itself to criticism, organized opposition, and periodic free elections? If defeated in those elections, would it relinquish power? No Marxist government of any country has ever done so. Yet Nicaragua's rulers say they are ready to meet the terms of the peace plan adopted at Esquipulas, Guatemala, by the presidents of the five Central American nations.

Do they mean it, or are they following Lenin's recommended tactic of "two steps forward, one step back," seeking to eliminate the contras with concessions that can be repealed later?

The peace plan calls for a cease-fire in internal wars of the region, full freedom of expression, and full political freedom—including free elections to be held in 1990.

The government of Nicaragua accepted the plan and has announced several steps to comply with its terms. It is said that Nicaragua's opposition newspaper, *La Prensa*, which the Sandinistas first submitted to heavy prior censorship and then shut down, will be permitted to operate freely. Radio Catolica and other independent radio stations also shut down by the government will be permitted to function, it is said.

These could be significant steps. And the government of Nicaragua has indicated additional liberalization should be expected between now and November 7, the deadline for compliance with the plan.

Do these steps mark the first democratic transition of a Marxist government? It is difficult to be certain. While announcing that the Nicaraguan government will no longer censor any media, Interior Minister Tomas Borge noted that the state of emergency remains in effect and that it will be the editor's responsibility not to publish anything that threatens the prospects for peace or tends to destabilize the Nicaraguan economy.

If Nicaragua's rulers keep their promises for democracy this time, then there will be democracy, peace, and development in Central America. It is as simple as that. A democratic Nicaragua would not continue to militarize Central America, nor arm guerrillas in El Salvador and Colombia, nor invite thousands of troops and advisers from Libya, the PLO, and elsewhere in the Soviet bloc, nor spend its resources building a 10,000-foot runway to accommodate heavy bombers. Costa Rica, El Salvador, Honduras, Colombia, and the United States would not need to fear the policies of a democratic Nicaragua. There would be no stream of refugees to burden the economies and disrupt the societies of neighbors.

It would be marvelous if the Arias plan were to bring democracy to Nicaragua. But many in Central America and Washington fear it will have very different consequences.

They worry that the junta will liberalize its practices just enough to ensure the end of support for the contras and then reinstitute repression once the resistance forces have been dismantled. There is also widespread concern that Costa Rican and congressional liberals will lower the standards for democracy to permit the Sandinistas a "passing grade."

Sen. Tom Harkin (D-Iowa) shocked his colleagues by urging Violeta Chamorro—owner of *La Prensa*—to agree to "moderate censorship" as a condition for reopening the newspaper. Sen. Christopher Dodd (D-Conn.) has already begun to advocate "flexible" standards for judging Sandinista compliance, and U.S. friends of the Sandinistas have recently suggested that it is excessive for the Reagan administration to insist on "complete democratization" of Nicaragua. Fears that standards of democracy will be stretched to cover Sandinista conduct were heightened when Costa Rica's President Oscar Arias, in his speech on Capitol Hill, advocated flexibility in judging compliance.

In Costa Rica, the man whom Arias narrowly defeated in the last presidential election charged that "more and more, the peace plan seems designed to disarm and dismantle the Nicaraguan resistance forces." Reports circulating in Washington suggest this may be the case, at least in part. It is known that the "Wright" plan was leaked to the Sandinistas five days before other governments in the region received it and that revisions were made to take account of Sandinista criticism. Reports also have it that Dodd and Democratic adviser Col. Edward King made significant contributions to the Arias plan.

Arias's clear opposition to U.S. funding for the contras mired the plan—and Costa Rica—still more deeply in U.S. partisan politics on the side of congressional liberals and aroused real resentment within the administration and among those in Congress who for seven years have led the fight to secure some $5 billion in U.S. assistance for Central America.

The peace plan has involved both Arias and El Salvador's José Napoleon Duarte in a dangerous game with Republicans as well as the Sandinistas. Rep. Jack Kemp (R-N.Y.) made this clear when he noted after Arias's speech that "it will be very difficult to get assistance to governments in Central America—particularly Costa Rica—if there is a lobbying effort by President Arias against U.S. assistance to the freedom fighters in Nicaragua."

Two things are very badly needed at this stage: some relatively clear criteria and bipartisan agreement on what constitutes democratization and some bipartisan agreement about what will happen if the commanders of Nicaragua's revolution once again renege on their promises of democracy.

Much Bravery Seen during Visit to Nicaragua

October 18, 1987

During a visit to Managua in October 1987, I was deeply impressed with the scarcity, repression, and fear that had become a normal part of everyday life. Nonetheless, as soon as the Sandinista regime began a tentative, cautious liberalization in late 1987, civil society struggled to reemerge. Two years later we saw a similar phenomenon in Poland and in the Soviet Union itself.

Life is grim today in Nicaragua. Nearly 10,000 Nicaraguans are political prisoners, more than the total in all other Central American countries. Half a million Nicaraguans have fled their nation of only 3 million. Inflation soars, last year at 750 percent, this year higher still. Everything is scarce—bread, corn, beans, eggs, chickens—everything. Nonetheless, there is hope.

"The People Triumph," *La Prensa*'s banner headline announced in the first issue published since the Nicaraguan government had shut it down 451 days earlier. Now, in the wake of the Central American accords, the paper is again being read.

But each day is a struggle, and each edition is a victory over multiple obstacles. Paper can be procured only from the government.

It is Russian, of inferior quality, and available only in strictly limited quantities. Distribution is complicated by the lack of subscriptions and vehicles for delivery. Each day's edition sells out, but it is not possible to print more copies because *La Prensa*'s circulation is not permitted to exceed that of the government's official newspaper, *Barricada*.

La Prensa publisher Violeta Chamorro and her editors, however, are not downhearted. She told me they are eager and determined to use the opportunity created by the Central American agreement. They do not know how long the freedom to publish will be available or when government censors may move in. But each day *La Prensa* makes it clear that government organs do not speak for all Nicaraguans, that an independent public opinion exists in that country even though its voice has been muffled by the heavy-handed "liberators" who took control in July 1979. That is why Venezuela's former president, Luis Herrera Campíns, declared: "Read and buy *La Prensa*. It is a vote for freedom, a plebiscite for democracy."

Nicaragua's democratic opposition parties, independent trade unions, and church organizations make the same point: that they are there, many thousands strong, that the *comandantes* do not speak for them, that the *comandantes'* unions do not represent the workers of Nicaragua, and that the FSLN does not speak for the nation. In these days when world attention is focused on their country, Nicaraguans are sending a message: Their nation requires plural voices because Nicaraguans do not all think alike.

It takes courage to voice unauthorized opinions in Nicaragua today. Eight years of one-party rule, of arbitrary arrests, long sentences, and "divine mobs" have taken their toll on Nicaraguan spirits. "We are afraid," conservative leader Mario Rappaccioli was brave enough to admit in comments published by *La Prensa*. Rappaccioli's National Conservative party was excluded from the official dialogue authorized by the Sandinista government, and so were other leading Nicaraguan political parties despite appeals by Carlos Huembes, president of the umbrella group Coordinadora Democratica Nicaragüense, and by other Central American presidents.

So far the government of Nicaragua has refused all requests to broaden the dialogues to include the major opposition parties. They are even less willing to speak to leaders of the democratic resistance forces (contras), some 16,000 of whom fight today inside Nicaragua.

How can there be reconciliation or democracy in Nicaragua if government leaders refuse even to speak to their opponents? This is the question that confronts hopes for freedom and peace in Central America.

There will not be peace in El Salvador unless there is democracy in Nicaragua, and there cannot be democracy in Nicaragua without amnesty, internal reconciliation, free expression, free assembly, and free elections—precisely the conditions required by the Central American peace accords.

Will the Sandinistas comply? Nobody knows. All that is required of them is that they forgo the use of force in dealing with other Nicaraguans.

Is the Nicaraguan Government Ready to Comply with the Esquipulas Agreement?

October 25, 1987

We now know the answer to the question I posed at the start of this column. The Sandinistas violated a cease-fire agreement with the contras, periodically shut down and harassed independent new media such as La Prensa *and* Radio Catolica, *hectored opponents and disrupted opposition marches, and continued to hold thousands of political prisoners.*

But Oscar Arias and his Central American colleagues repeatedly extended deadlines, hoping that a little more "moral pressure" would induce the Sandinistas to jettison their Marxism-Leninism and become good democrats.

The Sandinista dictatorship was ultimately defeated in early 1990 in the elections held under the accords and under the scrutiny of a thousand international observers.

Time flies. We are nearing the date for compliance with the Central American Accords signed by the presidents of Nicaragua, El Salvador, Honduras, Costa Rica, and Guatemala on August 7.

Will the government of Nicaragua comply with the terms of the agreement it signed at Esquipulas? Will the government stand aside while Radio Catolica broadcasts news as well as prayers and the dozen other radio stations shut down by the FSLN *comandantes* go back on the air? Will the opposition parties be able to hold meetings and peaceful marches without disruption? Will the government negotiate a cease-fire with the resistance (the contras)? Will it free nine to ten thousand political prisoners held in Nicaragua's jails?

We will know the answer to these and other questions by November 7, the deadline. We will not know whether Nicaragua's ruling junta will submit to free elections in 1990, but we will know whether they have abandoned the use of force against Nicaraguans with different ideas about how the country should be organized and governed.

That, finally, is the issue in Nicaragua and elsewhere in Central America: whether governments and groups contending for power (including Marxist-Leninists and "death squads") are willing to work out the future of their country without killing, kidnapping, and taking hostage those with different ideas about what that future should be. The Central American Accords commit the governments of the region to amnesty and to free expression, assembly, and elections—to internal dialogue and external peace. The accords, however, do not commit them to any particular economic, social, or political form of organization but to a particular political method—to the method of dialogue and consent rather than the method of violence. And in politics, as George Orwell wrote, the choice of method is the definitive act.

The Sandinistas are not finding it easy to forgo force in dealing with opponents. Eight days after the accords were signed, police with dogs, batons, and electric cattle prods broke up a peaceful demonstration and arrested and jailed the president of the Nicaraguan Bar Association and the head of the Nicaraguan Human Rights Commission. The clear purpose was to intimidate not only those who participated in the march but also all those who were aware of what happened to the marchers.

A week later, eighteen Nicaraguan youths were arrested en route to an anniversary celebration of the Social Christian party in Managua. They were tried, and some are still in jail. Again the clear purpose was intimidation.

Outside Managua arbitrary arrests of *campesinos* continue unabated.

The habits of violence and intimidation are strong in Nicaragua. They are sustained by the Sandinista *comandantes'* belief that force is an acceptable method for dealing with fellow Nicaraguans. Obviously they find it morally permissible to govern by force—they are part of a great world revolution that itself proceeds mainly by force.

When Daniel Ortega spoke at the UN General Assembly on October 9, he commenced by noting that it was the twentieth anniversary of the death of Che Guevara. Ortega said that like Gandhi and Christ, Che "left everything to work for the people." Ortega seems not to have noticed that unlike Gandhi and Christ, Che

217

Guevara chose violence as his method of "working" for the people. The reminder came from Bolivia and El Salvador, where other guerrillas commemorated Che's anniversary with bombings. Ortega seems not to understand that while Christ and Gandhi affirmed the humanity of all, the method of violence requires dehumanizing opponents—seeing them as traitors, mercenaries, counterrevolutionaries, collaborationists, not as fellow citizens with different ideas about how best to live together.

Herein lies the reason that the dialogue prescribed by the accords is so crucial. The very act of discussing an issue with an opponent humanizes him. It gives respect both to the individual and his opinions. This is the reason, doubtless, that the government of Nicaragua has so far refused discussion with the leaders of the Nicaraguan resistance.

It is also the reason that El Salvador's president, José Napoleon Duarte, acted immediately to initiate negotiations with El Salvador's guerrilla forces, the FMLN. Duarte refuses to dehumanize, refuses to hate even the man whom he knows planned and supervised the kidnapping of his daughter. Duarte is therefore always ready to make peace with El Salvador's guerrillas.

In El Salvador, it is the guerrillas who are reluctant to talk peace. "Our confidence is in the total struggle of our people," said FMLN chief and Communist party leader Shafik Handal. "When the struggle has developed further there will be new possibilities for a just solution." For Marxists in El Salvador as in Nicaragua "struggle"—that is, violence—is the preferred, "historically correct" method.

But in signing the Central American Accords Daniel Ortega committed himself not only to democratic ends but to democratic means. He committed himself to eschewing violent "struggle" against the people of Nicaragua.

Now he is stuck with that commitment.

Moment of Truth for Central America
November 9, 1987

*Some people could not understand why Ronald Reagan—and others of
us—were so concerned about Nicaragua or El Salvador. What harm
could a small, poor Central American country do to the United States?
I believed—and believe—we had a special responsibility for their independence because they were small, poor neighboring countries and also
because the violence within them could spread to their neighbors.*

*Moreover, through aid to guerrilla forces and terrorists, the Sandi-
nistas could help provoke the collapse of the region's vulnerable democracies. A Communist Central America could then put great pressure on
Mexico.*

*The Central American democracies were front line states. They
knew it. At their regional summit in January 1988, called to follow up
on the previous summer's Esquipulas plan, they accused the Sandinistas
of noncompliance but still withheld support for the contras.*

"In Nicaraguan culture much more importance is placed on one's
ability to shine in the major media markets abroad than in the sorry
shallow outlets at home," Arturo Cruz, Jr., writes in *The New Republic*
(November 16). "To be known among one's own tribe is no particular
accomplishment. What is important is to maintain one's pertinence
abroad," says the distinguished Nicaraguan in exile.

If Nicaraguans are all that interested in world attention, they
must feel pleased indeed with Daniel Ortega. In less than a decade
Ortega not only has established his preeminence over the eight other
theoretically equal Sandinista *comandantes* but has known how to
project himself onto the world stage and into the world press—
including *The New York Times*, where he was most recently photo-
graphed alongside Erich Honecker, Gen. Wojciech Jaruzelski, and
other big-time Communist leaders in Moscow to hear and cheer the
Soviet anniversary celebration.

Ortega is not the first leader of a small, poor Central American
country who has wanted to link his nation's struggle to global
political processes and purposes. Most major Central American parties have tried to interest the world in their struggle through ties with
Socialist International or the Christian Democratic International.
Costa Rican President Oscar Arias's Nobel Prize testifies to their
success.

Today the whole political world has heard of the Arias plan for

219

Central American peace. This global interest must be satisfying to the leaders and peoples of these countries that were so long ignored, disdained, and even despised by great powers that could not be bothered to learn the names of Central American states.

It is time the world took notice. But as Cruz's comment suggests, there are pitfalls. There is a danger that, at this crucial moment in the history of Central America, the glare of international attention may distract Central American leaders from the hard realities of their concrete situation. This is the moment at which the governments of Central America must ask themselves (and tell the rest of us) how the peace plan is actually working.

That plan differs in crucial respects from all other peace proposals offered for this troubled region. It is more interesting and more promising.

It gives priority to democracy with its centerpiece of "an authentic democratic process." It commits each government to provide within ninety days of signature free expression and free association— including the right of radio and television stations and newspapers to operate without censorship or intimidation. It recognizes the right of political parties and others to organize marches, meetings, and demonstrations geared toward the free elections that each president promised to his people.

The peace plan reflects the belief widely held throughout the region that the future of Central America—its security and development—depends on Nicaragua's becoming a democracy. Although the Arias plan does not require free elections in Nicaragua until 1990 and does not require that the Sandinista government share power or dismantle the infrastructure of repression before the resistance is disbanded, it does require that the Nicaraguan government provide full and prompt respect for democratic freedoms. It bets that freedom has its own momentum, which, once established, can carry Nicaragua through to free elections.

As Susan Purcell points out in her recent penetrating analysis in *Foreign Affairs*, the Arias plan "gives a big advantage to the Sandinistas" but takes major risks because Arias and his fellow democratic presidents were determined "to test once and for all the Sandinistas' willingness to democratize." Purcell continues: "When asked what would happen if the Sandinistas did not carry out democratic reforms, [Arias replied] that the world would then know what the Sandinistas were really like."

But it is not the world that will suffer the direct consequences if the Sandinistas fail to comply. It is the people of Central America.

Repeated polls in Central American countries outside Nicaragua (which of course does not permit public opinion polls) show that large majorities believe Nicaragua is governed by a repressive regime that rules by force, is opposed by its own people, and constitutes a threat to other countries in the region. The same large majorities believe it would be better for Nicaragua and the region if the resistance wins. Still larger majorities approve U.S. military and humanitarian aid to the contras.

Eventually Oscar Arias and the other presidents will have to face Sandinista realities. So far they have only taken bows on the world stage. Arias has won additional applause for saying he will "never" support the use of force (read contras) in Nicaragua. But if the resistance is dismantled and the Nicaraguan military regime is left intact, there will be no peace, no stability, no development, and finally no freedom in Central America—not in El Salvador, nor in Guatemala, nor in Costa Rica.

Now, with the need to report on compliance with the plan, it is the moment of truth for Central America's presidents. The consequences of their decisions will be felt in the daily lives of Central Americans long after the world's attention has moved on to some other political melodrama.

The Prisoners of Nicaragua
September 26, 1988

The Sandinistas have made many promises. On the edge of victory in June 1979 they promised elections; on the eve of defeat in 1987 they promised elections again. Repeatedly, they have promised that freedom and reneged. After the Central American Accords, FSLN goons attacked a peaceful opposition march at Nandaime, beating and arresting. Several leaders of the traditional parties were jailed under harsh conditions, held for months, and denied fundamental rights.

Nandaime became a symbol of Sandinista lawlessness.

It has been just over a year since the government of Nicaragua signed the Central American Peace Accords promising democracy. But democracy has not come to Nicaragua.

Instead, a campaign of repression and intimidation against the opposition is in full swing. On September 17, Managua police turned down an opposition request to hold a march later this month. This way, at least, the opposition will not be arrested, as forty were at a Nandaime march on July 10. Those forty are still being held at La Granja prison under extremely harsh conditions—each in a crowded cell with fifty to sixty common criminals.

Most of these civilian political, trade union, and business leaders are already suffering the effects of malnutrition and skin fungus. The health of several has deteriorated seriously. The wife of the secretary general of the Democratic Coordinating Board, Roger Guevara Mena, reported recently after visiting her husband that the food is adulterated as well as inadequate, that many prisoners have developed skin ailments and throat infections, and that most receive no medical care. Trade union leader Carlos Huembes has lost thirty pounds since his imprisonment and is still losing weight.

Most serious is the condition of conservative party leader Dr. Miriam Arguello, who was one of those arrested at Nandaime. Seized while she spoke, jailed and paraded in prison garb before TV cameras, consigned to a crowded cell with common criminals, and restricted to her bunk, Arguello suffered rapid deterioration of her physical condition.

Her private physician, Dr. José Maria Morales, who examined her on September 9, said Arguello was permitted to get up from her jail bunk only when a guard was standing in front of the cell door and then was permitted to walk around the cell only for the length of time that the guard stood at the door.

Morales said Arguello appeared "dazed and in a fog." He said her history of circulatory problems, lack of proper nourishment, and the continuous psychological pressure had caused her blood pressure to rise and the loss of some control in her hands.

The Sandinista government and its newspapers, Barricada and El Nuevo Diario, denied that any of the imprisoned political leaders had health problems. Sandinista physician Dr. Miguel Aragon pronounced Arguello "in good health" and requiring no medical attention. She and other political leaders were, he said, in "perfect condition." But such claims are not credible. Too many Nicaraguans have seen the prisoners.

The political leaders arrested at Nandaime were held for three weeks without being charged and are now being tried for the "crime" of peaceful opposition. The Puebla Institute, which tracks human rights problems in Nicaragua, is especially disturbed by the denial of due process in their trials. Puebla Institute's president, Nina Shea, emphasizes that the prisoners are denied visits by foreign human rights groups, including the International Red Cross; that they are permitted only extremely infrequent visits by their families; that neither they nor their lawyers are allowed to be present throughout the trials against them—nor even provided a full list of the charges they face. Nor are they provided adequate time to work with their counsel to prepare an effective defense.

Arguello, Huembes, Guevara, and their colleagues are not the only Nicaraguans to suffer such treatment. A soon-to-be-released report by the Nicaraguan Association for Human Rights documents the widespread existence of harsh conditions, poor food, inadequate medical care, and extremely restricted contact with the outside world throughout Nicaragua's overcrowded prisons.

They also document the existence of more than 7,500 political prisoners in Nicaragua. A remarkable list of these prisoners has been prepared by the association and is expected to be included in the report.

Perhaps its publication will provoke some response from a largely indifferent world. So far, the international community has remained essentially quiet about the Sandinistas' denial of free speech and assembly, arbitrary arrests and imprisonment, denial of due process, failure to grant amnesty to political prisoners, and violations of other promises made in the Central American Peace Accords.

Nicaragua's Central American neighbors, the Contadora countries, the Europeans, the Democrats in the U.S. Congress—all of whom were enthusiastic about the accords—seem little disturbed by their violation. And Costa Rican President Oscar Arias himself has had little to say about violations of the accords for which he was so widely celebrated and for which he received a Nobel Prize.

Meanwhile, Nicaragua's economy is deteriorating almost as quickly as the health of its political prisoners. Inflation, stagnation, and scarcity are the order of the day. The democratic resistance, denied essential aid by Congress, is without arms, food, and shoes and has been forced to abandon its strategic positions inside Nicaragua.

No one, however, should imagine that Sandinista consolidation of power will bring peace to Central America. It will merely preface a new round of civil war.

Their Style of Democracy
January 25, 1988

From the time of their arrival in power the Sandinistas refused to share power, refused to open processes, and did their best to intimidate domestic opponents. But they never stopped holding out the prospect that they might improve.

Again and again their promises were used to oppose U.S. aid for the Nicaraguan resistance on grounds that it was necessary to take a "risk for peace."

The risks proved quite high, and the losses of the Nicaraguan people, large.

The Central American Peace Accord signed in Guatemala last August was a plan, not just an expression of good intentions. It committed its signatories, the five presidents of Central America, to establish authentic democratic processes and carry out national reconciliation. A time frame for compliance was provided. Then time ran out.

When the presidents met in Costa Rica a week ago to examine the question of compliance, it was clear to all (except possibly Daniel Ortega) that Nicaragua had not fulfilled its promises. There had been no general amnesty, no cease-fire, no internal reconciliation. Controls over speech, press, and assembly had been relaxed, but freedom in all domains remained sharply limited. Central America's presidents said as much. Now they said Nicaragua must either comply or give up the pretense, and must do so at a time when the U.S. Congress would be considering continued aid to the contras.

The pressure precipitated an interesting and often contradictory scramble in Nicaragua that has already produced new promises, new punitive actions, and new proposals for peace talks. The Sandinista response—including its latest proposal Thursday for urgent talks with the contras—makes it clear the Nicaraguan government does not relish the choice with which it has been confronted.

The contradictory actions of the Sandinistas were reflected in last week's headlines. "Nicaragua Cancels State of Emergency," *The Washington Post* announced on page one of its January 17 edition. "Five More in Nicaraguan Opposition Are Arrested by the Security Police," *The New York Times* said on the same page on the same day. Both headlines were accurate.

On the same day that Managua announced the lifting of a state of emergency, police arrested leaders of Nicaragua's democratic trade unions, private sector, independent press, and democratic political parties. They were interrogated for some thirty-six hours and released.

This was not the first time opposition leaders were arrested at the same time the government sought to convince the world of its democratization. It also happened eight days after the signing of the accords, when the Nicaraguan government forcibly broke up a peaceful demonstration and arrested Lino Hernandez, director of the independent Permanent Commission on Human Rights, and Alberto Saborio, president of the Nicaraguan Bar Association. Both arrests were clearly designed to intimidate.

Now Hernandez, Saborio, and ten associates once again are victims of the Sandinista desire to proclaim freedom and control its use.

It is not the only contradiction. An amnesty was declared for 3,500 political prisoners *providing* they are accepted by the United States. While the state of emergency was lifted and the constitution restored, the official newspaper *Barricada* warned that the restoration of civil rights "should not be misinterpreted as a blank check for irresponsibility and subversion."

"They are telling us that this is their style of democracy," said *La Prensa* Director Violeta Chamorro, whose brother-in-law, *La Prensa* editor Jaime Chamorro, was arrested.

Is this "style of democracy" acceptable to the U.S. congressmen who have tied their support for aid to the contras to Nicaragua's compliance with the Central American Accords? The vote is scheduled for the first week in February, and some Democratic leaders have indicated they will make an all-out effort to block further aid to the contras. They call their policy "a risk for peace."

But it is necessary to ask what is being risked.

The most recent Sandinista proposal for peace talks is clearly designed as a further measure to influence the U.S. Congress against providing additional aid. Still, Congress cannot avoid the fundamental questions—which are unchanged by the Sandinistas' latest overture.

Is there a chance for democracy in Nicaragua without continued pressure on these would-be totalitarians?

Is there a chance for peace in El Salvador while the Sandinista regime rules Nicaragua?

Is there a chance for economic development in Central America while the region is thus afflicted by repression, revolution, and civil war?

Is there any good reason for Democrats who do not desire a

Communist Central America to oppose aid to the contras?

But opponents of aid have a question of their own: is it morally justifiable for those who believe in peace and democracy to support the use of force by Nicaraguans against the Nicaraguan government?

El Salvador's president, José Napoleon Duarte, provided the answer to this last question in a speech before the United Nations General Assembly: "Force can only be acceptable," Duarte argued, "when there are no institutional processes available to open the political system, and then should only be used for the purpose of opening that system."

Supporters of democracy must agree. There still remain no institutional processes through which internal or external opposition to the Sandinistas can effectively participate in the country's political system. It is therefore up to Congress to help the rulers of Nicaragua understand that democracy is their only alternative.

Nicaragua's Flawed Election Law

May 1, 1989

The Sandinistas' electoral law gave the regime control of the electoral process and made a truly fair vote impossible. It is a measure of how unpopular the regime had become that Violeta Chamorro won anyway, despite the advantages that the Sandinistas reserved for themselves and the hardships they imposed on Chamorro's UNO coalition.

"We ask free men and women to look carefully at what is happening in Nicaragua and not to be distracted by short time frames or government spotlights shining on selected voices, while others are silently suffocated in the darkness."

Jaime Chamorro Cardenal, senior editor of *La Prensa*, Nicaragua's beleaguered independent newspaper, asks a lot in his new book on Nicaragua's long struggle for freedom (*La Prensa*, Freedom House, 1989). He asks free people to look beyond the orderly, hopeful processes of international diplomacy to the bitter realities of daily life in his country.

Watching a people suffocate is unpleasant business. It is so much more agreeable to view Nicaragua from a distance, through the solemn promises made—to international applause—by the five Central American presidents, including Daniel Ortega. These presidents committed themselves to "authentic democratic processes," "respect for human rights," "total freedom for television, radio and press," and "genuine freedom of electoral processes."

Ortega hopes that if the world keeps its attention fixed on the agreements or on his current tour of Western European capitals, it may not notice that the Sandinistas' new election laws make a mockery of the international agreements and the commitment to democracy.

The agreements have one great virtue: specificity. Not only do they agree to democratization and democratic elections for Nicaragua, but also they provide timetables and other specifics:

• That Nicaragua's election of a president, vice president, national assembly, municipal governments, and delegates to a Central American parliament should take place no later than February 25, 1990.

• That Nicaraguan electoral laws should be reformed to provide balanced participation and representation of opposition parties on the Supreme Electoral Council.

• That Nicaraguan law should be reformed to guarantee equal access on state television and radio stations for all parties.

• That adequate time should be allowed for the opposition's preparation for and organization of an electoral campaign.

But the election laws passed last week by the Sandinista-dominated legislature were a far cry from those Ortega agreed to on February 14.

First, the new law guarantees government domination of the Supreme Electoral Council, which will oversee the elections by promising the Sandinistas three of five seats on the council.

Second, it sharply limits the opposition's access to television.

Third, it gives the government an overwhelming financial advantage and provides that the electoral council will receive one-half of any foreign funds provided to the opposition parties.

Fourth, it prohibits absentee voting by the nearly 1 million Nicaraguans who are temporarily living outside their country.

Fifth, although the elections provided by the Sandinistas will be held within the promised time frame, a provision of the new law decrees that those elected will not take office for a full ten and a half months after the election date.

Nicaragua's democratic opposition was disappointed but not surprised by the new electoral law. Their calls for a national dialogue had gone unheeded. They have few resources except their own courage. But that is substantial. Some of them, like Carlos Huembes,

227

president of the Coordinadora, and Miriam Arguello of the Conservative party have already endured six months of prison and mistreatment after they were arrested in Nicaragua's most recent peaceful demonstration last summer. Others, such as Joaquin Mejia, of *La Prensa* and the independent Liberal party, have been badly beaten by Sandinista "turbas"—mobs that operate outside the Sandinistas' own legal system.

These leaders know too that to save their country they must continue to fight. And they hope for help from other countries in Central America and from the United States.

They even hope for help from the leaders of Western Europe, with whom Daniel Ortega is currently speaking. From Paris, Ortega said he was told by François Mitterrand that France would help bring peace to Nicaragua. Presumably, the French will recall Oscar Arias's caution: "Without democracy there can be no peace in Central America."

Nicaragua's Flawed Election Process
January 22, 1990

"It does not cross the FSLN [Sandinista] members' minds that the opposition will win the elections. . . . This would be a return to the Middle Ages. It would be a return to the cave," Nicaragua's interior minister, Tomas Borge, commented last October.

The Marxist military junta that has ruled Nicaragua for a decade does not intend to lose the election. It has organized every phase of the elections to favor its candidate. It wrote the election laws. It controls the election commission, the police, courts, and media. It has the power to decide who will and will not be permitted to observe the election. The Supreme Electoral Council, which will administer the election, was created by the government and is largely stacked with its supporters.

Almost none of the preconditions for an honest election exists in Nicaragua, and we should not fudge that fact. Yet, the Sandinistas and Daniel Ortega *could* lose. UNO and its candidate, Violeta Barrios de Chamorro, could win.

Any fair election requires that opposition parties enjoy equal protection of law, equal access to media, and equal freedom to organize meetings, solicit funds, and spend them. It requires an adequate opportunity for voters to register and vote, to have their votes counted honestly, and to participate in a campaign without fear of reprisal.

Few of these conditions exist in Nicaragua. The registration process was too brief. It was marked by bureaucratic delays and complications and, worse, by harassment and violent intimidation. An UNO rally at Masatepe was attacked so viciously that one person was killed and several injured.

Chamorro has received anonymous death threats. Her vice presidential running mate, Virgilio Godoy, has been subjected to repeated death threats and other pressures to withdraw from the campaign. Some of UNO's candidates for the National Assembly and municipal offices have been forced to resign. Others have been heavily pressured to withdraw.

The government, which enjoys a monopoly of television and radio, saturates both media with "news" favorable to its candidate and its case and unfavorable to the opposition. There are two wholly state-controlled television channels. UNO gets ten minutes every three days on Channel 2, a weak black-and-white channel that can be received only in the Managua area. Channel 6 is a strong color channel, received throughout the country, and is saturated by Sandinista campaign propaganda throughout the day.

But all this may not be enough. Daniel Ortega just might lose the election anyway, much in the way Communist candidates were swept to defeat in Poland. It has been more than a decade since the *comandantes* of the FSLN seized power in Nicaragua. During that decade, the Nicaraguan people have learned firsthand hard lessons about "the dictatorship of the proletariat." Of a total population of fewer than 3 million, more than 600,000 have gone into exile. Thousands who remained have spent time in jail for political offenses. The economy is a shambles. There are shortages of bread and beef, of rice and beans, and even of coffee. Above all, there is a shortage of hard currency.

The economy of Nicaragua has been destroyed—not by the contras but by the mismanagement of young *comandantes* who imagined they were competent to direct it.

The president of Nicaragua's private sector, Gilberto Cuadra, said last week the private sector had lived through a tragic year in 1989 and that the future had "disappeared." The production of milk, he said, is one-sixth what it once was because Sandinistas have heedlessly slaughtered cows to get hard currency.

By 1989 Nicaragua had also become heavily dependent on the charity of neighbors. In that year, 39 percent of the rice consumed by

229

Nicaraguans was donated (and later sold by the government to the people). Ortega said in his year's-end address, "Democracy cannot be separated from economic issues." If the voters judge the government by its economic policies, Ortega will be defeated, despite the lack of a fair campaign, adequate registration and election procedures, and protection of citizens.

But for this to happen there will have to be an honest count. And if it is not honest, will the world know the difference? The government of Nicaragua has so far refused to number ballots, so there will be no way of ascertaining whether ballot boxes have been stuffed. No measures have yet been taken to prevent multiple voting.

Freedom House's representative, John McAward, has written: "Many of the concerns . . . about the election can be allayed by the presence of large numbers of observers from democratic groups and governments in the United States and around the world. . . . This is the key to a successful election."

So far, however, it appears that the government is determined to use visas as an instrument to screen out "provocative" and "negative" observers.

We should not be surprised that a government ready to rig an election is also eager to rig its observers. The world must not let it succeed.

Election Surprise
March 5, 1990

After the election the Sandinistas' North American apologists complained that "the Nicaraguan people voted with their bellies, not with their hearts." I think they voted with their hearts, minds, and bellies. No people anywhere vote to keep in office a regime that has deprived them of basic rights for ten years.

The Sandinistas' electoral defeat in February 1990 followed on the heels of a series of Communist defeats in Eastern Europe. These defeats underscore the point made by Aristotle, Bentham, and others: the people know best when the shoe pinches (and government represses), and the great virtue of democracy is that it gives to the people the opportunity to rid themselves of those responsible.

Violeta Chamorro is a strong, elegant woman who gives credit for victory where credit is due: to the people of Nicaragua, who—without the help of foreign consultants or advisers—listened to campaign promises, reflected on their ten years of experience with a Sandinista government, and cast their votes.

"We have shown the world an example of civic duty, demonstrating that we Nicaraguans want to live in democracy, want to live in peace and, above all, that we want to live in liberty," Chamorro said in an impeccable victory statement. "We have achieved the first democratic election in the history of this country."

Like the other people of Central America—Salvadorans, Guatemalans, Hondurans, and Costa Ricans—Nicaraguans demonstrated a resounding preference for democratic elections over violent revolution. The performance of the people of all these small countries should silence forever demeaning doubts about whether they need democracy or are finally "ready" for self-government.

No sooner were the elections over than the scramble for credit began. But there is credit enough for all. And, given the importance of the event, it is appropriate to reflect a bit on whose good work was in fact involved.

Deserving credit as great as that of the voters themselves were Violeta Chamorro and those who ran as opposition candidates, hanging in the race after repeated threats, in a context where their opponents controlled the police, the army, the economy, and repeatedly used force to silence opposition. They also deserve credit for their discipline and restraint in uniting in a single coalition behind a single slate of candidates. The tradition of schismatic politics is strong in Nicaragua. Both the Somoza and the Sandinista regimes have practiced the strategy of divide and rule to prevent the coalescence of opposition. So the leaders of Nicaragua's traditional parties have had no opportunity to acquire the skills of compromise and the habits of cooperation so important to success in democratic politics.

But though they lacked experience with democratic politics, they have experience enough with the Sandinistas. All had been severely mistreated by the Sandinistas. Some were beaten, some imprisoned, all were threatened. So, although each of the fourteen parties in UNO had its own ideas about who should be the presidential candidate, each understood it was necessary first to beat the Sandinistas and then to settle the differences among themselves peaceably.

Many other Nicaraguans deserve credit as well, prominent among them Cardinal Miguel Obando y Bravo, whose clarity and personal courage were bulwarks against the subversion of truth and the establishment of political control over religion. These Nicaraguans

231

also include the young men whose armed resistance provided Sandinista comandantes with the incentive to negotiate, to promise elections, and finally to fulfill their promises. These contras risked their lives in a clear-cut freedom fight and, with the transition to democracy, will have attained their goals. I do not doubt that the contribution of this largely peasant army will be honored by their countrymen. So will the contribution of the contra leaders, who for a decade endured the frustrations of American politics to win support for their struggle. Nicaraguans will also understand and appreciate the special solidarity of the Honduran government in providing them refuge.

The contras were the "fight" in a successful, though uncoordinated, strategy of "fight and talk." The Central American presidents provided the other element—the "talk." The presidents of Central America—especially El Salvador's José Napoleon Duarte, Costa Rica's Oscar Arias, and Honduras's José Azcona—persisted in negotiations that extracted ever more specific commitments from the Sandinistas for free and fair elections.

Mikhail Gorbachev deserves credit for recommending to the Sandinistas the paths of moderation and negotiation, political pluralism, and a mixed economy. It is truly no accident that, throughout the campaign and in his concession speech, Daniel Ortega used language identical with that of Soviet recommendations. Ortega, who identified heavily with the Socialist International camp, could not have been indifferent to the Soviet leader's new revolution of democracy.

Actually, Ortega himself deserves some credit for following the lead of Gorbachev rather than Fidel Castro and credit as well for conducting a free election with an honest count. And he deserves a lot of credit for a graceful concession in defeat.

Last but not least, some credit is due the North and South Americans who supported democracy in Central America, helping where they could with diplomacy, money, guns, refuge, and encouragement. Ronald Reagan was steadfast in this effort, as were George Bush, William Casey, and dozens of others. Those who have helped in the past will need to help again.

The task of consolidating free institutions and rebuilding and restoring economies in Central America is enormous. But the prospects are magnificent.

Democracy At Last

April 30, 1990

Violeta Chamorro's government faces daunting challenges: an economy wrecked by ten years of Sandinista mismanagement, top-heavy armed forces still commanded by Sandinista officers, a weak and fractious political base, the problem of reintegrating resistance force (and thousands of returning refugees) into Nicaragua's domestic life, and a U.S. Congress disinclined to offer substantial economic assistance. Although Daniel Ortega stood aside in accordance with the people's vote, Sandinista militants continue to make trouble for the government, organizing labor strikes and resisting removal from their civil service redoubts.

Nevertheless, Doña Violeta boasts two key assets: democratic legitimacy, enjoyed by no previous Nicaraguan government, and freedom from the Soviet sphere of influence. The Sandinistas' fall does not ensure a happy future for Nicaragua but makes it conceivable. That's progress.

Violeta Chamorro called it a "democratic fiesta," the long, hot ceremony during which Daniel Ortega relinquished the presidency.

It was an altogether extraordinary inauguration or *toma de posesion* (taking possession) as the tickets called it. Held at the National Stadium in the presence of the world press and representatives from a dozen foreign governments, it featured the active participation of Sandinista and UNO activists.

The inauguration marked the acceptance by Sandinistas of democratic elections as the basis of government legitimacy. This alone made it a remarkable occasion. Until recently, Sandinistas have claimed that their leadership of the revolution gave them all the right they needed to permanent power.

It was perhaps to recall this other claim that most of the Sandinista *comandantes* showed up in military uniform for the inauguration. But Daniel Ortega, who has learned many lessons of image politics, arrived carrying a baby and wearing a dark red open-collared shirt with a Sandinista kerchief around his neck. His trim, jeans-clad wife and numerous children were at his side. He presented the very model of young civilian leadership.

Carefully, Chamorro embraced both Ortegas and each of their children, while reminding watchers that she has known "Daniel" most of his life. Like Nicaragua's Cardinal Miguel Obando y Bravo, she is well acquainted with all the *comandantes,* because Nicaragua is a small country and because they were all allies in the fight to bring down Anastasio Somoza. Neither the cardinal nor Chamorro is a hater. Both are eager to get on with the business of national reconciliation.

But the many embraces could not hide the deep political cleavages that divide Nicaraguans.

The long speeches of Ortega and Chamorro were a study in clashing political symbols, philosophies, and styles.

Ortega's speech was structured around the long rhetorical questions, self-evident answers, and escalating charges made famous by Fidel Castro. The revolution was still present in his speech, but so was a new claim: that the Sandinistas brought democracy to Nicaragua. As Ortega sees it, the Sandinista revolution succeeded because it ended *Somocismo*. It made the Sandinistas the principal democratic force in Nicaragua. Sandinista opponents are mainly *Somocistas*. The contras are North American mercenaries and dupes. The economy failed because of the U.S. boycott.

In Ortega's speech there were no apologies, no regrets. As he sees it, in voting for UNO Nicaraguans did not reject "the revolution." They simply voted for "peace"—for contra demobilization and an end to the American embargo.

For Violeta Chamorro, Nicaraguan democracy began with the elections of February 25 and proceeds under a guardian angel—*Santa Libertad* (St. Liberty). The decade of Sandinista rule was part of the 100 years of dictatorship through which Nicaraguans longed for democracy. Now, Chamorro emphasized, Nicaraguans are determined that "never again" will the people permit tyrants to impose themselves upon the nation. Now policies can be adopted that will reverse the damage of "the revolution." Now there can be an end to regulations that stifle the economy and policies that foment war and exile.

She promised unconditional amnesty, deregulation, and demilitarization and emphasized national reconciliation. But it was clear even during the inauguration that reconciliation would not be easy. The opponents of the Sandinistas are already divided among themselves.

Chamorro's decision to retain in her cabinet Sandinista Defense Chief Humberto Ortega split the shaky coalition of fourteen parties in whose name (UNO) Chamorro campaigned. It precipitated three resignations from her planned cabinet and widespread charges that she is already bypassing the parties in favor of a highly personal, familial style of decision making involving close family members as principal counselors.

Listening to Nicaraguans discuss the Chamorro presidency, one realizes how quickly a traditional schismatic, familial-style of politics has reasserted itself.

For a decade Nicaragua was a battlefield in a global struggle—with Karl Marx postage stamps, swarms of *internacionalistas*, totalitarian aspirations, and maximum participation in the "world Socialist revolution."

Now it is only a small, poor Central American country whose meager public resources have been depleted by profligate policies and hurried plundering during the Sandinistas' last weeks in power, as they appropriated for themselves and their party the vehicles, typewriters, and light fixtures of the government offices.

Violeta Chamorro's minister for economic affairs said to me that Chamorro's crutches, which she uses while a broken leg mends, are a good symbol of Nicaragua's condition—damaged, in need of a helping hand, but courageous and capable of recovery.

El Salvador . . .

Some observers in the early 1980s could not understand why the Reagan administration gave so much attention to El Salvador. In their view, neither the weak democratic credentials of its leaders nor the small U.S. security stake there justified millions of dollars annually in U.S. economic and military aid.

I disagreed. El Salvador was the vanguard of the democratic resurgence that swept Latin America. It was also a test case for the violent Left, which was determined to seize power by force and create a Communist Central America.

A victory by the Communist and Cuban-backed FMLN guerrillas would have denied self-government to Salvadorans, tarnished the appeal of democratic institutions in neighboring countries, and generated momentum for further violence in the region. The Reagan administration believed that consolidation of democracy under the leadership of José Napoleon Duarte would strengthen democratic legitimacy and further undercut the resort to force.

As of 1990 democracy is winning over violence in El Salvador. Two democratic transfers of power have taken place, and the guerrillas are increasingly demoralized and isolated. They continue to exacerbate the country's grave economic problems, but the future looks increasingly bright.

The Suffering of a Father/President

October 6, 1985

*There are laws of war, and they do not permit kidnapping the daughter
of a president. That is terrorism.*

*Napoleon Duarte was a good man who more than any single person
brought democracy to his country. He had suffered jail, exile, torture.
He told me nothing had been so hard for him to bear as the kidnapping
of his daughter—whose release was eventually bargained for along with
that of other prisoners and hostages.*

The kidnapping of Salvadoran President José Napoleon Duarte's
daughter, Ines, three weeks ago has created shock and consternation
in that nation and embarrassed various guerrilla sympathizers. It has
also prompted new political problems, as well as personal suffering,
for President Duarte, who must do his best to save his daughter
without violating the public trust.

Salvadoran officials close to the case believe Ines Duarte Duran
was abducted by a special commando unit of the country's principal
guerrilla group, the FMLN (Farabundo Marti National Liberation).
They hold that belief even though credit for the kidnapping has been
claimed not by the FMLN but by the Pedro Pablo Castillo Front—of
whom no one had previously heard.

Those officials are also convinced that Ines, who was seized
while riding in a microbus to attend a class in downtown San
Salvador, is still alive. A heavily armed band intercepted the bus,
killed two security guards, and dragged the thirty-five-year-old
mother of three into another vehicle.

There have been strong indications of direct FMLN involvement
from the outset.

First, there was the manner of the kidnapping. Four vehicles
used in the attack had been stolen two hours earlier by persons who
identified themselves as members of the FMLN. The kidnappers'
ability to vanish without a trace in a matter of minutes from downtown San Salvador suggested to experts a sophisticated network of
hideouts and communication.

The FMLN link was further confirmed by the fact that radio
communications from the kidnappers originate in a zone of El Salvador controlled by the rebels.

Finally, negotiations with the kidnappers also point directly to
the FMLN. First came sweeping demands with which President

Duarte could not conceivably comply: cease all military operations against the guerrillas and impose a strict blackout on news and commentary about the case. Next came the more specific demand that the government release some thirty-four persons who, the kidnappers claim, are currently held in El Salvador's prisons.

Some of the names on the list are not known to the government, but most have clear FMLN connections and are in prison because they were tried and found guilty of violence against persons and property.

Perhaps the strongest evidence of all was provided by the leader of a neighboring state who had personal confirmation of the FMLN role.

The kidnapping has posed both personal and political problems for President Duarte.

The FMLN is also now holding captive thirteen mayors whom they have kidnapped in recent months. Obviously, President Duarte must not win Ines's release with concessions he would not make to free the mayors. So, the government is working hard to secure the release of all.

President Duarte, a good man, deeply devoted to his family, has spoken frankly of his own feelings:

> If the promoters of this horrible action . . . thought to torment a father who is also president of the republic, they have indeed succeeded. I have never experienced greater sorrow than now, not even during the tortures and mistreatment to which I was subjected in 1972 for fighting with my people; not even during the sorrowful moments when I lost my parents, whom I loved so much.

The kidnapping produced more sympathy for El Salvador's president and more international condemnation than was expected. So it has created new problems for the guerrillas as well.

The FMLN has not been content to attack villages, bomb electrical power stations, and mount military actions. It is a new-style guerrilla group that has adopted all the trappings of a "national liberation movement." Like the PLO, SWAPO, and the Polisario, the FMLN has civilian leaders who travel about the world, visit the United Nations, make presentations before the Socialist International, confer with heads of sympathetic governments, and generally seek to create an aura of legitimacy around their violent efforts to seize power.

Guillermo Ungo and Rubén Zamora have helped the El Salvadoran guerrillas cultivate the impression that the FMLN is broader based, more civilized, less brutal than it is. The personal standing of

Ungo and Zamora and their activities on behalf of the FMLN have created some real confusion among Europe's democratic Left about who stands for democracy in El Salvador. Now evidence linking the kidnapping to the FMLN has confronted Ungo and Zamora with a stark choice: either condemn such tactics or stand revealed as supporting them.

When a vice president of the Socialist International, José Francisco Pena Gomez, appealed to Ungo to guarantee Ines Duarte's safety, Ungo denied knowledge of the kidnapping without condemning it. But this position becomes less tenable by the day.

The FMLN was having major problems even before the kidnapping. Its image suffered a major blow when France and Mexico decided to establish diplomatic relations with El Salvador's democratic government. FMLN military strength has also suffered one setback after another until today it is no longer capable of mounting large-scale military operations.

Its diminished forces still have the capacity to sabotage El Salvador's economy, kidnap civilians, and terrorize isolated hamlets. Their new tactics, specifically adapted to their reduced circumstances, rely heavily on terrorist acts and the "propaganda of the deed." But, as with other forms of propaganda, the medium is the message.

It is a grim message that reveals El Salvador's guerrillas for what they are: a band of violent men bent on denying the people of that country the right to govern themselves.

Duarte's Departure
June 6, 1988

Obviously, I both liked and admired Napoleon Duarte—his personal and political courage, his intelligence, and his indefatigable fight for democracy in El Salvador. Nonetheless, his party succumbed to factionalisms that remain the most familiar weakness of political groups.

Duarte's party lost the March 1989 elections, but President Alfredo Cristiani has pleasantly surprised those who had feared that Arena meant hard-right lawlessness. Cristiani has demonstrated commitment to law enforcement and even the government's critics are speaking positively about him. But moral support is not enough. El Salvador still needs U.S. economic and military aid for the elected government to stave off the violent traditionalists and revolutionaries.

El Salvador has been the premier target of Fidel Castro and the FSLN, who targeted El Salvador's elected government, hoping to show that socialism and not democracy was the more resilient force. The Communist FMLN might still win, but today—as one of its patrons cedes power and the other looks increasingly shaky—FMLN victory looks less and less likely.

"You all know I am a man of crisis, a man of battle and struggle, and have fought against dictatorship to establish democracy," President José Napoleon Duarte said as he left El Salvador on Tuesday for medical treatment in the United States, "Now God has given me this additional test, and I will fight and, if God wills, go ahead.

"What I have," Duarte said with characteristic candor, "is a bleeding ulcer of seven centimeters in my stomach that is malignant."

Duarte, in visible pain, made careful plans for his departure. He met with leaders of the church, the military, the government, and his party. He caused his vice president to be named acting president and made a strong appeal for unity to the two men—Julio Adolfo Rey Prendes and Fidel Chavez Mena—locked in a bitter struggle to succeed him. No amount of preparation fills the vacuum left by his departure.

Duarte's lifelong struggle against dictatorship and his personal courage and commitment to democracy are widely known and respected outside El Salvador. El Salvador has no other leader who commands comparable respect in the United States, Latin America, and the world.

His illness deprives that poor country of its major international asset at a particularly difficult time. "It could not have come at a worse time," said one of Duarte's close associates. "We have a political crisis, polarization, late rain and failing crops. It seems like God is angry at us."

It would appear that God has been angry at El Salvador and at the people of Central America for some time. The guerrilla FMLN's relentless attack on El Salvador's economy cost more than a billion dollars last year. And the FMLN leaders understand the damage they wreak.

To those leaders, the Central American Peace Accords constituted an opportunity to step up their activities. "We should strengthen and enlarge the feeling of mass discouragement and despair through intense propaganda and agitation through every medium," a captured FMLN document directed last spring. Since then, FMLN attacks have multiplied. Duarte has seen his generous offers of amnesty and negotiations rejected by the FMLN, one by one.

Duarte's own Christian Democratic party is rent by rivalries so deep that Duarte lamented recently: "Today our existence is threatened from within the party itself." Already, he said, internal divisions have caused the party to lose its legislative majority to the opposition Arena party, which has serious problems of its own.

Arena is a legitimate political party that espouses market approaches, private ownership, personal initiative, and deregulation—the sorts of things Margaret Thatcher and Ronald Reagan have built their careers on. But Arena's international image suffers from the reputation of its last presidential candidate, Roberto d'Aubuisson, whom rumor has long linked to the infamous death squads.

Arena's new leader, Alfredo Cristiani, is a prominent civic and business leader of excellent reputation. Unfortunately for El Salvador, Cristiani is unknown outside his country, and longtime opponents of U.S. aid to El Salvador are poised to attack that assistance.

El Salvador's economic prospects depend on an end to its civil war, and that, in turn, depends on cutting off the flow of arms from Nicaragua. But U.S. intelligence officials know arms are flowing despite Sandinista commitments to the contrary in the Esquipulas accords.

FMLN leaders believe their most important problems will disappear with the end of the Reagan administration, the contras, and Napoleon Duarte. They could be right.

"We will win in Nicaragua and El Salvador will follow," Sandinista brigades chant, emphasizing the link between the civil war in Nicaragua and El Salvador, between Marxism in Nicaragua and El Salvador—and, by implication, between democracy in Nicaragua and El Salvador.

Almost everyone who follows the problem understands these relations—except House Democrats.

Last week, House Democrats acted again to prevent the CIA from aiding Nicaragua's resistance forces. They did so at a time when preparations were under way for a major offensive against the contras and when Sandinista aid to the FMLN had been stepped up.

Presumably, there are a few—but only a few—Democrats in the House who would actually welcome the consolidation of power by the Communist government of Nicaragua. It is easy enough to understand why *they* are mobilized to prevent assistance to the contras. But why many other Democrats have agreed to make this issue a litmus test of party loyalty surpasses understanding.

Is it possible that they do not understand the contagion of

violence in culturally and linguistically homogeneous Central America? Or that they do not finally understand the importance of Central America's proximity to U.S. national security?

It is a puzzlement that some Democrats some day will need to explain to the rest of us, because the consequences for Central America and for the United States will be large and expensive.

The Marxists' Game in El Salvador
February 6, 1989

The Salvadoran rebels have learned many lessons from their Cuban and Soviet mentors—among them, the traditional Communist two-track strategy of talking and fighting. For them negotiation is more an opportunity to disseminate propaganda than a means to resolve conflict. By continuing to employ force—terrorism, sabotage, and warfare—as it talks with the government about peace, the FMLN has shown that it is not serious about peace.

A new, most destructive offensive launched at the end of 1989 demonstrated that the guerrillas were still determined to win.

From time to time, it has seemed as though democracy and peace have come to El Salvador. But El Salvador's Marxist guerrillas have never lost faith in their ultimate victory.

"We have time," FMLN commander Ferman Cienfuegos has said of their fifteen-year-long struggle to win power over Central America's smallest, most overcrowded, deeply divided country. "All the time it takes."

Now, six weeks before El Salvador's presidential election, the FMLN has launched a new "strategic offensive." The FMLN representative to Cuba, Farid Handal, explained that their struggle had entered a new phase. Now the guerrillas would simultaneously accelerate military activities *and* enter the electoral arena "but without making any electoral commitments." Each tactic reinforced the other: the strategic offensive targeted mayors and the accompanying "peace proposal" promised that—for a price—the murder of mayors could be called off.

By the time the so-called peace proposal was offered (January 24), several dozen mayors had already been killed, and more were

resigning daily in the face of deadly serious threats—three in Usulu-
tan Department on January 18 after being given forty-eight hours to
leave their posts or die, several more in Ahuachupan Department,
and another in Santa Ana, where the lives of the mayor's family were
threatened along with his own.

"The resignation of mayors in several of our country's munici-
palities is nothing more than an expression that the FMLN is an
alternate power in El Salvador," guerrilla spokesman Javier Castillo
bragged.

But the FMLN is not interested just in murder. Out of respect for
the "current trend in the international field" where "most wars are
being solved by negotiations," El Salvador's guerrillas announced
that they would not kill mayors who refused all cooperation from the
government. The FMLN would "respect those who abandoned resistance."

As further proof of their flexibility, the five commanders of the
FMLN also offered in their January 24 proposal to participate in
national elections *providing* the presidential election be postponed for
six months, from March 19 to September 15, and held under a new
electoral law adopted by *consensus* by a new electoral commission in
which the FMLN would be represented.

During this six-month period El Salvador's army would be required to cease all attacks on guerrilla forces in return for which the
FMLN would observe a five-day cease-fire (from two days before the
election until two days after).

No prescience was required to see that this was an offer that no
government could accept.

"The president's term is set by the constitution," El Salvador's
President Napoleon Duarte commented on January 26. "It is not
possible to extend the presidential term of office by a single day. I am
not going to stay one day more in the presidency, so this document
that proposes I remain in the presidency is neither valid nor acceptable at all."

Opposition leader Alfredo Cristiani struck a similar note: "The
people do not want a mere two days of truce before and after the
elections. If the FMLN is seeking peace it should declare its decision
and accept a permanent and verifiable cease-fire."

Duarte's chosen successor, Christian Democratic candidate Fidel
Chavez Mena, agreed. Like Duarte, he welcomed the fact that for the
first time ever the FMLN had spoken of elections, but he said the
proposal raised insurmountable legal problems: "If they agree in
supporting the elections, why not do it now, without waiting any
longer?"

Why indeed? Because the FMLN—like the PLO—understands how to pursue power by violence and propaganda: seeking now to terrorize, now to legitimize its own intentions, now to delegitimize existing processes and opponents.

Speaking always of peace while making war confuses the easily confused and provides a fig leaf for those who would like to see the Marxists win. Meanwhile, the violence is spilling across the borders of the region.

The same day Duarte rejected the FMLN proposal, Honduran Gen. Gustavo Alvarez Martinez and his driver were shot dead in Tegucigalpa. Within fifteen minutes, the Cinchonero Peoples Movement had claimed credit for his murder. "The execution of Gustavo Alvarez Martinez was assigned to our heroic Lempira command. Long live our martyrs, their ideas and their practices! Let us all organize better to wage the people's revolutionary war! Those who know how to die always win."

Meanwhile in Managua, Nicaraguan President Daniel Ortega offered a visitor from the German Democratic Republic a tour of the Karl Marx Hospital and transmitted revolutionary congratulations to comrade Heng Samrin, Vietnam's puppet ruler of Cambodia.

And the slow slide to a Marxist Central America continues.

A Trap in El Salvador
February 28, 1989

The FMLN believed it could trick a new American administration into undermining El Salvador's constitutional processes and could use the Christian Democrats' desire to win the elections to undermine the election process.
Napoleon Duarte refused to be tempted.

It would appear that the Bush administration, including Secretary of State James Baker, has been lured into a trap regarding El Salvador— a trap that has been baited as usual with what some mistake as a proposal to bring peace to the deeply troubled region.

El Salvador's FMLN guerrillas have presented two new "peace" proposals in the past two weeks. The first was an offer to participate in elections—for a price. The second, which followed a week later, is a broader proposal that offers "definitively" to end El Salvador's war.

El Salvador's government and all its major political parties promptly rejected the FMLN's initial offer to participate in the presidential election, and for good reason. It called for postponing the election for six months (in clear violation of El Salvador's constitution), required that government forces cease actions against guerrillas, and provided for an FMLN veto on electoral arrangements. In return, the FMLN offered a five-day cease-fire and promised to stop assassinating mayors if mayors ceased cooperating with the government.

It was an offer no government could accept. But the Bush administration has let it be known that it acted—through the person of Vice President Dan Quayle—to encourage reconsideration, thus justifying the FMLN expectation that the "new team" might prove more flexible than Ronald Reagan, George Shultz, and Elliott Abrams.

"We wanted to wait until the end of the Reagan administration" to present the new plan, one guerrilla commander commented. Like Yasser Arafat and Daniel Ortega, FMLN leaders expect that the new administration will be more "open" and less informed about what has gone before and will therefore perhaps be more accommodating.

Although some in the media describe the FMLN's second proposal as a "new" and "important" departure from its longstanding position, in fact all that is new is the packaging. El Salvador's Communist party leader, Shafik Jorge Handal, was more accurate when he said: "This is not a new proposal," it is a "further development" of the FMLN's previous offer.

Following the traditional FMLN position, the new proposal still calls for "dissolution of the current security force": the national police, the national guard, and the treasury police, and for reducing El Salvador's army from 55,000 to 12,000.

There is, however, some new language. In the past, the FMLN explicitly insisted on integration of the guerrilla forces into El Salvador's army. Now it is willing "to recognize the existence of a single army" (which means a single, much smaller army into which FMLN forces would be integrated).

Where previously it demanded a share of power in a reconstituted interim government, now it demands the establishment of three joint commissions: one on cessation of hostilities and withdrawal of military forces, one on revision of the electoral code, and a third to organize international oversight of implementation. In these commissions, power would be shared, and decisions would be made by consensus.

El Salvador's political parties responded to this latest offer by agreeing to meet with FMLN leaders on "neutral" ground in Mexico last week. After the meeting, the political parties concluded that the government should respond to the repackaged FMLN demands.

There is no question how Salvadoran President Napoleon Duarte will respond. His whole life has been a struggle to give his country constitutional government. He will not in his final days dismantle the legacy he has worked so painstakingly to construct.

He understands—if the Bush administration does not—that it is not possible to "suspend" El Salvador's Constitution and still preserve democratic government. He understands that for a decade the prime target of the FMLN has been to dismantle and take control of El Salvador's armed forces and that for a decade those sympathetic with the guerrillas have sought to paralyze El Salvador's army under the guise of its "permanent reorganization."

And he knows that for a decade the FMLN has sought by all means and ruses to prevent the development and implementation of a democratic constitution, not only by denying the legitimacy of elections and refusing to participate, but by attacking polling places and voters as well.

Duarte understands that El Salvador's armed forces, which have so painstakingly learned restraint of power, would not be restrained if the Constitution were violated. Said Defense Minister Gen. Eugenio Vides Casanova: "Falling into the trap would mean anyone could have the opportunity for disrupting the democratic process simply for the sake of staying in the presidency longer."

Duarte will know how to deal with the FMLN proposal. Meanwhile, someone at a responsible level in the Bush administration with an interest in preserving democracy and serving U.S. foreign policy interests should do some cramming on the recent history of Central America.

And it wouldn't hurt American journalists covering the region to consult original documents rather than relying on government and guerrilla public relations handouts.

El Salvador: The Election Was Fair

March 27, 1989

In March 1989 Salvadorans elected the conservative Arena candidate, Alfredo Cristiani, as their president in spite of the manifest preferences of the U.S. State Department.

The many faces of U.S. interventionism in El Salvador—by which I mean here favoritism for particular political groups and policies— perpetuate the stereotype of the overbearing yanqui *imposing his will on small dependent nations.*

We should do better and limit our assistance to support for open democratic processes and rule of law.

When the U.S. government urged democracy on El Salvador, virtually no one in Washington thought El Salvadorans would choose the candidate of the Arena party as president. But that is what happened last week when Alfredo Cristiani scored a clear victory over Christian Democratic candidate Fidel Chavez Mena.

The election's outcome will not only test Arena's commitment to the rule of law, but also the commitment of the State Department and congressional liberals to democracy.

It was widely understood in El Salvador that the U.S. government wanted the Christian Democrats to win. Chavez Mena is well known and respected by many Americans, including me. And American distrust of the Arena party and disapproval of its former candidate, Roberto D'Aubuisson, have been openly expressed for years. Many people knew the U.S. government had funneled covert funds into El Salvador to help Napoleon Duarte defeat D'Aubuisson in the previous presidential election, and many knew that the State Department had urged President Duarte to postpone this year's election once public opinion polls showed Cristiani holding a large lead.

To make certain no one missed the point, U.S. officials hinted darkly at the consequences of an Arena victory. But El Salvadorans thought it was time for a change. They gave Cristiani more than 50 percent of the vote in a four-man field.

Now the United States confronts a democratically elected president who is not of its choosing. There was grumbling galore in Washington as disgruntled people sought to discredit an election that has been described by international observers as "free, fair and honest."

Those who always opposed U.S. aid to El Salvador believe

Cristiani's election is a cause for ending it. And those who were always skeptical about U.S. aid are now more so. This latter category includes a good many Democrats whose votes have been needed to send the country approximately $1.5 million a day in assistance.

Should the United States continue aid to El Salvador even though America's preferred candidate went down in defeat?

It depends, of course, on how Cristiani governs and on why we were giving aid in the first place.

Three factors loom large in the discussion.

First, the D'Aubuisson connection. D'Aubuisson, a founder of Arena and its first presidential candidate, is believed by the U.S. government (as well as by El Salvador's Christian Democrats) to have close ties to the infamous "death squads" and to have been personally involved in the 1980 murder of Archbishop Oscar Romero. The evidence Washington has collected on these matters is not adequate to convict D'Aubuisson in a court, but it was persuasive enough to convince the Reagan administration that D'Aubuisson would not be an acceptable president.

D'Aubuisson and Arena got the message. He stood aside, clearing the way for U.S.-educated businessman Cristiani. The big question is, Who is really in charge, Cristiani or D'Aubuisson?

Second is the land reform issue. Following the 1979 overthrow of El Salvador's military ruler, the United States strongly supported development of a plan for taking land from large landholders and redistributing it to landless peasants.

From time to time, the American government has made full implementation of a three-phase reform plan a precondition for further U.S. aid—in spite of the fact that land reform has not produced the desired results.

Cristiani has said he will respect the land reform that has taken place. No one expects that he will implement the remainder of the reform program.

Third is communism in Central America. The United States became involved in El Salvador because the Reagan administration and a majority of Congress judged the establishment of a second Communist government in Central America not to be in the U.S. interest and saw a Marxist guerrilla victory as a distinct possibility once the Sandinistas in Nicaragua stepped up shipment of weapons to the FMLN guerrillas.

When the United States encourages others to adopt democratic institutions, it incurs certain obligations—the most important of which is to respect the right of other people to make their own decisions through democratic processes. The U.S. government has no right to intervene in the elections of another country.

Americans also do not have the right to make decisions on other people's domestic policies. It is unseemly for the United States to try to impose on the people of El Salvador a land-redistribution program that could not conceivably be adopted in the United States.

It is, of course, the right of Americans to decide whether they will aid another country. This decision should also take into account both U.S. interests and U.S. values.

The United States has a continuing interest in having near its borders independent, democratic governments that will not permit their countries to be used by hostile powers. This gives the United States an irreducible stake in Central America.

The U.S. government should, therefore, congratulate the new president of El Salvador for a clear-cut electoral victory and should wish him well in tackling his nation's pressing military and economic problems. We should also carefully and clearly explain that the reason Americans oppose Communist governments is that they are too often contemptuous of law and human rights, and the reason we help other governments is to nurture respect for law and human rights.

Finally, the new American government should communicate to the new government of El Salvador that it looks forward to working together on these problems.

Cuba . . .

Our Cuban Misadventures: Half Measures, Half Deals

April 21, 1986

The lesson of our early dealings with Fidel Castro was that failure has consequences. A Communist Cuba became the base for training guerrillas and shipping arms to the countries of the Caribbean and Central America.

The 1962 Cuban missile crisis showed how agreements between democracies and Communist dictatorships can work against our side. We pledged not to invade Cuba, and Castro promised to stop subverting other governments. We kept our promise; Castro did not. Many in the

State Department argued that the United States was nonetheless bound by its commitment—as though it were a unilateral unconditional promise, rather than half a bargain.

This unilateralist logic leaves the United States helpless when confronted with noncompliance. Parallel arguments have been used to insist that the United States was bound by the terms of SALT I, ABM, and other arrangements—in spite of Soviet violations. The case for unilateral compliance is nearly identical with the case for unilateral disarmament.

It has been twenty-five years now since—on April 17, 1961—some 1,400 Cubans trained by the CIA at bases in Central America landed at the Bay of Pigs, where they fought bravely until, their ammunition and fuel exhausted, they were killed or captured by Fidel Castro's troops. In Miami the anniversary was commemorated by opening a museum dedicated to the event.

During the intervening twenty-five years, criticism of the U.S. government for not doing enough at the Bay of Pigs gave way to criticism for having tried to do anything at all. The Bay of Pigs joined the Vietnam War in the liberal's showcase of horrors concerning the disastrous consequences of U.S. attempts to oppose the consolidation of new Communist governments. I have no desire to rake over old questions about who was responsible for the failure at the Bay of Pigs, but it is worth pausing to wonder what would have happened had the rebel brigade been able to secure positions and mount an insurgency. What difference would it have made?

"Why," said a Nicaraguan refugee to whom I put the question, "I would be in Managua, not in Washington."

It is a question worth pondering in these days when support for Nicaragua's contras competes with Muammar Qaddafi for headlines and attention in the American media. Obviously the establishment of a Soviet client state ninety miles from Florida has had its consequences. And just as obviously there are lessons to be learned from the experience of the Bay of Pigs and its sequel, the Cuban missile crisis.

There are lessons in the landing itself: about the vulnerability of troops that are fired on from the air, whether from old planes such as Castro's or whether from Hind helicopters such as those used today in Nicaragua, Afghanistan, and Angola. Men on the ground are destroyed because they possess no defense against the attacking aircraft.

There is a broader lesson to be learned about the necessity of

249

adequate force where force is to be used.

The Kennedy team, never fully comfortable with the plan inherited from the Eisenhower administration, expressed its misgivings by adding on constraints. The cumulative effects of these constraints is believed by many to have been crippling. "We can be criticized," said CIA official Richard Bissell, "for allowing this chipping away to go on without insisting on the whole plan or cancellation."

One clear lesson of the Bay of Pigs (and the Vietnam War and the unsuccessful attempt to rescue American hostages held in Iran) is that diffuse responsibility, remote decision making, and inadequate force are deadly to successful military operations.

Two air strikes had been planned to wipe out Castro's small, old air force in advance of the rebels' landing and to prevent Castro's use of planes against the men on the beach. John Kennedy canceled the second strike after the first strike produced a flurry of protest at the United Nations. But the United Nations and the world being what they were then (and are now), the flap should have been expected and discounted. No military action should ever be undertaken unless it is clear that its tangible benefits outweight the intangible discomforts of international disapproval.

The fact that the Bay of Pigs operation did not succeed does not mean it could not have succeeded. And while we do not know what would have happened had the brigade established a beachhead, we know what happened because it did not. Consolidation of power by the Castro government was not inevitable, and it has been extremely costly—in human values and human lives, in military budgets and in continuing risks to our national security.

The first consequence of the failure was a dangerous, direct confrontation between the United States and the Soviet Union known as the Cuban missile crisis. That crisis—and the deal that ended it— was a costly operation for the United States, one which also offers lessons.

The crisis ended, we now know, with two deals: one below the table and one above it. The deal below the table committed the United States to remove U.S. missiles from Turkey when Khrushchev had removed Soviet missile installations from Cuba. It was contingent on the Soviet Union "remaining silent on the deal."

Of this covert arrangement, McGeorge Bundy said last summer, "We avoided the tremendous brouhaha of selling out our European friends" by removing the supposedly Turkish-owned Jupiter missiles, "but we did it keeping it secret. Not altogether a happy thing to do. It has costs, playing secret diplomacy." The secret deal was not confirmed until last year, when previously classified documents were released.

The U.S.–Soviet deal publicly affirmed by Kennedy and his secretary of state, Dean Rusk, was quite different. According to it, the Soviets agreed to remove offensive weapons systems and not to install offensive weapons in Cuba. In exchange the United States agreed to lift the blockade and not to invade Cuba.

Kennedy asserted, "As for our part, if all offensive weapons systems are removed from Cuba and kept out of the hemisphere in the future, under adequate verification and safeguards, and if Cuba is not used for the export of aggressive communist purposes, there will be peace in the Caribbean. And as I said in September, we shall neither initiate nor permit aggression in this hemisphere."

In effect, Kennedy believed the United States had secured a commitment that Cuba would not be used as a forward base for Soviet military power or for Marxist revolution and that in exchange the United States became the guarantor of Cuba's Communist government. Obviously, we kept our part of the bargain. The United States has not invaded Cuba, nor encouraged, nor assisted others in doing so. Just as obviously, the Soviets and Cubans have not kept their bargain.

So, the Bay of Pigs did not produce the desired outcome. Neither did the Kennedy-Khrushchev negotiation ending the Cuban missile crisis. This experience teaches that neither force nor negotiation can be relied on to achieve desired goals in foreign policy. It all depends on how they are used.

While "Pawns" Rot in Cuban Jails
August 11, 1986

The human rights record of Fidel Castro's Cuba is present in the experiences of the plantados, *the prisoners who for decades were submitted to inhuman pressures. Their stories have been told again and again—unbearable stories of torture and degradation.*

Armando Valladares speaks for legions in his moving account of more than two decades in Fidel's jails.

Armando Valladares's account of his twenty-two years in Cuba's jails is the most compelling prison memoir since Alexander Solzhenitsyn's

Gulag Archipelago. Like Solzhenitsyn, Valladares not only describes appalling, wrenching personal experiences, but depicts a world of organized corruption and brutality. He reminds us that one man of clarity and courage can defeat an army of tormentors.

Against all Hope is Valladares's witness to an experience incredible to him and incredible to us. He neither expected nor feared problems with Cuba's political police—right down to the night in 1962 when he awoke with the muzzle of a machine gun pressed against his temple.

"My life until the day of my detention," he writes, "had passed in a perfectly conventional way, like the life of any young man my age, unremarkable for any adventures or unusual circumstances, lacking anything worth other people's attention."

Valladares was not a political activist. He worked as a clerk in a postal savings bank connected to the Ministry of Communications and attended a university. He was not a Communist, however, and he criticized Marxism and declined to have placed on his desk a plaque asserting, "If Fidel is a Communist, then put me on the list. He's got the right idea."

Valladares tells us, "It never occurred to me that because I expressed my opinions, because I spoke out against Marxism, they would drag me off to jail." The Cuban government had not even declared itself Marxist at that time.

Valladares assured his mother and sister he would soon be back home. But it was twenty-two years before he was finally released and then only after a worldwide campaign by the Cuban-American National Foundation, Amnesty International, the international writers' organization PEN, and a personal appeal from French President François Mitterrand to Fidel Castro.

During those twenty-two years, Valladares was starved, beaten, crippled, burned, and kept in "drawers" without light and rooms without night where fluorescent bulbs were never turned off. He was bitten by rats, covered with roaches, drenched in excrement, starved of protein and vitamin C. He was kept sometimes wet and cold, sometimes hot and dehydrated. He was beaten again and again and again. He watched friends suffer and bleed and die.

"How does it feel to be a free man?" I heard a Washington reporter ask Valladares at the first press conference after his release in 1984. "I was always a free man," he replied. "I never lost my freedom in Cuba's jails." Valladares's jailers damaged him, but in twenty-two years they never conquered him.

The violent politics of our era has spawned a new category of literature—the prison memoir—and a new hero, one who survives with integrity a total assault on his body, mind, and psyche. Occasionally, one of these heroes is also a great writer and his memoir is a great book. Valladares is such a man.

Valladares has not forgotten, any more than Huber Matos has forgotten or Andres Vargas Gomes has forgotten. During a brief visit to Washington, D.C., in July, he insisted that we remember his fellow prisoners still suffering in the jails he described. Especially, he insisted that the U.S. government act to gain the freedom and emigration to America of some seventy-five long-term political prisoners now in Cuba's jails.

He reminded everyone he saw that last October Castro promised visiting U.S. bishops he would release the seventy-five prisoners if the United States would admit them. But nine months later the United States has still not acted.

The reasons for this failure are bureaucratic. The State Department and the Immigration and Naturalization Service are trying to work out a new immigration agreement with Cuba under which the Cuban government accepts the 2,500 criminals and criminally insane persons whom Castro palmed off on us several years ago in Mariel, in return for U.S. acceptance of up to 20,000 Cubans a year, plus 3,000 political prisoners and their families. When Castro terminated the agreement to protest the inauguration of Radio Marti earlier this year, he announced he would not accept the 2,500 undesirables. The U.S. government announced that the United States would accept no more political prisoners. Presumably, we were "retaliating."

But as Valladares said during his visit, "This so-called punishment against Castro is not punishment at all. Castro is happy to see that the United States would not accept his political prisoners because this is a further way of humiliating them." Now the State Department has indicated that it is really the INS that is blocking the admission of political prisoners, and an INS spokesman admits, "The prisoners have become pawns in this international power play . . . the issue is not the people, it is the Cuban government that refuses to address a fair immigration policy."

The INS is wrong. The issue *is* the people. We can do better. We can change our policy. One hears in Washington that a change is in the works. It's about time.

A Cuban Hero
October 5, 1986

In totalitarian regimes heroes are those who resist compliance with demeaning demands. Reasonable men are those who resist unreasonable demands. Moral men are those who resist immoral demands to become complicitous in their own dehumanization.

This column celebrates such a man—the kind called "difficult"—so difficult as to wish that his humanity be respected.

"What happened, I think," commented America's premier Soviet specialist, Richard Pipes, "is that the Daniloff case intruded, and both sides tried to set it aside."

Nothing is more inconvenient from the perspective of great power politics than the intrusion of particular individuals whose lives become entangled in dramatic ways with carefully laid plans and historic events such as summits.

From the latest intrusion—the arrest of Nicholas Daniloff—Americans relearned important, disturbing facts about Soviet attitudes toward evidence, fairness, and individual rights.

To prevent such facts from upsetting the placid course of its diplomacy, the Soviet Union goes to great lengths to close its society and to control information about how its government deals with its citizens. To prevent such facts from being collected, discussed, and published, the Soviet government condemns such men as Yuri Orlov to forced labor and Siberian exile. And it demands ransom to let them emigrate.

Men like Orlov, Andrei Sakharov, Alexander Solzhenitsyn, and Anatoly Shcharansky are a very special problem for a repressive government. They are also its most impressive product. The Soviet system is now old enough to have produced a large crop of such home-grown heroes who have honed their sense of reality against official "truths," their courage against daily intimidation, and their integrity against temptations of success and safety. These are the men who intrude into the carefully laid diplomatic plans of governments.

On the other side of the world, another such man has intruded into France's congenial relationship with Castro's Cuba. He is Ricardo Bofill Pages, president of the Cuban Commission for Human Rights.

For the second time, Bofill has taken refuge in France's embassy in Havana, where he is once again creating a problem for French

254

diplomats, a *cause célèbre* for Paris's large population of political exiles, and a challenge for France's newly established Bureau of Human Rights.

Bofill must be a special embarrassment to Fidel Castro's government. First, because he was a professor of Marxism, of all things. Second, because he was successful, having become vice rector of the University of Havana at an early age. Third, because neither imprisonment, nor long stretches in solitary confinement, nor incarceration in a mental hospital, nor separation from wife and son, nor hunger and harsh treatment have broken his spirit.

Bofill was first arrested in 1967, charged with ideological deviations, and sentenced to twelve years at hard labor. When he was released in 1972, the Cuban government, ever solicitous for the well-being of its citizens, found him a job sweeping out a factory in Havana. Bofill persisted in protesting human rights violations and was arrested again in 1980, charged again with dissidence and sentenced to five years in the Combinado del Este prison—where he met Armando Valladares, author of the recent widely acclaimed book on Cuban prisons, *Against All Hope.*

After two years Bofill was again released for reasons of health but was stripped of civil rights, denied a job, and kept under heavy surveillance. Still he continued to speak out. He did not, however, desire to return to Castro's prison. Sensing that he was about to be arrested, in April 1983 Bofill took refuge in the French Embassy in Havana.

It was a time of warm relations between France's Socialist government and the Castro regime. Regis Debray, special adviser to President François Mitterrand, was a close personal friend of Castro. Three French ministers had visited Havana, including Foreign Minister Claude Cheysson, and all had been warmly received. Therefore, when Cuban Vice President Carlos Rafael Rodriguez offered personal assurances that Bofill would be allowed to go into exile in France, the French government was delighted to see an end to the inconvenient episode.

But on September 3, 1983, Bofill was again arrested, held in a psychiatric hospital, then sent back to Combinado del Este. By now, however, his health had deteriorated seriously. He was again released and again intruded into Franco-Cuban relations, once more seeking refuge in France's embassy in Havana. Now, however, the Franco-Cuban honeymoon may be over.

France has a new government with a new Gaullist prime minister, Jacques Chirac, and a new Bureau of Human Rights headed by Claude Malhuret, former director of the distinguished French humanitarian organization, Medecins Sans Frontiers. It will be extremely interesting to see how the new French team handles the inconvenient intrusion of the heroic Ricardo Bofill.[1]

Castro's Nightmare
February 27, 1990

For years Cuba has lived off of economic subsidies and services from the Soviet Union and Eastern Europe, while it focused on the more glamorous tasks of world revolution. The consequence was growing dependence on the Socialist economic system. That dependence has become a serious vulnerability, as was demonstrated in January 1990 when the Soviets delayed expected grain shipments for a month.

I believe the Cuban regime is likely to collapse in the relatively near future.

Nothing is what it used to be for Fidel Castro. His faithful allies— Maurice Bishop in Grenada, Manuel Noriega in Panama, and now Daniel Ortega in Nicaragua—have passed from power. The very foundations of the world Socialist bloc have crumbled. As he complained to the Congress of Cuba's Working People: "Whereas previously it was customary to hear the word 'comrade' at meetings of the socialist countries . . . now they say 'ladies and gentlemen.'

"The building of capitalism has become the openly declared goal of some of these countries," he continued. "There is already talk of the market, private ownership, a market economy. Anti-Communist sentiments are gaining strength in almost all these countries." He was speaking, of course, of Eastern Europe and was sharing his concerns with "the masses." Where will all these reforms leave Cuba? he asked:

> We hope that certain trade agreements will be fulfilled in 1990. . . . Nevertheless we are not sure of this. . . . What price will they pay for our sugar? Perhaps they will try to pay for it at the price of the international garbage pit which is the world sugar market.

---

1. Bofill's second stay in the French Embassy ended on January 28, 1987. He now lives in Miami, where he is foreign representative of the Havana-based Cuban Commission for Human Rights.

For thirty years, Fidel Castro had no doubt that the economic and social problems of Cuba and the world were due to imperialism and imperialist exploitation, the principal offender being, of course, the United States. But lately Castro's problems have been coming not just from the United States but from the Soviet Union as well, whose delayed grain shipments have caused severe shortages, long lines, hungry cows, and a good deal of trepidation. "For 20 years now," Castro said, "grain and certain foodstuffs and raw materials for the year have arrived from the Soviet Union ahead of schedule in November and December." However, he said, the shipments needed for January had still not arrived at the end of the month.

Rationing was imposed for bread and other wheat products. The use of feed grain for cattle was completely stopped. It was cut back for poultry farming, threatening to make necessary the slaughter of millions of chickens, with a consequent drop in egg production. The government was forced to spend hard currency to buy wheat from Canada because Cuban reserves had already been used up.

Fidel Castro and his colleagues believe their problems are a consequence of *perestroika*. Soviet deliveries are no longer as reliable as they always have been, he says, because of "disturbances, strikes, distortions and stoppages of production." Cuban fruit has been left to rot or has been consumed at home, because merchant ships from East Germany, Poland, and the Soviet Union that should have taken the fruit to market have been unavailable.

Not surprisingly, Soviet spokesmen have a different view of who is to blame. First, the Soviets insist there was no shortfall in Soviet grain deliveries to Cuba in 1989. Planned shipments for 1989 were 100 percent fulfilled, they say. Second, there has been no cut in Soviet grain shipments to Cuba in 1990, but a "slight one-month delay" in the arrival of "advanced shipments" of Soviet foodstuffs and raw materials. Castro, they suggest, is overreacting, doubtless because of his fear of change in the Socialist camp.

Ever so gently, Soviet spokesmen suggest that there are Cuban causes for Cuba's economic problems: "Adverse weather" (to which Socialist agriculture is so uniquely prone) has reduced the sugar cane harvest; the slow pace of construction in Cuba has hampered work on needed dock facilities; archaic equipment at Cuban ports and chronic scarcity of transportation and warehouse facilities have forced Soviet ships to dock for long periods.

Soviet spokesmen flatly deny that the economic pressure felt in Cuba is a tactic designed to force Castro to reconsider his opposition to Mikhail Gorbachev's leadership. "There is no such pressure on Cuba," said Vladimir Shalalov, president of the Soviet-Cuban Friendship Society. "But there is currently a need for reorganization, just as we are doing in the Soviet Union." While some Soviet economists charge that the Soviet Union cannot afford to continue forever its wholesale subsidization of the Cuban economy, official spokesmen deny that "Soviet aid to Cuba is like throwing money down the drain," and in denying it, they give further credibility to the charge.

Castro calls this "the most decisive period in Cuba's history." And indeed recent events must lead him to wonder about which way history is moving after all. With Manuel Noriega's fall, he lost a valuable ally in Panama. With Daniel Ortega's defeat he loses his best friend in the hemisphere. With *perestroika*, he risks losing the system of reliable subsidies that delivered Cuba from the disciplines of the market. With the transformation of Eastern Europe, he risks losing the sense of membership in a great global system of power that ensures him a role in the vanguard of history.

On January 29, Castro ended a speech with: "Do we want the newest reforms? No. Do we want bourgeois reforms? No. Do we want neo-liberal reforms? No. We don't even want that in our dreams." Now Fidel is having nightmares.

Several days ago, he announced a plan for "perfecting" Cuba's Communist party. The sentimental break with the Soviet Union has already come. The political break is on the horizon.

Cuba, the United Nations, and the Vanishing "Socialist Bloc"
March 12, 1990

The UN Human Rights Commission's vote to censure Cuba for human rights crimes demonstrated Cuba's increasing isolation within the Socialist bloc.

Unfortunately, the vote also reminded us how far Latin America has drifted away from the United States. Once upon a time all members of the Organization of American States—founded to promote democracy in this hemisphere—voted to isolate Castro diplomatically. This time several important Latin countries abstained from the censure, and one— Mexico—voted with Cuba. The UN vote, combined with widespread nonrecognition of Panama's democratically elected Endara government (installed with U.S. assistance) and with calls by some Latin states for a new hemispheric organization excluding the United States, indicate that the United States and its hemispheric partners have drifted far apart.

"What happened to the Socialist world?" Cuban Foreign Minister Raul Roa was reported to have said minutes after the United Nations Human Rights Commission handed his country a stinging defeat.

By a vote of 19-12, the commission expressed its grave concern about the Cuban government's reprisals against people who had testified before the commission during the previous year and resolved to keep Cuba's human rights practices on its agenda.

Raul Roa understood perfectly what has happened. In the Human Rights Commission, as in its economic affairs, Cuba is feeling the consequences of dramatic change in the Socialist world.

In the commission, the outcome of a vote is determined not only by the merits of any given case but also by the size and cohesion of blocs. For decades, the "Socialist bloc" was so large, so perfectly cohesive, and so influential in the third world that it could protect its members against condemnation, or even investigation, of anything— however heinous.

These countries were never cited for human rights violations, not even during the worst periods of repression and mass murder—not Cambodia under Pol Pot, not Ethiopia, not Cuba, not Romania, not Afghanistan, not Vietnam, not China. They stuck together in interlocking, overlapping blocs with the other great human rights violators. They and their camp followers protected each other.

So great was their power, and so dispirited and indifferent were the Western democracies, that, though the facts about Cuba's treatment of dissenters and political prisoners were well known, the Castro regime was not even brought into UN human rights arenas until the United States finally managed it midway through the Reagan years.

Today, the Socialist bloc in the United Nations is reduced in size, cohesion, and clout. Two former members, Bulgaria and Hungary, voted with the Western democracies to continue the investigation of Cuba's very real record of intimidation and abuse. Two others, Poland and Czechoslovakia, cosponsored the resolution—even though as nonvoting members of the commission they were unable to cast ballots for it. Panama, also a faithful Cuban ally in the past, joined the Western democracies this year. So did pro-Western Morocco, Senegal, Gambia, and Bangladesh.

The facts on Cuba's continuing violations of the human rights of its citizens are clear and have been spelled out most recently in a just-released U.S. State Department report that says Cuba's "human rights situation in 1989 worsened significantly from the previous year."

The Human Rights Commission votes are welcome evidence of the continuing reorientation of the new democracies' foreign policies. But they also illustrate the limits of reform in the Soviet government on key questions of morality in politics.

Mikhail Gorbachev's government voted exactly the same as the unreformed governments of his predecessors—to block investigation of a fellow Socialist country. Only the Soviets, their associated "autonomous republic" of the Ukraine, and a few reliable friends and fellow violators stood with Cuba.

Latin American votes were again especially disappointing. Mexico, which almost always votes with Cuba in the United Nations, voted with Cuba again. Argentina, Brazil, Colombia, Peru, and Venezuela abstained again, demonstrating that Latin solidarity is stronger than their solidarity with human rights victims. These priorities are particularly disappointing for the people of such nations as Argentina and Brazil—who have themselves suffered under arbitrary, nondemocratic governments within the past decade—and Venezuela, a country that claims to hold serious democratic commitments.

Their votes reflect anachronistic priorities in this time of rapid democratization of the South American continent. It is ironic that this Latin unity is demonstrated at a time when previously solid blocs in Asia, Africa, and the Middle East begin to crumble and when Fidel Castro's Cuba finds itself progressively out of step with global trends, including those in the Soviet bloc.

One wonders why the Czech, Polish, Hungarian, and Bulgarian foreign offices are so much clearer than the Argentine and Brazilian foreign offices about where they stand with regard to one-party dictatorship and totalitarian controls in Cuba.

Whatever the explanation of Latin behavior, it is clear that the East Europeans are not neutral about totalitarianism and arbitrary government. It is also clear that the reorientation of their foreign policies is being felt in Cuba, which is rapidly becoming a less-favored trading partner; in the Middle East, where terrorist groups are feeling the cutoff of East European support systems; in Nicaragua, where East Europeans joined international election observers; and in the Soviet Union, whose military power in Europe has relied in part on the power of allied East European armies.

What has happened to the Socialist world? Its member states are beginning to make their own decisions, as befits self-governing democratic countries.

Castro's Last Cheerleaders
July 30, 1990

Pity Fidel Castro—so many friends have deserted him. His East European cronies have been pitched out of power. The Moscow media complain that he is expensive and rigid. And the Soviet Union has told him that in the future it will pay market prices for Cuban sugar. The fall of Daniel Ortega and Manuel Noriega left him isolated in Central America. More than a hundred Latin American intellectuals have petitioned him to allow a plebiscite. Even Gabriel Garcia Marquez has urged Castro to enact "profound reforms."

Incredible! At a time when repression in Cuba hardens and international problems mount, when human rights activists on the island are sentenced to long prison terms and Cubans seek asylum in half a dozen Western embassies—at just that time—a popular French novelist, Jean-Edern Hallier, delivers a paean of praise to Fidel Castro.

Castro, he says, is a "medieval knight" whose "island is too small for him," a "great man" in a historic role. Cuba itself, he says, exemplifies a kind of "Rousseauism," with what Jean-Paul Sartre once called "direct democracy and warm lemonade."

Castro has always had a kind of magnetic appeal for certain writers and intellectuals, especially Europeans and especially the French. He has courted them, read their books and letters, played host to such internationally esteemed writers as Graham Greene and Gabriel Garcia Marquez.

But now the whole world knows the facts on Cuba's political prisons, economic failure, military adventurism, and abject dependence on the Soviet Union. Castro's appeal as a charismatic revolutionary leader has waned even as the appeal of revolution itself has dimmed. It obviously has not disappeared entirely, however.

The long interview by Hallier in the French Communist daily *L'Humanite'* demonstrates that, for at least one writer of the Left, Fidel Castro retains his magnetism.

He tells us Castro is a man of "moving, true simplicity," devoted

261

to a life-long "quest," a man "who questions himself." He says Castro is a veritable embodiment of the "universal spirit of resistance," a man "who has never accepted the discovery that human nature is not good."

We have heard before testimonials concerning the Caribbean Caudillo, his Rousseauistic island and his personal charisma. "If Fidel Castro had not had this charisma for the masses, the arms that he distributed to the people would have been turned against him long ago," Hallier assures us.

Writers more distinguished than Hallier have testified to the attraction felt for remote despots by Western intellectuals who also have insatiable appetites for freedom in their own societies.

This pathology of the Left has been recently reviewed by another French writer, Jeannine Verdes-Leroux, in *The Moon and the Caudillo* (Gallimard, 1989). Like the monkeys who hear no evil, see no evil, and speak no evil, generations of intellectuals of the Left guarded the Castro myth, testifying in the midst of squalor and tyranny to Castro's solemn commitment "to give the moon to the Cuban people, if they need it" (Sartre, 1960).

How could such smart people make such dumb mistakes about a "liberating" revolution that has filled Cuba with prisons, driven one Cuban in nine into exile, and has reduced the Cuban gross national product from third among the twenty countries of Latin America in 1952 to near the bottom today? The long romance of Western intellectuals with tyrannies is still not fully understood and remains potentially dangerous.

What is it that makes smiling tyrants attractive to free men and women? Is it, as Erich Fromm once argued, that they find freedom too difficult to bear, the multiple choices of democracy too difficult to make? Or is it because of an abiding, unacknowledged hunger for power and the conviction that they know better than the masses themselves what the masses need?

Is this why they find it so difficult to understand George Orwell's fundamental insight about dictatorship and revolution—that power is an end, that one does not establish a dictatorship to make a revolution, but one makes a revolution to establish a dictatorship?

Castro made a revolution and established a dictatorship and claimed the special relationship to history that Hallier ascribes to him today. For more than three decades, he has exercised supreme power. He has trained guerrillas from around the world and exported guns, drugs, revolution—and especially uniformed Cubans.

He counted on the Soviet Union and Eastern Europe to provide life's more mundane necessities. When it worked, it worked. As long as the Soviet Union was governed by men interested chiefly in world revolution and military power, Castro prospered—even if Cubans suffered.

He could count on reliable support from the Soviet Union, Czechoslovakia, and the rest of Eastern Europe. Now, with the Soviet Union busy with internal change and Eastern Europe free, about all he can count on from Czechoslovakia is a lecture on human rights.

Fidel Castro thinks he knows all he cares to about how to handle people who raise the issue of human rights—arrest them, as he did recently when eleven Cuban activists in the Youth Association for the Rights of Man were sentenced to up to fifteen years in prison. That's not so bad by Cuban standards. Two political prisoners, workers Mario Chanes de Armas and Ernesto Diaz Rodriquez, have been held in Cuban prisons for twenty-eight and twenty-six years respectively.

Not many people find Fidel's claims as interesting or as persuasive as they used to. He must have really enjoyed the ten-hour conversation with Jean-Edern Hallier.

Totalitarianism and Terror . . .

Ideological Crimes and the Beijing Spring
June 29, 1987

The relationship between totalitarianism and terror is integral. The totalitarian vision seeks transformation of human nature by way of *politics and government. The totalitarian ruler is prepared to use force to secure conformity to his vision. The use of force to impose a broad agenda finally saturates the society with force.*

The defining fact about Communist regimes has been the use of force to implement a comprehensive "revolution" in human behavior that only begins *with the seizure of power and continues until Utopia is finally reached.*

The totalitarian vision provides the moral certainty that justifies the use of force against citizens without rights. The relationship between totalitarian vision and terror explains why all Communist regimes have been characterized by broad violation of the rights of their citizens.

263

Klaus Barbie, the infamous Nazi "Butcher of Lyon," thinks it outrageous that he is being tried for crimes against humanity. He claims that in beating, torturing, and shooting prisoners and in shipping Jewish children to their deaths at Auschwitz, he acted as any German officer would have acted in wartime. Barbie complains, through his attorneys, that he is being illegally tried for his heinous policies as SS chief in Lyon during the Nazi occupation of France. He says he was fighting a war. He says war produces atrocities—in Algeria, in Vietnam. He says his side lost and now he is being tried under the law of the victor.

But sending Jewish children to be killed at Auschwitz is not "normal" war. Rounding up Jews for deportation, ripping babies from their mothers' arms, disfiguring young women to extract information from their fathers is not "normal" war. It is something different and far worse. What differentiates Barbie's brutality from other instances of sadistic behavior in war is that, first, there was much more of it and, second, for the Nazi occupiers, sadism was official policy.

Barbie is the first person to be tried under a twenty-three-year-old French law adopted unanimously by the parliament. The law incorporated into French statute the various understandings of wartime allies that Nazi officers and soldiers responsible for abominable crimes against humanity "should be pursued to the ends of the earth, and returned to the country where their crimes were committed and tried under the law of that country."

At his trial, Barbie and his counsel deny that there were "crimes against humanity." So, in addition to hearing testimony from a grim procession of Barbie's victims, there has been a good deal of discussion in the courtroom about the nature and meaning of "crimes against humanity."

The argument of prosecuting attorney Bernard de Bigault du Granrut has attracted approving commentary. According to Granrut, a crime against humanity (against which there can be no statute of limitations) is "not simply a violation of laws and customs of war," "but an attack on the fundamental rights of man" and "the right to equality without regard to race, color, or nationality, religious or political opinions." Such a crime, Granrut noted, "does not merely maim or kill, it deliberately deprives its victim of human dignity because he belongs to a category of humanity which is different than that of the hangman—or because he refuses to submit to domination."

God knows Klaus Barbie violated—in every way cited by Granrut—the human rights and human dignity of the victims he is now forced to face. Barbie's zealous, determined pursuit of France's Jews and their deportation to death camps remind anyone who needs reminding that he and his Nazi colleagues were implementing a profoundly mistaken and immoral racist ideology.

But the prosecutors of the French court are taking great pains to establish Barbie's personal responsibility for specific crimes. Each charge against Barbie is meticulously examined. Maimed, disfigured witnesses have testified to their torture at Barbie's hands day after day, and to their personal knowledge of murders for which Barbie was directly responsible. The names of each Jewish child shipped to Auschwitz have been read. The careful examination of evidence and the establishment of personal responsibility contrast sharply with the practices of Nazis and others who treat individual persons merely as instances of an ideological category.

Barbie will be convicted not because of his associations or beliefs, but because of his sadistic treatment of specific persons. He will not be convicted for holding a despicable ideology, but for implementing it.

There is a larger lesson here. When those who hold a sinister ideology gain control of a government and use its power to impose their policies on hapless populations, human tragedies follow. It is terribly important that those who believe in human dignity, equality, and freedom be aware of the human consequences of political ideologies. But crimes committed in the name of an ideology do not thereby become "ideological crimes." They are simply crimes. The damage done to a battered, tortured kidnap victim is not morally different if perpetrated in the name of politics rather than by a psychopath.

The long, grim procession of witnesses against Klaus Barbie reminds everyone that "crimes against humanity" have concrete human victims—as "the final solution of the Jewish question" meant deportation and death to the children of Izieu and millions of other Jews, as the "de-Kulakization" meant starvation to millions of Ukrainians, and as "village-ization" recently has brought starvation to hundreds of thousands of Ethiopians.

In holding Barbie personally responsible, French courts are reaffirming his humanity—and that of his victims.

June 13, 1989

"Reason will prevail over brute force," a banner in Tiananmen Square proclaimed right down to the moment when tanks and troops demonstrated that, in China, power still comes from the barrel of a gun—just as Mao said it did.

No one, including the experts, expected the great uprising in the square, nor the brutality with which it was suppressed. The Beijing Spring contained so many surprises of such great importance for China and the world. It is worthwhile to note what we didn't know, and when we didn't know it.

First, there was the uprising itself—whose occurrence, strength, and duration came as a continuing surprise. Why did so many know so little about an event involving so many people.

The most likely answer is that the demonstrations were a truly spontaneous occurrence, triggered by another unpredictable event, the death of Hu Yaobang and by the arrival of Mikhail Gorbachev in Beijing. No one could be expected to know when a man will die, but it is reasonable to ask why so many experts failed to perceive the explosive atmosphere from which the demonstrations materialized.

Was it because the government provides no opportunity for the expression of opinion, permits no polls, sponsors no elections, tolerates little dissent? Did the experts know so little about the Chinese students' attitudes because the traditional culture discourages the expression of feelings and opinions? Were the experts taken by surprise because they underestimated the appeal of democratic ideas to Chinese universities?

Did the experts discount the possibility of an uprising because they believed that government controls were so effective as to render such an event impossible—even though uprisings in Hungary (1956), Czechoslovakia (1968), and Poland (1981) showed that mass demonstrations could take place in Communist countries?

A second factor concerns what we didn't know, or didn't guess, about the People's Republic of China's response to the demonstrations.

Why were the experts so surprised when units of the military fired on demonstrators point-blank? Why did the experts underestimate the government's readiness to use force? Or to eliminate dissent? Did they underestimate Deng Xiaoping's capacity for rage against the students (who were again and again called "his children") when they called for his resignation? Did they underestimate the government's capacity and inclination to use maximum force when it felt its power threatened?

And what of other governments that have altered significant aspects of their China policies in protest against the PRC's brutal use of force—the United States, the United Kingdom, Australia, West Germany? Why were they so surprised? Did they not know about China's brutal repression of Tibetans in recent years?

Why were the experts so relatively uninformed about the power struggles and relative power positions in the Chinese Politburo? Few Westerners seemed to have guessed that Deng—who himself had suffered greatly under repression—would throw his weight behind those advocating tough measures, even when the demonstrations themselves were peaceable.

In spite of the fate of the prior liberal heir apparent, Hu Yaobang, almost no one foresaw that the other leading reformer, Zhao Ziyang, would so quickly disappear from the inner circle. Still fewer predicted that Politburo member Qiao Shi was the man to watch in the competition for succession. And no one is now ready to tell us how seriously to take the talk of a return to "class struggle" and the rhetoric of the Cultural Revolution.

There are good reasons the world does not know the answers to these questions. Despite the significant "openings" of recent years, politics in the PRC are still conducted behind a heavy veil of secrecy. And political competition is still not institutionalized. There are no established public procedures for choosing leaders, debating issues, and making policy.

Moreover, what is true of China is true of every Communist system.

As long as these regimes have not institutionalized and limited power—tamed power—their governance will be vulnerable. And we will be vulnerable as well to sudden, even terrible shifts in the composition and policies of leadership.

Until reason and law prevail over brute force, in Tiananmen Square, in Georgia, Uzbekistan, Warsaw, and Moscow, power will continue to come out of the barrel of the gun.

Realism and Chinese Repression

October 13, 1989

Dealing with the Chinese government poses a difficult problem for the United States. In this column I emphasize that the oppression at Tiananmen Square was not an isolated example of Chinese support for brutal policy but a manifestation of continuing support for brutal policies. Still, there are good reasons to maintain such contact and protect our interests at the expense of moral commitments.

I think the two positions are not always mutually exclusive. We can make clear in a variety of ways our revulsion at the June 1989 crackdown and at the same time seek to encourage positive changes in Chinese behavior. China is not immune to outside influence.

We should also remember that although "realism" sometimes requires us to engage with distasteful regimes, systems built upon a utopian, unnatural ideology such as communism are themselves "unrealistic."

The foreign minister of the People's Republic of China, Qian Qichen, took advantage of his trip to the United Nations to chide Americans for their "interference" in China's internal affairs. Though the Bush administration's low-key response to China's repression of the democracy movement has frustrated a good many Americans, it did not satisfy the Chinese government. Irritated by continuing criticism of China in the U.S. Congress, Qian said plainly, "At present Sino-U.S. relations are at a crossroad. We hope to see our bilateral relations repaired and developed. But that will depend on the policy and action of the U.S. government."

Americans' continued concern about repression of the prodemocracy movement is not compatible with a good relationship between the two countries, Qian added. Instead, Americans should build their relations with China on the basis of shared economic and strategic concerns.

Once again China offers a choice especially difficult for Americans: between a foreign policy based on moral concerns and one that gives priority to geostrategic factors. Again the U.S. relationship with China poses a head-on conflict between *Realpolitik* and human rights.

China's size, population, and location have always made it a prime candidate for exemption from U.S. standards. The Nixon administration explicitly chose "realism" over moral concerns when it opened relations with the People's Republic. Even Sen. Henry

"Scoop" Jackson (D-Wash.), author of the doctrine of link between human rights and foreign relations, applauded. Both the Carter and the Reagan administrations honored "the China exception" to their human rights policies. The Bush administration reaction to the Tiananmen Square massacre stood squarely in this tradition. Now the Chinese are demanding silence from Congress as well.

The repression at Tiananmen Square was not the most brutal event in the history of the Chinese revolution. The consolidation of power and the Cultural Revolution both involved the brutal elimination of millions. But they did not take place on television. The events of Tiananmen Square are unique because the demonstrators' high hopes, reasonable demands, and ruthless repression were watched by millions.

"Realists" cannot deny the "reality" of these events. This reality confronts any U.S. government with a starker choice and less opportunity for obfuscation than has hitherto been the case. This time the U.S. government makes its policies in broad daylight before citizens who know the nature of the Chinese regime.

The situation is further complicated by the PRC's policies in Tibet and Cambodia.

The massacre at Tiananmen Square was in fact only a reapplication in Peking of techniques already used against Tibetans at Lhasa. The slaughter of Chinese students who demanded only dialogue had been foreshadowed by the slaughter of Tibetans who demonstrated against Chinese rule in March 1989. The repression of Tibet continues and is made harder to forget by Tibetans, who have become more skilled at reminding the world of their suffering.

The Khmer Rouge bid for power in Cambodia is another extremely unwelcome reminder of the Chinese government's indifference to human rights. Pol Pot is one of the champion killers of all time. The Khmer Rouge government he headed specialized in slave labor and mass murder of its subjects. Most observers believe that at least 2 million Cambodians were starved, shot, or worked to death in the Khmer Rouge killing fields. Just as did Joseph Stalin and Adolf Hitler, the Khmer Rouge systematically wiped out whole classes of society.

The Khmer Rouge is a subsidiary of China. Without Chinese money and material and subtle pressure on Thailand, the Khmer Rouge would have shriveled and died after the Vietnamese invasion dislodged it from power. With Chinese help it is once again a contender for supreme power in Cambodia. The Vietnamese army, which was the only important obstacle to the Khmer Rouge return to power, has been removed. The Cambodian people are now confronted with reestablishment of the genocide that symbolized Pol Pot's rule.

The Khmer Rouge say they will behave differently should they return to power. They say they have revised their beliefs and goals and changed their leadership. But refugees report that in the border communities controlled by the Khmer Rouge, they rule as they ruled in Cambodia—by terror—and that no matter who has the title, Pol Pot still has the power.

Can the United States have a good relationship with a country that makes war on its own dissidents and arms the Khmer Rouge? Henry Kissinger says the brutality of the attacks at Tiananmen Square was "shocking and even more so the trials and Stalinist-style propaganda that followed. Nevertheless, China remains too important for Americans and national security to risk the relationship on the emotion of the moment."

Milovan Djilas says to the contrary: "The true political realists in the West and East are only those who refuse to accept tyranny."

I think they are both right. We should maintain a relationship with China while facing squarely both moral and geopolitical realities. China *is* important, and it is in our interest to have normal relations with a major regional power. But realism does not require us to enhance the power of that government—or any whose practices violate democratic values.

PART FIVE

Reflections on the New Soviet Revolution

Reflections on the
New Soviet Revolution

The speed with which the Soviet Union and Eastern Europe were transformed was itself a great shock. A chief characteristic of Marxist-Leninist states had always been the skill of their elites not only in seizing and consolidating power but also in preserving power. None had ever been overthrown by its own military, although several existed in countries with a tradition of military coups and intrigue. None had ever fallen because of dissension in its ranks, although several were found in countries with a tradition of factionalism. None had been overthrown from within nor evolved into any other kind of government, although several existed in countries where there was a long tradition of regime instability. These regimes were called totalitarian because they claimed total jurisdiction over all aspects of the society.

Change of a regime most often comes from some group with a power base outside the state. English barons were able to wrest concessions from King John in 1215 because they had the money he needed to finance his policies. They owned the land, produced the food, raised the armies, paid the taxes. Their land, rank, and wealth were the power base from which they bargained with the king. By the time of the French Revolution, the rising industrial and commercial classes of France were the largest source of revenue for the government. Those who brought down the shah of Iran has organized support from the bazaars and the mullah. Anastasio Somoza was toppled by a coalition that included the church, much of the business community, and the trade unions. Ferdinand Marcos resigned after he lost the support of most of the business, banking, planting, and labor communities and incurred the active opposition of the Philippine Catholic hierarchy. And so forth. This, or something much like it, is how entrenched authoritarian states fall. It can happen because these governments do not control all the power bases in the society.

But the central characteristic of the modern totalitarian state is the absence of independent power bases and power contenders.

Marxist-Leninist leaders did their best to ensure that all was within the state, and nothing outside the state. How then could change occur?

Virtually everyone believed the Soviet Union and the Eastern European states would prove more resistant to changes than they turned out to be. Students of totalitarianism believed the conviction and discipline of Party cadres spread through the system would reinforce it at every level. Or that the absence of independent institutions would prevent the association of people into opposition movements. Or that the ubiquity of the secret police and the habit of using force would prevent the spread of opposition. Or that control of speech, press, and assembly would make it impossible for opponents to discuss their views or learn about one another or coordinate response. We thought the centralization in the state of control over food, shelter, income, news, communication, and police would prevent the rapid spread of opposition.

But those of us who thought such a totalitarian state would be extremely resistant to change mistakenly assumed that the impetus of change must come from below. We never seriously considered the possibility that change would be initiated from the top by a leader who first managed to gain power in this most centralized power structure, then use his power to change the system.

We assumed without much thought that long years of socialization in the society and the Party—the years of preparation, screening, and scrutiny—would preclude the arrival of a maverick or dissident at the top. We should have reflected more on the models of regime changes offered by Plato, Pareto, or Harold Lasswell, which insist that regime change begins with the ruling elite, and less about those offered by the European revolutionary tradition, which sees change as precipitated by mass discontent.

What happened, of course, was that a leader with different goals, experiences, and temperament made his way to the top. The revolution in the Soviet Union should remind us again of the irreducible importance of individual persons in history. Mikhail Gorbachev changed the world. His policies loosened the reins of power that have controlled Soviet society since 1917 and held in subjection the peoples of Eastern Europe.

Obviously Gorbachev was not the only source of change in the world, in the West, or in the Soviet Union. Alexander Solzhenitsyn, the late Andrei Sakharov, Anatoly Shcharansky, the refuseniks, and generations of dissidents have articulated alternatives to the stifling official Soviet prescription and have provided models of courage and honesty. Ronald Reagan and the Reagan administration dramatized the need for change and made the case for freedom. The democracies of Western Europe provided nearby examples of the benefits of freedom. The Information Age, the Strategic Defense Initiative, CO-COM, the decision to deploy Pershing missiles in Europe, and the promise of the European Community also contributed to the Soviet motivation to change. Stagnation and the worsening economic situation were important too. The fact that the Soviet Union was the only industrial nation in the world with rising infant mortality rates and declining life expectancy statistics as well as falling living standards contributed to the felt need for change.

But it was Gorbachev who saw stagnation in the Soviet economy, a growing gap between the Soviet Union and the West, an escalating arms race, deadlock in Europe, and a costly war in Afghanistan as a reason to undertake reform. From the apex of the Soviet system he acted. The Soviet Union, founded on the decisions of a single man, is being reshaped by the decisions of another. Gorbachev is a lawyer, more oriented to legal concerns than his predecessors, a curious man who traveled with his wife and friend to Western Europe on a vacation—a most unusual step for an ambitious apparatchik. He is a modern man who desired to rule a modern country. He is obviously more pragmatic than ideological by temperament. When he asked of the Soviet economy, Does it work?, he faced the fact it did not, tried a Leninist measure or two (saying to Soviet workers, "Sober up, shape up, show up for work, work harder") and, finding it did not bring results, tried something else.

With a sure sense of tactics and great political skill, he managed to win the assent of colleagues in the government he sought to reform, and to retain power long enough to transform the system.

Initially, it appeared that the *"perestroika* revolution," as Gorbachev called it, aimed to dismantle the police state, shake up the bureaucracy, reorganize many aspects of social life including work, the workplace, and property but also to preserve the state, socialism, and a leading role for the Communist party. But by 1990 even these fundamentals had also been caught up in the surge of change, and Soviet leaders proposed they be dropped. Gorbachev admitted that the goals themselves were being revised:

> We usually used to take a negative attitude to the very term "democratic socialism," which was identified with the expression of a reformist and opportunist line in the socialist movement. Now we are talking about the democratization

275

not only of the state system but of all of social life—a democratization that is a powerful incentive for increasing and creating the conditions for the masses' social activeness and independent activity.

The idea of building a socialist rule-of-law state, an idea which means the supremacy of the law, the granting to each individual of a wide range of social and political rights and freedoms in conjunction with a high degree of responsibility and discipline, and the creation of effective management mechanisms, is organically linked with the development of freedom.

Democracy and freedom are great values of human civilization which we have inherited and are filling with the development of freedom.

Great values, yes. Marxist values? No. Leninist values? Of course not. But as the reform process developed, there was more and more talk of universal human values and less of class struggle.

"In the Beginning Was the Word"

The Soviet Union was a country patterned on a theory—the theory that history is propelled on a predetermined course by a conflict between exploiters and exploited that rages across centuries. According to the theory, that struggle *and everything else* reflect the unequal distribution of property. Eliminate private property—the theory advised—and everything changes, including the moral sentiments of human beings and the relations among them. Egoism and conflict give way to altruism and harmony.

It was not an original idea. Plato also believed that division of property was the source of egoism and conflict in society and that common property (among the ruling elite) would abolish these unwelcome human characteristics. But Plato had no Lenin to organize a party to which everything would be permitted.

While Marxism is a complex body of ideas, just three concepts have been essential to the political movement: the *class struggle* as the engine of history; *property*, whose distribution determines everything else including human consciousness; and the *Party*, vanguard and guide of the revolution. With these concepts, Soviet leaders (and those who followed them) based the claim to power. On these concepts, the *legitimacy* of Communist rule and the Soviet state has depended.

I began to take the Soviet reform process seriously—as something other than a superficial tactical change—when I perceived that it included major revisions of the basic concepts of Marxism-Leninism. These reinterpretations gave Gorbachev doctrinal permission to change and eroded the foundations of the Soviet state.

Major departures were already present in his book, *Perestroika*, where Gorbachev announced that Soviet economic problems were rooted in Soviet society and that broad restructuring was needed. The *perestroika* revolution, he wrote, was required "not only in the economy but in all other sides of social life: social relations, the political system, the spiritual and ideological sphere, the style and work methods of the Party and all our cadres." *Perestroika* would be a "genuine revolution in the minds and hearts of people," abandoning the "dogmatic approach" and replacing it with "socialist pluralism" and "socialist democracy."

Socialist Pluralism

"Socialist pluralism," however, required a major reinterpretation of doctrine to free culture from economic determinism. This was accomplished by redefining the class basis of ideology. According to Marx and Engels, religion, science, and ideas—in the whole of culture— were a reflection of a person's position in the continuing class war. They thought that after "the revolution," when classes and class conflict had been destroyed, there would be no conflicts, only harmony. Thus, a conflict of opinion was a manifestation of class war, and a person with whom one disagreed was a class enemy—whom the state could appropriately silence, banish, or destroy.

With *glasnost* this doctrine of class struggle was not formally abandoned but was amended so that class was no longer the only possible basis of opinion. Now it was accepted that some opinions might have other bases (nationality, for example) and might persist after the revolution had abolished classes and ended the class struggle.

This very important change undermined the Communist party's claim to a monopoly on truth and made it possible for the government to admit what everyone knew: that differences of opinion exist in Socialist states. It was no longer necessary to pretend that all conflict had been eliminated or would be eliminated. Now it became possible to speak frankly about the actual conflicts in the Soviet Union. Tolerating differences of opinion was no longer tantamount to tolerating a deadly enemy. This revision also made it possible to search for a description of reality that was not simply the reflection of a class bias.

Real Marxists believe that bourgeois notions of truth and science reflect the interests of the bourgeoisie, and proletarian truth reflects

277

the interests of the proletariat. All descriptions of reality reflect the interests of some class. This makes it meaningless to speak of what is "true," as though some "truth" exists independently of its historical context and can be established by scientific investigation. But shortly after announcing *glasnost*, Gorbachev appointed a commission to investigate the matter of Nikolai Bukharin's guilt, to determine whether *it was true* that Bukharin and other Old Bolsheviks purged by Stalin were in fact guilty of the treason of which they had been convicted. Then Gorbachev appointed another commission to investigate the Hitler-Stalin Pact, including its secret provision regarding the Baltic States. When these commissions completed their investigations, Bukharin was posthumously declared innocent of the treason for which he had been executed, and the secret protocols providing for Soviet annexation of the Baltic States were published. Correcting the record undermined the ideological version of history of which these instances were part and eliminated any trace of legitimacy in the Soviet claim to the Baltics and stimulated demands for Baltic independence.

Is it true? is not a Bolshevik kind of question. Investigation is not a Bolshevik means for settling debate. Appeal to the authority of the Party and its leader is the Bolshevik means of settling questions of truth. Once authority is rejected in favor of scholarship and critical analysis, anything can happen. In fact, the process of "filling in the blanks" of Soviet history led from criticism of Brezhnev, Stalin, and the Stalinist era to criticism of the Communist system and to Lenin himself.

No sooner had Soviet historians publicly acknowledged the full extent of Stalin's terror than Alexander Tsipko charged in the Moscow monthly *Science and Life* that Stalinist terror was not an aberration but a product of Marxist doctrine itself. With an analysis that could have been borrowed from Friedrich von Hayek, Tsipko argued that the suppression of a free market and the imposition of a centrally planned economy led directly to tyranny. The problem was not the event but the structure. "How could a commission go about establishing the reasons for cracks in a recently completed building?" he asked. "Naturally, by looking at the architectural plan of the building itself." In the Soviet Union, he argued, the architectural plan is itself deficient. Lenin, not Stalin, was the first Soviet leader to resort to terror. The Red Terror broke out in 1919 in the city now called Leningrad when Lenin governed the Soviet Union. "Officers of the Czarist army were killed simply because they were officers," wrote Tsipko. "Priests because they were priests. . . . Persons were executed merely by being of 'non-proletariat origins.' " Tsipko was not alone in making such charges. Soviet historian and deputy Yuri Afanasiev charged that the Soviet regime "was brought into being through bloodshed, with the aid of murder and crimes against humanity." In other words, the very foundation of the regime was illegitimate.

Gorbachev and his colleagues had put their foot on a slippery slope. The future as well as the past was at stake in these debates. If the architectural plan—Marxism—was responsible for Stalinism, then so were the Party, state, and socialism itself.

Rethinking Economic Relations

Does it work? is also a non-Bolshevik question, but it is the question to which Marxist economic policies have been submitted. Gorbachev himself posed it at the special meeting of the Communist Party Central Committee held in February 1989 to discuss agriculture. The answer was clear: Soviet agriculture did not work. At that time, Gorbachev argued that the Soviet Union's chronic agricultural failure made it necessary to dissolve unproductive farms and that state enterprises should be disbanded in favor of new forms of land leasing and free-market cooperatives. "To maintain them further at the expense of the state budget through credits they don't pay back is not only impossible but makes no sense," he observed.

Noting that in the Soviet Union more than 98 percent of Soviet farmland is owned and operated by state collectives and that the 1.6 percent of arable land privately farmed produces 30 percent of the country's food, former Politburo ideologist Vadim Medvedev argued that the Soviet Union must lift the ban on leasing imposed in 1930.

"It was not for this that we established Soviet power," replied Gorbachev's chief rival, Yegor Ligachev. Of course, Ligachev was right. They did not make a revolution to raise production but to revolutionize distribution and to make fundamental changes in the workers' relation to property. But the reformers were not deterred. "Today, few doubt that socialism requires profound renovation," Medvedev said, adding that "the key to reform is restructuring property relations and ending the state of alienation between people and public property." But Marx's doctrine of property is the foundation stone of Marxism-Leninism, and the elimination of private property was a raison d'être of the Soviet state. The belief that socialism would end alienation of workers from one another and from themselves was a basic belief. Yet now, drawing on the experience of all Socialist countries, Medvedev argued, "We must now admit our previous concepts of public property have proven untenable."

The next year Gorbachev himself went all the way in revising

279

Marx's conception of property and alienation saying, "Production relations which have served as a source of the workers' alienation from property and from the results of their labor, are being dismantled. The conditions for free competition among socialist producers are being created" (July 3, 1990).

Economic reform has proceeded more slowly, more cautiously, and least successfully of all aspects of the reform program—in part because literally no one knows how to transform a fully centralized Socialist state into something else and in part because resistance to economic change has been strongest. "Mounting a struggle against alcoholism we thoughtlessly destroyed vineyards," Supreme Soviet Vice Chairman Igor Belorisov warned. The basic issues of socialism are involved here as Ligachev made clear in his argument against Gorbachev's proposals for private ownership of industry: "Public property unites people's interests and private property separates them, and stratifies society socially." The new concept of labor private property will not eliminate the social consequences of private property, he insisted.

Nothing has been easy: neither expanded cooperatives, nor reforms permitting leasing, nor joint ventures, nor other economic reforms have produced hoped-for increases in production. By the end of 1989, however, Gorbachev made the shocking suggestion that gains in freedom offset the slow movement of the economy. He told the Congress of People's Deputies:

> We are estimating the results of *perestroika*. It is true that it has not brought us economic results on the whole, but it has provided freedom of expression and creativity and freedoms in the political sphere. Only recently we all said that we had been suffocating under paralyzed ideas and deeds. Didn't we dream of freedom as the most cherished thing?

Freedom more important than ownership of the means of production in the view of the general secretary of the Communist party? This is revolution.

From this position it was a short step to economic freedom and the market. In 1990 Lenin's heirs admitted that the Soviet Union should work toward a market economy, of all things. "The advantages of the market economy had been proven on a world scale," Gorbachev himself said. "Workers are more productive, nations more prosperous."

"It would be a ruinous mistake to throw the country into the arms of the elemental force of the market," former KGB Chief Vladimir Kryuchkov warned. But Gorbachev had his answer ready.

The market is not what it used to be, he assured the Party congress. The modern market economy has evolved from "uncontrolled evolution" to a "highly organized mechanism," which is compatible with social security.

To his report of July 2, 1990, to the Twenty-eighth Congress of the Communist Party of the Soviet Union, Gorbachev went on to say: "In the conditions of the market the possibility presents itself of realistically ascertaining needs and finding ways of satisfying them effectively, balancing out demand and supply, and creating a normal and natural environment for the development of production." The modern market, he said, is not incompatible with socialism: "Moving toward the market we are not moving aside from socialism but to a fuller realization of society's possibilities."

Justice Minister Veniamin Yakovlev explained that there is a "civilized market that is regulated by law, and so it is not a speculators' market, but a fair and honest market."

But the tentative half-steps toward a market economy have so far produced little but disorganization and decline. Production of most goods is down, productivity is down, distribution has been disrupted, scarcities multiply, and it becomes clearer than ever that force made Soviet socialism work as force held the empire together.

Revolution, Public Opinion, and the Party

Lenin had said, "The Bolsheviks must learn to trade." As of 1990, Bolsheviks still had not but as the economy worsened Mikhail Gorbachev began to associate himself more and more closely with the demands of Boris Yeltsin for rapid transition to a market system.

Marxism-Leninism is not a seamless web but a system of thought whose various parts hang together. The reinterpretations of *perestroika* ripped apart key elements of the system. The dogmatism that *glasnost* targeted was the very foundation of the Party's claim to a monopoly of power. The Communist party's authority to exercise power on behalf of the proletariat derives from its "scientific" understanding of history. This so-called scientific understanding of the laws and the dynamics of history enables the Party to transcend its class position and escape the false consciousness that renders everyone else a prisoner of history. This is why the Party knows better than the proletariat itself what the proletariat needs. As Marx wrote, "It is not a question of what this or that proletarian, or even the entire proletariat imagines to be its goal. It is a matter of what it is . . . and what it will be historically forced to do." The Party knows the goal—or so the theory goes.

Because the Party alone knows, the Party alone should rule. And rule it has—claiming and exercising a monopoly of power, eliminating opposition, and denying the legitimacy of any insight or interests outside itself. Even Trotsky said (at the Thirteenth Party Congress in 1924), "I cannot be right against the party . . . for history has not created other ways for realizing what is right."

From the elimination of the Mensheviks till the Gorbachev reforms, there were debates about how the Party should be organized and how power could be exercised more effectively, but there were no debates about the Party's "privileged position," because the Party's role is the very heart of Leninism.

From the time of his split with the Mensheviks (before the revolution, while all were still in exile), Lenin had insisted that the revolution depended on a small, professional "cadre" Party to serve as a vanguard of the proletariat and of revolution. Lenin justified the seizure of power and the dismissal of Russia's elected parliament (the Duma) in 1917 on the grounds that legitimate power belonged to the Party by virtue of the laws of history, not to the Duma by virtue of elections. "Leninism" is a doctrine that sees the Party as the vanguard, the engine, the executive of the revolution.

Now Mikhail Gorbachev was saying that the Party had erred and needed to purge itself of everything that had linked it with an authoritarian bureaucratic system. Invoking the "great legacy of Marx, Engels and Lenin," he said the Communist party should "rid itself of ideological dogmatism ingrained in past decades, of obsolete stereotypes of domestic policies, and the outmoded views of the world revolutionary process and world developments as a whole, everything that led to socialist countries being isolated within the common flow of world civilization."

"We reject the notion that it is possible to build socialism according to a preconceived scheme," proclaimed the leader of a society built according to just such a preconceived scheme.

Gorbachev's reforms weakened the Communist party in several ways: by direct criticism, by doctrinal revisions, and by constitutional and legal changes that reduce its monopoly on power. By permitting open discussion of public issues, organizing elections, and demanding that officials win the approval of voters, Gorbachev reopened the question about the legitimate relationship between the people, the Party, and the government. The elections of February 1989, limited as they were, challenged the Party's privileged role in government, enhanced the role of public opinion, and undermined the Party's claim to a monopoly of power. At the same time, however, Gorbachev formally supported the Party's privileged position and argued that there was no need for multiple parties in the Soviet Union, because now all points of view could be discussed *inside* the Communist party.

Meanwhile, the public criticism of the Party continued. The Party, said Alexander Yakovlev, "still remains a captive of the system of social stagnation generated by the regime of personal power." Politburo alternate member Boris Pugo said, "The party is sick. It has been undermined from within by instances of corruption, parochialism, bureaucracy, servility, and lies. That is why the problem of curing the party has come to the forefront."

Still, as late as December 1989, the Congress of People's Deputies upheld the privileged position of the Communist party and retained Article Six of the Soviet Constitution (which guaranteeed that privileged position), but parties could not be indefinitely prohibited once criticism and debate were tolerated. So, early in 1990, after debate by the Congress of People's Deputies, the role of the Party was formally altered. On February 5, 1990, Gorbachev announced,

> In a society that is renewing itself the party can . . . fulfill its vanguard role only as a democratically acknowledged force. . . . The CPSU naturally intends to fight for the position of being a ruling party, but it intends to do this strictly within the framework of the democratic process, renouncing any and all legal and political advantages, putting forward its own program, defending it in discussions, cooperating with other public and political forces, constantly working among the masses, living their interests and needs.

And at the July 1990, Twenty-eighth Party Congress, Gorbachev went further, suggesting that the Party must become a democratic party in a democratic Soviet Union. The Party, he envisions,

> strives to play an initiating role in political and ideological processes using methods of persuasion, and of propaganda . . . and developing relations with all progressive, social, and political forces of the country. . . . We believe that one cannot force a vanguard role on society, it can only be won by an active struggle for the interests of the working people, by practical deeds, and by our whole political and moral image.
>
> The party will pursue its policy and fight to maintain its mandate as the ruling party within the framework of the democratic process and elections to the central and local legislative bodies . . . acting as a parliamentary party.

This statement embodies a revolution. Now the Party's power should derive from the confidence of the people, not from "history."

Now the Party must compete for power, not seize it. In view of the defeat of Communist candidates in Eastern Europe and the rejection of the Party's preferred candidates in the Soviet Union, Gorbachev has indicated he is ready to risk the Party's position and his own power to win a new kind of legitimacy.

He has also strengthened the government at the expense of the Party—by creating the post of executive president, establishing a cabinet, and making decisions through it rather than through the Politburo. At the Congress of the Communist Party of the Soviet Socialist Republic of July 1990, the power of the Party was further diminished and that of the government enlarged. Key officials (including top adviser Alexander Yakovlev) resigned from the Politburo "to devote full time to government," which is, of course, precisely what the Politburo had done in the Party state.

The Party had created the totalitarian state and has held together, driven, and directed its interlocking bureaucracies. The Party had made the claim for total control of the society and the people in it. The Party headed the state that administered economic, social, and political life and tried hard to bend all associations to political purposes. Its penetration of all institutions deprived them of autonomy. Thus, neither the army nor the police nor the captains of Soviet industry could act independently. This political penetration of all institutions by the Party is the hallmark of the totalitarian state. For that state to be dismantled, other institutions must be liberated from Party control. There was, therefore, recurring discussion at the Twenty-eighth Party Congress of diminishing or ending the role of the Party in the army and the KGB, in the workplace, and elsewhere in the government itself. No definitive reforms took place, but a clear intention was expressed to break the Party's stranglehold on Soviet society.

At every stage there has been consistent, sometimes bitter, resistance to these changes. Early in 1989, Yegor Ligachev worried aloud about attacks on the Party:

> The denunciation of Stalin's personality cult and its pernicious consequences and also of the stagnation phenomenon have cleared the path for democratization, working people's initiatives, and the enhancement of their role in the management of the state . . . and the people have duly appreciated this. However, at the same time, a campaign has been launched to slander everything that Soviet people hold dear and to negate the role of the Party and the work of whole generations of communists. The history of our country has always served as a source of pride for our people and a

source of strength, especially in the most difficult times. Now they have been largely deprived of this.

Do not deprive the people of pride in their history, the Soviet conservatives insist. Do not weaken the Party.

"So many accusations have been brought against the Party both in our country and abroad," Ligachev asserts. "The authority of Party cadres and the Party's regional committees and primary organizations is being undermined before our very eyes."

"Why is the Communist Party making concession after concession and surrendering one position after another?" said V. S. Belorisov, a delegate to the Twenty-eighth Party Congress, who spoke for many. "I have the impression that someone is subtly and cleverly gradually chipping away at the party from within and undermining its ideological and organizational foundations." Finally, however, conservative Party members responsive to appeals to Party discipline, accustomed to following the leader, voted for Mikhail Gorbachev— although they had criticized his policies. And Gorbachev offered them reassurances at the same time that he reduced the Party's power. "The Communist Party of the Soviet Union lives and will continue to live," he told them.

Perhaps. But the Party that emerged from the Twenty-eighth Congress is not the Leninist Party that denied elections as a source of legitimacy, seized power, eliminated opponents, stifled criticism, denied the very existence of universal values, and saw itself only as the instrument of a global class struggle.

This new Party, he said, "pay(s) tribute to all the generations of Soviet people which have drawn inspiration from the socialist ideal" but has dramatically departed from its goals. He continued:

In place of the Stalinist model of socialism we are becoming a citizens' society of free people. The political system is being transformed radically, genuine democracy with free elections, the existence of many parties and human rights is becoming established, and real people's power is being revived.

The End of the Cold War

The cold war could not be understood as a contest between two superpowers for global dominance or preeminence nor in conventional balance-of-power terms—that is, merely as a contest for power. It was grounded in the Soviet will to empire and in the use of force, both of which were driven by the conviction of the Soviet elites that Marxism was the key to history and that the Soviet Union was the leader of the international Communist movement. Marxism is a faith that provided certainty and direction. The cold war ended as its credibility faded.

Two Marxist myths supported Soviet power and Communist expansion: the myth that socialism is a superior recipe for economic development and the myth that dictatorship of the Party would lead to a superior form of democracy.

Both claims were taken extremely seriously. Khrushchev boasted in 1958 that during the lifetime of the generation alive in 1961 the Soviet Union would achieve the "world's highest standard of living" and would also create the world's most just and democratic society. Each time a new country was conquered by a Marxist elite, these claims were offered to comfort them for the ensuing repression and loss of independence.

It became a truism of Western historians and political scientists that the Soviet Union constituted a "model of development" that was one option for people seeking rapid modernization. This notion that "socialism" on the Soviet model was a viable strategy of development persisted well into the 1980s and has been abandoned only with the greatest reluctance by Western intellectuals.

Many in the West had as great a difficulty as the Soviet leaders themselves in accepting realities about these myths. Many could not accept the fact that the Marxist revolution created more human misery, was guilty of more mass murder, even than Adolf Hitler— and that it was not an effective strategy of modernization. While Korea, Taiwan, Singapore, and West Germany set new records for sustained growth, the Soviet economy stagnated and declined.

Eventually almost everyone has been forced to admit the truth. The result has changed the world.

The New Russian Revolution

The revolution that transformed the Soviet Union, Eastern Europe, and the politics of our times teaches many lessons—some new, some old but nearly forgotten.

Not only were people liberated and institutions transformed but, as always happens in revolutions, principles of legitimacy were transformed. Marxism-Leninism relied on the laws of history and the authority of Party for legitimacy, but to justify their positions, Mikhail Gorbachev and his allies more and more frequently invoked public opinion, elections, and freedom—reminding us that principles of legitimacy always change when a real revolution takes place.

We have also learned from the fact that it all happened *very* fast.

The world was surprised by the lightning speed with which these totalitarian or would-be totalitarian regimes collapsed. One-party rule, monolithic culture, closed borders, and isolation from the West were permanent characteristics of these regimes. All rapidly gave way when it became clear that massive force was no longer available to maintain them. The speed with which these institutions collapsed proved they had never struck root in the societies they ruled. But the conformity they commanded had misled almost everyone. There are two morals to the story: we should take care neither to underestimate nor to overestimate what can be accomplished with force. The second lesson, especially for our times, is, Expect change.

The existence of traditional and alternative identifications and practices beneath the surface of official Marxism also testified to weak internalization of the official ideology. The lack of a strong continuing interest in Marxism and socialism is more evidence of the failure of indoctrination.

Concerning the Soviet future, we must live with uncertainty. Although the absence of pluralism did not make change impossible, it makes the transition to some other kind of system more difficult. In the Soviet Union, more than seventy years of totalitarian rule largely eliminated the alternative bases of power and alternative elites one finds in pluralist societies. Considered objectively, the prospects for democracy and development in the Soviet Union are exciting but not promising. The institutions of civil society and the habits of free association are weak. Prior experience with democracy was brief.

It is true, however, that in recent years democracy has struck root in some societies with little or no previous experience with democratic institutions and without the conditions that we often think of as prerequisites to democracy. The Soviet people have had a searing experience with tyranny that doubtless sensitizes them to the dangers of uncontrolled power.

The situation is complicated by the chronic, deepening economic crisis and by structural and cultural aspects of Soviet society that impede development. Almost everything in Soviet society discourages and inhibits movement toward a more dynamic, market-oriented economy. The experience of various newly developed countries shows that full democratic freedoms are not necessary to make market economies work but that some profit incentives and free movement of labor are. The Soviet system still features public ownership of almost everything, limited freedom of movement for workers, and few opportunities to profit. For the Soviets to increase production, efficiency, and growth, material incentives are necessary but still lacking. To produce the goods that will serve as incentives to produce more, the Soviets need enterprise, flexibility, and decentralization—yet centralization, rigidity, and uncertainty prevail. To these, chaos has now been added.

As societies develop, more than the modes of production must change: people must change. Attitudes toward time, toward achievement, toward authority, and toward one's self and one's future are all associated with modernization. People must believe that their situation can get better before they will work to make it better. These human correlates of modernization drive economic development.

It seems unlikely that modernization can ever be achieved under conditions of socialism—including the modified socialism that now exists in the Soviet Union. The economic actors who drive the market system are individuals who make decisions for themselves about what is best to do: where to work and what to work at. Indeed, the explosion of the individual into history created the energy that powered the modernization process. But socialism is proudly, confidently based on opposite conceptions. It focuses on collectivities—on classes above all—and sees the individual as subordinated to collectivities. It makes calculations in terms of the impact of policy on the collectivity. The collective rewards it offers are almost surely less effective in stimulating and sustaining individual effort, as intangible rewards are usually less effective than tangible incentives. A society in which rewards are collective but discipline is individual can probably neither achieve nor establish and sustain genuine growth. No Socialist system has.

Several reasons prevent socialism from being an effective economic system. In a system of centralized Socialist planning, decision makers are remote from the consequences of their decisions, and unlikely to be informed about them or directly affected by them. A Socialist system does not eliminate the self-interest of the decision maker, but it changes the nature of that interest. The Socialist planner's success depends on good interpersonal bureaucratic relations, not on the goods produced or the profits achieved. The Socialist system tends, by its very nature, to make economic decisions on the basis of political criteria. This does not make for sound economic decisions.

Another basic obstacle hinders Soviet economic growth: the transition to a market economy must be managed by Socialist bureaucrats. Socialism of any kind requires decision makers who—at least in principle—make decisions that will be good for the whole, not for their own profit. Decision makers feel no direct economic consequences of their decisions. Thus they do not grow rich if they make good decisions or go without if they make bad ones. Can persons outside the market system design a market system and make it work?

How can the hierarchical, centralized, one-party state be persuaded to forgo comprehensive control over the economy—especially if those in power do not really want to do so? How can market incentives become an effective stimulus when the centralized planners tax away the lion's share of the resulting profits? How can workers be expected to work harder if there are no rewards for effort? What does it matter if, in any case, there is nothing to buy with money earned?

The fact is, no one knows how to do it. There is no prior experience with a peaceful transition from a fully controlled centralized economy to a market system. While books on the transition from capitalism to socialism would fill a library, there has been little speculation or analysis of the route from socialism "back" to a society and an economy that work.

Realities Reexamined

The surprises of the past year have illuminated some aspects of the political world that had grown murky with time, confusion, and obfuscation.

The speed with which Hungary, Poland, East Germany, and Czechoslovakia seized the opportunity to dump Communist rulers and communism, transform their regimes, and loosen ties to the Warsaw Pact settled once and for all outstanding questions about whether those people of Eastern Europe had "chosen" socialism, or whether they "accepted" it, or whether they constituted a European empire held together by force.

When Mikhail Gorbachev signaled Eastern European clients that Soviet troops would not be available to maintain them, those governments collapsed. Force and the threat of force were starkly revealed to be the keystone of an Eastern European Soviet empire—just as anti-Communists said it was.

It also became clearer than it had been for a long time that the American and Western response to Soviet expansion was just that—a response to a perceived Soviet threat to the independence or integrity of Western European nations. Revisionist theories of the cold war had denied the reality of Soviet expansion and Western defense. They denied that Communist governments in Eastern Europe had been imposed by force and were maintained by force and that Soviet expansionism had ever constituted a credible threat to Western Europe or made necessary or prudent a counterforce. They denied that the people of Eastern Europe and the Soviet Union preferred other institutions to those under which they lived. They saw the U.S. presence as reflecting an American imperial urge. But the end of the cold war made it clearer than ever that that was never true.

The End of the Cold War Era

The end of the cold war signaled the end of the postwar era that began with the Hitler-Stalin Pact and defined the past half-century.

That postwar era was characterized by a Soviet threat, grounded in Marxism and backed by Soviet military forces; by a divided Europe, symbolized by the Berlin Wall and the many miles of closed, fortified borders separating the Communist East from the democratic West; and by the U.S. presence as a superpower in an alliance designed to protect Western Europe from the Soviet threat. These were, of course, the principal characteristics of the decades after World War II. It was all over by 1990.

By the beginning of 1990 the Berlin Wall had become the object of souvenir salesmen. The Soviet military threat had faded as, in one Eastern European country after another, the Soviet government demonstrated that its will to empire had given way to other interests and needs. The end of the cold war marked Europe's recovery of its historic position. Through most of modern history Europe was the world's center of power, at least for those people rooted in a European civilization. With the emergence of the cold war and a bipolar power distribution, Europe lost its political predominance, and the center of political gravity shifted away from the heart of Europe. Europe became the object of a power struggle as well as a participant in it.

In the cold war, Europe's distinctive balance-of-power politics gave way to ideological politics; multipolarity gave way to bipolarity, and nations lost their customary scope to maneuver. Ideology and identity determined which side a nation could be on. The cold war dramatically limited available choices. It cast the United States in a central role in European politics and gave it a presence of unprecedented importance on the European continent.

The end of the cold war means the end of ideological politics on the grand scale and of bipolarity. It means the restoration of choice. Already, "the sides" have no clear borders. Neutrality and nonalignment have lost their meaning. Already the preoccupations of nations have changed.

The Soviets are absorbed in internal reforms. The Western Europeans are preoccupied with German reunification, European integration, and the development of Eastern Europe. These are not cold war kinds of questions. With the end of the cold war, governments must learn to think again about who they are and how they should relate to one another, now that they are no longer locked into roles in a global contest and now that a civilization is no longer at stake. Now no overarching struggle links events in small remote countries to a global contest to which no major power could remain indifferent. Power contests in small countries are once again just that: power contests in small countries. Contests over economic resources are that. They are not a conflict of civilization. Millions have been released from the grip of a utopian nightmare.

USSR

MARCH 11, 1985: Mikhail Gorbachev succeeds Konstantin Chernenko as general secretary of the Communist party of the Soviet Union.

FEBRUARY 1986: In one of his first statements of *glasnost*, Gorbachev tells the French Communist party newspaper *Humanité*: "We see as a crucial task the further development of intra-party democracy and of socialist democracy more generally, the strengthening of the principles of collegiality in our work, and the widening of publicity (*glasnost*)."

FEBRUARY 11, 1986: Refusenik Anatoly Shcharansky is freed in an East-West prisoner exchange.

NOVEMBER 19, 1986: The Supreme Soviet approves legislation allowing limited private sector business activities in the Soviet Union. Henceforth, individuals and families could start their own small businesses and offer their skills for a fee.

DECEMBER 19, 1986: Andrei Sakharov and Yelena Bonner are released from exile in Gorky.

FEBRUARY 10, 1987: The Soviet foreign ministry announces the pardon and release of 140 dissidents from prison and labor camps.

FEBRUARY 12, 1987: Tass announces that *Dr. Zhivago* will be published in the Soviet Union in 1988.

FEBRUARY 20, 1987: Josef Begun, a Hebrew teacher jailed since 1983 on a charge of anti-Soviet activities, is freed.

JUNE 21, 1987: Elections to local soviets are held, in which some races are contested by more than one candidate, although all were approved by the Communist party.

JUNE 30, 1987: The Supreme Soviet enacts a law permitting the election of managers by workers and allowing businesses to set their own pay scales, fire workers for poor performance, and determine the use of profits.

January 6, 1988: Tass reports that the name of Leonid Brezhnev will be removed from one city, one city district, and two local squares.

February 5, 1988: The Soviet Union announces the posthumous rehabilitation of Nikolai Bukharin and nineteen other Bolsheviks purged by Stalin.

March 22, 1988: More than 3,500 volumes are removed from restricted shelves of libraries and made available to all readers. Previously banned religious literature, including Bibles, will henceforth be available.

April 14, 1988: Pakistan and Afghanistan sign a UN-sponsored agreement calling for a phased withdrawal of Soviet troops from Afghanistan. The Soviet Union and the United States are guarantors of the agreement.

May 12, 1988: It is reported that parts of George Orwell's *Nineteen Eighty-four* have been excerpted in *Literaturnaya Gazeta* and that the entire novel will be published in full by the magazine *Novy Mir*.

June 1, 1988: It is reported in the West that Soviet elementary and secondary schools have canceled final examinations so that textbooks could be rewritten to reflect reformist economic concepts and more accurate versions of history.

June 13, 1988: Four more prominent Bolsheviks purged by Stalin— Grigory Zinoviev, Lev Kamenev, Karl Radek, and Grigory Pyatakov—are posthumously rehabilitated.

June 28, 1988: At the Nineteenth Communist Party Conference Gorbachev calls for a sweeping political reorganization of the Soviet state, including the creation of a 2,250-member Congress of People's Deputies, of which 1,150 would be elected in contested races at the local and regional level.

July 9, 1988: Bukharin and other Old Bolsheviks purged by Stalin are posthumously readmitted into the Communist party.

September 28, 1988: The Voice of America receives permission to open a permanent bureau in Moscow.

October 25, 1988: The state publishing company announces that Leon Trotsky's writings will be published in 1989.

November 30, 1988: Officials of the United States Information Agency announce that the Soviet Union has stopped jamming broadcasts of Radio Liberty and Radio Free Europe after thirty-five years.

DECEMBER 7, 1988: At the United Nations Gorbachev promises large unilateral reductions in Soviet conventional forces by 1991 and a shift to a defensive military posture.

DECEMBER 29, 1988: The Kremlin orders the renaming of all public buildings, landmarks, factories, institutions, and streets named after Brezhnev or Chernenko.

DECEMBER 30, 1988: A military tribunal sentences Yuri Churbanov, the son-in-law of Leonid Brezhnev, to twelve years of hard labor for corruption.

FEBRUARY 15, 1989: The Soviet troop withdrawal from Afghanistan is completed.

MARCH 26, 1989: Many official Communist candidates are defeated in the first multicandidate parliamentary elections in the Soviet Union since 1917.

MAY 25, 1989: The Congress of People's Deputies convenes its first session. Gorbachev is elected to the revamped Soviet presidency. Deputies severely criticize the Party's Stalinist past.

MAY 30, 1989: In his presidential acceptance speech, Gorbachev offers firm figures on Soviet military outlays for 1989, the first such indication of Soviet defense spending.

JULY 4–8, 1989: A U.S. delegation visiting the Soviet Union is allowed to inspect a Soviet cruise missile and visit two secret military facilities.

JULY 7–8, 1989: At the annual Warsaw Pact summit meeting in Bucharest, Gorbachev calls for a "new atmosphere" of tolerance among member states, an atmosphere that would accept "independent solutions of national problems." He states: "We recognize the specifics of our parties and peoples on their path to socialist democracy and further development."

JULY 30, 1989: Dissident lawmakers in the Congress of People's Deputies, led by Boris Yeltsin and Andrei Sakharov, formally constitute themselves as the Inter-Regional Group of People's Deputies.

AUGUST 18, 1989: Communist party foreign policy official Alexander Yakovlev acknowledges the secret protocols to the 1939 Hitler-Stalin Pact, which relegated the Baltic states to Soviet domination. He "unequivocally" condemns the 1939 pact as a "deviation from the

Leninist principles of foreign policy."

SEPTEMBER 20, 1989: Gorbachev purges the Politburo of five prominent opponents of his *perestroika* campaign.

OCTOBER 17, 1989: The World Psychiatric Association votes to readmit the Soviet Union after a public acknowledgment by the Soviets of previous abuses of psychiatry for political reasons.

OCTOBER 24, 1989: Foreign Minister Shevardnadze admits that the Soviet invasion of Afghanistan violated Soviet law and international norms of behavior and that the Krasnoyarsk phased-array radar is an "open violation" of the 1972 Anti-Ballistic Missile Treaty.

NOVEMBER 4, 1989: KGB chief Vladimir Kryuchkov concedes that the KGB had been one of the "mechanisms of repression" during the Stalinist period and pledges that such abuses will "never happen again."

DECEMBER 1, 1989: Gorbachev meets with Pope John Paul II in the Vatican. The two leaders agree to work toward diplomatic relations between the Soviet Union and the Holy See.

DECEMBER 4, 1989: The Warsaw Pact nations (except for Romania), meeting in Moscow, condemn the 1968 invasion of Czechoslovakia.

DECEMBER 8, 1989: *Pravda* questions one-party rule by the Soviet Communist party.

JANUARY 10, 1990: The member states of Comecon agree to adopt gradually free-market trade policies based on hard currency, world market prices, and bilateral trade agreements between countries.

JANUARY 12, 1990: In Lithuania Gorbachev acknowledges that under the Soviet Constitution constituent republics have a right to secede. He asserts procedures must be spelled out.

JANUARY 13, 1990: Gorbachev expresses a willingness to accept a multiparty political system in the Soviet Union, saying, "We should not be afraid of a multiparty system the way the devil is afraid of incense."

JANUARY 16, 1990: The Soviet government announces that the study of Marxism will no longer be required in Soviet universities.

FEBRUARY 4, 1990: Hundreds of thousands of people participate in a prodemocracy rally in Moscow.

FEBRUARY 7, 1990: The Central Committee renounces the Party's constitutionally guaranteed monopoly on power and approves a draft party platform for sweeping economic and political change.

FEBRUARY 13, 1990: The new Party platform is published. It plays down the role of doctrine in party politics, opens the door to a multiparty system, commits the Party to the "creation of a full-fledged market economy," calls for separation of government powers, and supports the right of "self-determination, including secession," of the union republics.

FEBRUARY 24, 1990: In the first true multiparty elections held in the Soviet Union, candidates backed by Lithuanian nationalist organization Sajudis win majority of open seats in voting for the Lithuanian Parliament.

FEBRUARY 28, 1990: The Supreme Soviet votes to allow individuals to lease land for farming, housing, and small businesses.

MARCH 4, 1990: Radical reformists and nationalists score major gains in local and legislative elections held in Russia, Byelorussia, and Ukraine.

MARCH 6, 1990: The Supreme Soviet allows individuals to own, rent, or lease factories and other means of production. It also allows private employers to hire workers.

MARCH 11, 1990: The Lithuanian Parliament formally declares the republic's independence from the Soviet Union; Gorbachev calls the declaration illegal. Although the Kremlin rules out force in preventing Lithuanian independence, it subsequently sends tanks through Vilnius and seizes deserting Lithuanian soldiers, the Lithuanian Communist party headquarters, and government buildings.

MARCH 13–15, 1990: The Congress of People's Deputies repeals the Communist party's constitutional monopoly on power, creates a new presidential office, and elects Gorbachev to a five-year term as executive president. Gorbachev pledges to "radicalize economic reform" and hints that he might resign as Party chief to devote his time to the presidency.

MARCH 15, 1990: The Soviet Union and the Vatican reestablish limited diplomatic relations.

MARCH 17, 1990: Lithuania forms a non-Communist coalition government under Prime Minister Kazimiera Prunskiene.

MARCH 30, 1990: The Estonian Parliament declares the republic in a "transitional" stage toward independence.

April 9–10, 1990: Gorbachev and top economic adviser Leonid Abalkin outline an accelerated economic reform program based on dismantling the central pricing system, creating a stock market and joint-stock ventures, reducing restrictions on foreign investment, closing unprofitable state companies, and ruble convertibility with Western currencies.

April 13, 1990: The Soviet government admits that Stalin's secret police murdered more than 4,000 Polish officers in the Katyn Forest in 1940.

April 18, 1990: Moscow imposes an economic blockade of Lithuania, cutting off oil, natural gas, coal, and raw materials. On April 24 Bush indefinitely delays imposition of U.S. protest sanctions against the Soviet Union.

May 1, 1990: Gorbachev and Politburo are jeered by thousands of protestors at May Day parade in Red Square. For the first time, independent and unofficial organizations have been allowed to participate in the annual parade.

May 4, 1990: Latvian Parliament declares the republic's independence, with an unspecified transition period. On May 14 Gorbachev formally condemns the Latvian and Estonian declarations as illegal.

May 11–12, 1990: The three Baltic leaders meet in Tallinn, Estonia, and agree to coordinate political and economic strategy on winning independence.

May 16, 1990: Lithuania offers to suspend all laws passed since the declaration of independence and to discuss a transition period to full independence.

May 20, 1990: Gorbachev orders creation of a private housing market, directing the government to let private individuals build, buy, and sell their own houses and the lots on which they are built.

May 21, 1990: The Soviet Parliament enacts legislation making it a crime punishable by prison to insult the Soviet president "in an indecent way."

May 22, 1990: Gorbachev announces plans to double average food prices as part of a five-year transition to a "regulated market economy." On May 25 Muscovites begin panic food buying in anticipation of the price increases.

May 29, 1990: The Russian republican Parliament elects political maverick Boris Yeltsin as president of Russia.

JUNE 8, 1990: The Russian Parliament asserts that its own laws take precedence over Soviet laws within Russia.

JUNE 12, 1990: The Soviet Parliament approves a law on press freedom intended to end government censorship and allow individual citizens to start their own newspapers. Gorbachev also meets with the Baltic leaders and offers terms for negotiations on independence and for ending economic sanctions, and he calls for a new Soviet federation that would treat all republics as "sovereign states" with virtually full control over their own affairs. Lithuanian Prime Minister Prunskiene later says that Moscow has agreed to relax sanctions and that both sides are headed toward a negotiated settlement.

JUNE 14, 1990: The Supreme Soviet rejects Gorbachev's plan to raise bread prices as part of a shift to a market system but approves a corporate income tax.

JULY 2–12, 1990: Gorbachev weathers series of conservative challenges at twenty-eighth Communist Party Congress; his ally Vladimir Ivashko elected to new post of Party deputy leader; Politburo expanded to include republican Party chiefs. Yeltsin resigns from Party on July 12; mayors of Moscow and Leningrad follow.

JULY 15, 1990: Gorbachev decrees end to Communist monopoly on radio and television broadcasts.

JULY 16, 1990: Ukraine becomes tenth Soviet republic to declare sovereignty from central Soviet government.

JULY 27, 1990: Byelorussia's Parliament declares the republic's sovereignty, demanding its "share in Soviet riches."

AUGUST 1, 1990: Gorbachev agrees to join Yeltsin in creating commission to produce an economic reform program by September 1.

SEPTEMBER 3, 1990: Yeltsin releases a "500-day" plan for free-market reform, reportedly backed by Gorbachev.

HUNGARY

MAY 20–22, 1988: A special conference of the (Communist) Hungarian Socialist Workers party (the first national conference held since 1957) approves major changes in personnel and policy. Janos Kadar is replaced as party general secretary by Premier Karoly Grosz. About 40 percent of the Central Committee members are replaced. Grosz declares support for radical economic and political reforms but dismisses proposal for a multiparty system.

NOVEMBER 24, 1988: Miklos Nemeth, advocate of free market reforms, replaces Grosz as premier.

DECEMBER 7, 1988: Gorbachev promises in a UN speech to withdraw 10,000 Soviet tanks, 8,500 artillery pieces, and 800 combat aircraft from Hungary, East Germany, and Czechoslovakia by 1991.

JANUARY 11, 1989: Parliament approves legislation guaranteeing the rights to demonstrate and to form independent associations and political parties.

FEBRUARY 8, 1989: Gorbachev adviser Oleg Bogomolov affirms that Moscow could accept a neutral Hungary modeled after Austria or Sweden.

FEBRUARY 11, 1989: The Communist party Central Committee approves creation of independent political parties and agrees to a multiparty system. It also issues a compromise judgment on the 1956 Hungarian uprising, asserting it began as a popular revolt but degenerated into a counterrevolution.

MARCH 29, 1989: On return from Moscow, Grosz announces Gorbachev pledge not to interfere with reform in Hungary and elsewhere in Eastern Europe.

MARCH 31, 1989: State's media monopoly ends.

APRIL 12, 1989: The Central Committee removes four Politburo members, including one-time hard-liner Janos Berecz.

APRIL 25, 1989: The Soviet Union begins the formal withdrawal of military forces from Hungary.

MAY 2, 1989: Hungary begins dismantling the barbed wire and other fortifications along its border with neutral Austria.

MAY 30, 1989: The Communist party Central Committee announces that Imre Nagy's trial was "judicially unlawful."

JUNE 13, 1989: Formal talks begin on transition to multiparty politics.

JUNE 16, 1989: The remains of Imre Nagy (exhumed on March 29) and four of his closest aides are reburied in a solemn memorial ceremony in Budapest.

JUNE 24, 1989: The Central Committee establishes a collective presidency or Presidium. Of four members, three are from the Party's reformist wing.

JULY 6, 1989: Hungary's Supreme Court posthumously declares the innocence of Imre Nagy and eight associates.

JULY 6, 1989: Gorbachev speaks to the Council of Europe at Strasbourg, pledges noninterference in East European liberalization, and warns the West against trying to "overcome socialism" in the East bloc.

SEPTEMBER 26, 1989: Parliament affirms the right of Hungarians to possess a passport, travel abroad, and emigrate. The new law is intended to satisfy President Bush's requirement for a more liberal emigration policy before the United States can grant most-favored-nation status.

OCTOBER 6–7, 1989: Communist party congress votes to dissolve the Party and create a new one, the Hungarian Socialist party, committed to a market economy and parliamentary democracy.

OCTOBER 9, 1989: "Reformers" triumph over "conservatives" within the ruling party, as a new twenty-four-member Presidium is voted into power, of which at least fourteen members are radical reformers allied with reform Communist Imre Pozsgay.

OCTOBER 18, 1989: Parliament abolishes the Hungarian People's Republic, founded in 1949, and approves the Constitution of the new Republic of Hungary. The new charter contains no reference to the Communists' leading role or commitment to maintain socialism, and it establishes a powerful new presidency.

OCTOBER 19, 1989: The ruling party condemns the Soviet Union for crushing the 1956 Hungarian uprising and approves multiparty parliamentary elections to be held by June 1990.

OCTOBER 23, 1989: Acting President Matyas Szuros declares Hungary an independent democratic republic.

NOVEMBER 26, 1989: Hungarians vote to postpone election of a new president until after 1990 parliamentary elections (expected to be held March 18), to allow the fledgling opposition more time to prepare.

JANUARY 24, 1990: Hungarian Parliament guarantees freedom of religion and freedom of conscience.

FEBRUARY 9, 1990: Hungary restores diplomatic relations with the Vatican.

FEBRUARY 20, 1990: Foreign Minister Gyula Horn suggests a nonmilitary role for Hungary in NATO.

MARCH 1, 1990: To boost the presidential prospects of Imre Poszgay, the Socialist (formerly Communist)–dominated Parliament amends Constitution to allow direct presidential elections.

MARCH 11, 1990: Soviet military forces begin a full withdrawal from Hungary.

MARCH 18, 1990: The center-right Hungarian Democratic Forum, led by Joszef Antall, wins narrow plurality over the liberal Alliance of Free Democrats in Hungary's first free multiparty election since 1945. The HDF widens its margin in the April 8 runoff and subsequently forms a government with two smaller center-right parties.

JUNE 21, 1990: The Budapest Stock Exchange, the first stock exchange in Eastern Europe, officially opens.

JUNE 26, 1990: Parliament votes 232-0 (with four abstentions) to have government negotiate Hungary's withdrawal from Warsaw Pact.

AUGUST 3, 1990: Parliament elects writer Arpad Goncz as president.

POLAND

FEBRUARY 6, 1989: Round-table talks centering on political liberalization and legalization of Solidarity begin between the government and opposition, amid noisy demonstrations by militant students. The regime agreed to enter the talks in September 1988, after several months of unrest and industrial strikes.

APRIL 5, 1989: Round-table negotiations end, agreement signed mandating sweeping political reforms and allowing legalization of Solidarity. The Polish Parliament creates a new Senate and a strong presidency. New laws adopted giving citizens the right to form independent associations. Opposition could win control of the relatively powerless Senate but no more than 35 percent of Sejm seats in free elections scheduled for June.

APRIL 17, 1989: Solidarity, outlawed since 1982, is returned to legal status.

MAY 17, 1989: The Polish government legalizes the Roman Catholic church.

JUNE 4, 1989: In parliamentary elections Solidarity wins virtually all Senate seats and its allotted share of Sejm seats; most Communists nominated for the remaining parliamentary seats fail to win the required majority.

JUNE 18, 1989: Solidarity rejects Communist overtures for a coalition; a runoff election is held for the remaining unfilled Sejm seats, of which Solidarity wins all but one of those open to non-Communists.

JULY 4, 1989: The new Parliament convenes, and Premier Rakowski and his cabinet resign.

JULY 6, 1989: Gorbachev speaks to the Council of Europe at Strasbourg, indicates that he will not intervene in liberalizations in Poland and Hungary: "Any interference in domestic affairs and any attempt to restrict the sovereignty of states—friends, allies, or any others—are inadmissible."

JULY 19, 1989: Jaruzelski elected president by Polish Parliament.

JULY 26, 1989: Solidarity's parliamentary caucus refuses to join Communists in a coalition government.

JULY 29, 1989: Jaruzelski resigns as general secretary of the Communist party and as a member of the Politburo and Central Committee. He is replaced by Mieczyslaw Rakowski.

JULY 31, 1989: Gen. Czeslaw Kiszczak succeeds Rakowski as premier.

AUGUST 17, 1989: Kiszczak resigns as premier after failing to form a new government. Walesa assembles a coalition of Solidarity and two small parties formerly allied with the Communists; the Communists are offered the interior and defense ministries.

AUGUST 18, 1989: Jaruzelski names long-time Catholic activist and Solidarity adviser Tadeusz Mazowiecki to lead Poland's first non-Communist government in more than forty years.

SEPTEMBER 12, 1989: Parliament confirms a twenty-three-member coalition cabinet with eleven Solidarity members and four Communists.

OCTOBER 12, 1989: The Solidarity-led government announces a detailed program to create a free market economy.

JANUARY 27–28, 1990: The Polish United Workers' (Communist) party dissolves itself and then reforms itself under a new name, the Social Democratic party.

FEBRUARY 27, 1990: Poland restores full diplomatic relations with Israel.

MAY 9, 1990: Walesa declares "permanent political war" on the government, accusing it of timidity on economic and political reform.

MAY 27, 1990: In Poland's first fully free election since World War II, Solidarity triumphs in nationwide voting for community councils independent of Warsaw.

MAY 28, 1990: After two nights of impassioned persuasion by Lech Walesa, Polish rail workers agree to halt their two-week strike, the most serious threat to date to the government's economic reform plan.

JUNE 4, 1990: Walesa tries unsuccessfully to fire a leading critic, Adam Michnik, as editor of Solidarity daily *Gazeta Wyborcza*.

JUNE 24, 1990: Prominent Solidarity leaders allied with Mazowiecki break with Walesa over union leader's drive to become Polish president before end of 1990.

JULY 6, 1990: Mazowiecki drops opposition to early free national elections (by spring 1991) and dismisses three ex-Communist ministers from cabinet in effort to blunt Walesa's complaints about continuing Communist influence.

JULY 11, 1990: Rural Solidarity organizes nationwide protest by farmers angry about consequences of economic reform program.

CZECHOSLOVAKIA

OCTOBER 4, 1989: Foreign Minister Jaromir Johanes announces that Czechoslovakia will implement "deep-rooted" changes aimed at economic stabilization and creating a "deeply democratic political system."

NOVEMBER 12, 1989: Communist party General Secretary Milos Jakes tells a Communist youth conference that the Party will not tolerate street demonstrations or relax its control over the population.

NOVEMBER 17, 1989: Tens of thousands of demonstrators march through the streets of Prague in the largest antigovernment protest since 1968. Police disperse the protestors.

NOVEMBER 19, 1989: Opposition groups form the Civic Forum and demand the resignations of Czechoslovak Communist officials responsible for the 1968 Soviet invasion.

NOVEMBER 20, 1989: More than 200,000 protestors in Prague's Wenceslaus Square demand free elections and the resignation of hard-line Communist leaders. Protests spread to other cities.

NOVEMBER 24, 1989: Jakes and five other high Communist Presidium officials associated with the 1968 invasion resign; Karel Urbanek becomes Communist general secretary. Alexander Dubcek addresses a crowd of 300,000 in Wenceslaus Square.

NOVEMBER 27, 1989: Millions of people across Czechoslovakia walk off their jobs at midday in a two-hour general strike to protest Communist rule.

NOVEMBER 28, 1989: The government opens formal power-sharing talks with the Civic Forum. Premier Ladislav Adamec agrees to form a government with non-Communist representation by December 3.

NOVEMBER 29, 1989: A Communist official declares that free elections could take place within a year. The Communist-dominated Parliament votes unanimously to eliminate the Communist party's constitutionally guaranteed leading role in society and to remove another constitutional provision mandating Marxism-Leninism as the foundation of public education.

NOVEMBER 30, 1989: The government announces that it will open Czechoslovakia's border with Austria and remove virtually all restrictions on travel to the West.

DECEMBER 1, 1989: The new Communist party Politburo declares that the 1968 Soviet invasion was wrong. Gorbachev acknowledges that the Prague Spring resulted from a yearning for democracy.

DECEMBER 3, 1989: Premier Adamec, meeting a deadline set by the Civic Forum, announces new cabinet including five non-Communist ministers. Opposition calls for resumption of protests, threatens another general strike.

DECEMBER 7, 1989: Adamec resigns as prime minister, complaining of "ultimatums" from the Civic Forum. He is replaced by Marian Calfa, a little-known deputy.

DECEMBER 10, 1989: President Gustav Husak swears in a cabinet with a non-Communist majority and then immediately resigns.

DECEMBER 14, 1989: Jiri Dienstbier, a former leading dissident and the new foreign minister, declares that the agreement under which Soviet troops are stationed in Czechoslovakia was concluded under duress and is therefore invalid.

DECEMBER 28, 1989: Alexander Dubcek is elected chairman of Parliament.

DECEMBER 29, 1989: Parliament elects Vaclav Havel as president of Czechoslovakia.

JANUARY 1, 1990: Communist Premier Calfa announces that the government intends to adopt free market principles and increase ties with Western Europe.

JANUARY 18, 1990: Calfa resigns from the Communist party while continuing as head of government, leaving the Communists with only seven seats in the twenty-one-member coalition cabinet.

JANUARY 30, 1990: The Communist party loses its majority in Parliament.

FEBRUARY 19, 1990: It is reported that the Communist party has expelled former General Secretary Gustav Husak and twenty-one other members of the Party's old guard.

FEBRUARY 26, 1990: The withdrawal of 80,000 Soviet troops from Czechoslovakia begins.

APRIL 21–22, 1990: Pope John Paul II visits Czechoslovakia; diplomatic ties restored with the Vatican.

JUNE 8–9, 1990: The Communists are routed in Czechoslovakia's first free election since 1946. Havel's Civic Forum and Public against Violence win sweeping majorities in both houses of Parliament.

JULY 5, 1990: Havel is reelected to a two-year term as president.

GERMANY

AUGUST 1989: Hundreds of East Germans take refuge in three West German diplomatic facilities in hopes of receiving asylum in West Germany.

SEPTEMBER 11–14, 1989: More than 13,000 East Germans leave Hungary for West Germany via Austria. East Germany protests to Hungary, demands halt to exodus.

SEPTEMBER 18, 1989: Large-scale weekly protests begin in Leipzig.

SEPTEMBER 19, 1989: A new East German umbrella opposition group, New Forum, is formed to challenge Communist rule. On September 21 the East German Interior Ministry declares New Forum illegal.

SEPTEMBER 30, 1989: More than 17,000 East German refugees in West German embassies in Prague and Warsaw begin emigrating to West Germany.

OCTOBER 3, 1989: East Germany closes its border with Czechoslovakia in an effort to stem the refugee flow.

OCTOBER 6–7, 1989: Gorbachev attends East Germany's fortieth anniversary celebrations amid escalating protests, urges reform.

OCTOBER 18, 1989: Communist party chief Erich Honecker steps down as Party leader and head of state. Egon Krenz, security police chief and youngest Politburo member, becomes Party leader.

OCTOBER 24, 1989: Parliament approves Krenz as head of state, and government approves right to travel abroad.

NOVEMBER 1, 1989: Krenz meets with Gorbachev in Moscow, backs *perestroika* for East Germany.

NOVEMBER 3, 1989: Krenz purges five hard-liners from the East German Politburo and urges East Germans not to flee the country. Czechoslovakia opens its border to East Germans traveling west, and the exodus resumes. Krenz promises sweeping reforms.

NOVEMBER 4, 1989: In the largest political protest since 1953, at least half a million East Germans demonstrate in East Berlin for democracy.

NOVEMBER 6, 1989: Hundreds of thousands of demonstrators in eight East German cities demand free elections and travel.

NOVEMBER 7, 1989: Willi Stoph, East German premier since 1964, resigns with his cabinet.

NOVEMBER 8, 1989: Chancellor Helmut Kohl promises massive aid if East German leaders offer free elections. Politburo resigns. Krenz reelected as Party leader; Hans Modrow proposed as prime minister.

NOVEMBER 9, 1989: The Berlin Wall is opened and citizens are allowed to travel freely. More than 2 million East Germans visit West Berlin and West Germany.

NOVEMBER 17, 1989: Modrow includes eleven non-Communists in a new twenty-eight-member cabinet.

NOVEMBER 23, 1989: The East German Communist party launches a corruption investigation of Honecker.

NOVEMBER 28, 1989: Kohl calls for German federation as a first step toward reunification.

DECEMBER 1, 1989: The East German Parliament eliminates the constitutional guarantees of control by the Communist party and lifts the immunity of deputies from corruption investigations.

DECEMBER 3, 1989: Krenz resigns with the Politburo and the entire Central Committee in the midst of a swiftly widening corruption scandal. Honecker is expelled from the Party.

DECEMBER 5, 1989: Honecker and other senior East German officials are placed under house arrest, and top secret police officials resign over corruption charges. Crowds surround secret police headquarters in several cities in attempts to prevent removal of incriminating documents and illicit cash.

DECEMBER 6, 1989: Krenz resigns as head of state and chairman of the National Defense Council. Manfred Gerlach, a non-Communist, replaces him as acting head of state.

DECEMBER 7, 1989: The regime and the opposition hold power-sharing talks and call for free elections in 1990.

DECEMBER 9, 1989: The Communist party chooses Gregor Gysi as new Party chief.

DECEMBER 12, 1989: Secretary of State James Baker visits East Berlin, supports reform efforts.

DECEMBER 14, 1989: Secret police agency is abolished.

DECEMBER 16, 1989: Communist party changes its name to the Socialist Unity party of Germany–Party of Democratic Socialism in a continuing effort to remake its image.

JANUARY 4, 1990: Six opposition groups form a united front to challenge the Communists in elections scheduled for May 1990.

JANUARY 15, 1990: Thousands of angry protestors storm the secret police headquarters in East Berlin.

JANUARY 28, 1990: Parliament frees state media from Communist control and ends state censorship.

JANUARY 29, 1990: The East German government agrees to advance free elections by two months to stem the outflow of 3,000 citizens daily. Modrow and opposition groups create a broad, largely non-Communist coalition government to rule until elections now scheduled for March 18.

JANUARY 30, 1990: The Communist party drops opposition to reunification.

FEBRUARY 1, 1990: Modrow offers a plan for a unified, neutral Germany. Kohl rejects the proposal, defers negotiations until after March 18 East German general elections.

FEBRUARY 5, 1990: The Communists lose their majority in the East German cabinet.

FEBRUARY 6, 1990: The West German government outlines a plan to establish the deutsche mark as the single currency for East and West Germany.

MARCH 6, 1990: Gorbachev rejects membership of a unified Germany in NATO.

MARCH 14, 1990: The two German states and four victorious World War II allied powers open talks in Bonn on German reunification.

MARCH 18, 1990: The Alliance for Germany, a three-party alliance backed by West German Chancellor Kohl and headed by the Christian Democratic Union, wins general elections in East Germany. CDU leader Lothar de Maiziere subsequently forms a "grand coalition" government, sworn in on April 12.

APRIL 11, 1990: The United States rejects a Soviet proposal for a unified Germany to belong to both NATO and the Warsaw Pact.

APRIL 12, 1990: The East German Parliament asks forgiveness from Jews and the Soviet Union for Nazi atrocities during World War II.

311

APRIL 23, 1990: The West German government offers to exchange most East German marks for West German marks at one-to-one.

MAY 5, 1990: At "two-plus-four" talks in Bonn, the Soviets offer to delink German reunification from the resolution of external issues; Genscher initially welcomes the offer but Kohl rejects it.

MAY 17, 1990: Bush announces that he and Kohl agree that a unified Germany must remain in NATO and the rights of the allied victors ended. The Soviet Union has opposed NATO membership for Germany and said that the Allies should retain residual rights.

MAY 18, 1990: The East and West German finance ministers sign a state treaty to merge the two economies and make the West German mark the sole legal tender by July 2, 1990.

JUNE 12, 1990: Gorbachev drops a major Soviet condition for German reunification, agreeing that West German troops can stay in NATO without a corresponding role for East German troops in the Warsaw Pact (although he proposes an ill-defined "associate membership" for East Germany in the pact).

JUNE 21–22, 1990: The East German and West German Parliaments separately ratify the monetary union treaty.

JULY 1, 1990: German monetary union takes effect; next day East German coalition government agrees to West German call for all-German parliamentary election in December.

JULY 16, 1990: After two days of talks with Kohl, Gorbachev agrees to allow a reunified Germany to join NATO, removing last major external obstacle to reunification.

AUGUST 1, 1990: Governments and major political parties in East and West Germany agree on rules for December election.

OCTOBER 3, 1990: The four World War II victors abrogate all authority over Germany, the East German state is dissolved, and German unification takes place.

ROMANIA

JULY 7–8, 1989: Romanian dictator Nicolae Ceausescu is host to annual Warsaw Pact summit meeting in Bucharest. While Gorbachev calls for "independent solutions of national problems" among pact states, Ceausescu complains about disharmony within the alliance.

NOVEMBER 17, 1989: Romania seals border with Hungary.

NOVEMBER 20, 1989: Ceausescu opens the Fourteenth Congress of the Romanian Communist party, rejects reforms spreading across Eastern Europe.

NOVEMBER 24, 1989: Ceausescu is unanimously reelected as Communist party general secretary.

DECEMBER 15, 1989: Demonstrators surround a church in Timisoara, in western Romania, to prevent police from arresting a clergyman prominent in promoting rights of ethnic Hungarians.

DECEMBER 16–17, 1989: Security forces in Timisoara open fire on thousands of demonstrators demanding freedom and economic reform. Hundreds are killed and buried in mass graves.

DECEMBER 20, 1989: Ceausescu, returning from visit to Iran, declares state of emergency in western Romania and blames unrest on "fascist, reactionary groups." Demonstrations spread to at least eight other cities.

DECEMBER 21, 1989: Revolt spreads to Bucharest, where security forces open fire on demonstrators. A shocked Ceausescu is shouted down while addressing what he thought would be an orchestrated rally.

DECEMBER 22, 1989: Army units join the rebellion, and a group known as the Council of National Salvation announces that it has overthrown the Ceausescu regime. The council pledges to form a provisional government, try regime leaders, and restore democracy. Ceausescu and his wife Elena flee the presidential palace.

DECEMBER 23, 1989: The provisional government announces capture of the Ceausescus north of Bucharest. Fierce street fighting in Bucharest between the army, which backs the new government, and elements of the secret police loyal to Ceausescu.

DECEMBER 25, 1989: State radio announces execution of the Ceausescus after a secret trial finds them guilty of genocide and plundering the state treasury. The United States and the Soviet Union recognize the provisional government. Ceausescu's secret police battle the military and civilian rebels in Bucharest, Timisoara, and other cities until December 28, the provisional regime's deadline for security forces to surrender or face summary execution.

DECEMBER 26, 1989: The ruling front names the country's interim leaders and vows to hold free elections in April 1990. Ion Iliescu, a former Party official, is named interim president.

DECEMBER 27, 1989: The ruling front abolishes limits on the amount of food Romanians can buy and legalizes birth control and abortion.

DECEMBER 30, 1989: Rebel forces gain control throughout the country.

JANUARY 1, 1990: Interim President Iliescu announces that farmers can own up to 1.5 acres of land each and sell their produce on the free market. The provisional government announces the formal disbanding of the Securitate.

JANUARY 7, 1990: Thousands of Romanians throughout the country protest continuing presence of ex-Communists in high government posts. Demonstrations continue through January and February.

JANUARY 9, 1990: The provisional government lifts travel restrictions for Romanians.

JANUARY 23, 1990: The National Salvation Front formally decides to compete as a political party in upcoming national elections.

FEBRUARY 1, 1990: The National Salvation Front agrees to ease its control over Romania and govern in coalition with other political parties until expected elections in May 1990.

FEBRUARY 5, 1990: Interim President Iliescu signs a decree allowing businesses with up to twenty employees to operate for profit.

FEBRUARY 9, 1990: The new provisional Parliament, the Council for National Unity, convenes its first session.

MAY 20, 1990: In Romania's first free election in fifty years, Iliescu's National Salvation Front of ex-Communists wins a decisive victory amid fraud allegations.

JUNE 13–15, 1990: Student-led antigovernment protestors riot in Bucharest; proregime coal miners rampage against them in Eastern Europe's worst violence since Romania's 1989 revolution.

JULY 13, 1990: More than 20,000 people rally against the government in Bucharest's Victory Square.

BULGARIA

OCTOBER 30, 1989: Facing unprecedented public dissent, Bulgaria's Communist leadership announces new efforts at reform, particularly government reorganization and reducing the power of the Communist party Central Committee.

NOVEMBER 3, 1989: More than 4,000 Bulgarians in Sofia demand democracy and *glasnost* in the country's first mass protest under Communist rule.

NOVEMBER 10, 1989: Bulgarian President Todor Zhivkov unexpectedly resigns after thirty-five years in power. Foreign Minister Petar Mladenov replaces Zhivkov as Communist party chief.

NOVEMBER 16, 1989: Three hard-line Politburo members are forced into retirement as part of a major Party shakeup.

NOVEMBER 18, 1989: With full approval of the new Communist leadership, more than 50,000 people peacefully demonstrate in Sofia for immediate free elections, parliamentary rule, and the trial of Zhivkov for corruption.

DECEMBER 11, 1989: Mladenov proposes free elections in June 1990 and removal of the Party's constitutional guarantee of exclusive power.

DECEMBER 13, 1989: The Communist party Central Committee renounces its constitutionally guaranteed monopoly on political power and expels Zhivkov from the Party.

DECEMBER 27, 1989: The Communist party and the opposition Union of Democratic Forces agree to begin detailed power-sharing talks in January 1990.

JANUARY 15, 1990: Parliament revokes the constitutionally guaranteed dominant role of the Communist party.

JANUARY 16, 1990: The government begins round-table talks with the Union of Democratic Forces.

JANUARY 18, 1990: Former Communist leader Zhivkov is placed under house arrest (on January 29 he is formally arrested).

JANUARY 26, 1990: Communist party control over Bulgaria's military and police forces is eliminated.

FEBRUARY 1, 1990: Communist Prime Minister Georgi Atanasov's government resigns. An extraordinary party congress endorses multiparty democracy and minority rights within the Party. The opposition Union of Democratic Forces reiterates its refusal to join coalition government with Communists.

FEBRUARY 2, 1990: Alexander Lilov is elected to new post of Party chairman, replacing Mladenov (who remains head of state). Lilov promises to speed democratic reform. Party congress votes to replace the Central Committee with a smaller Supreme Council to be chosen by the delegates.

FEBRUARY 3, 1990: Parliament unanimously confirms Andrei Lukanov as premier, replacing Atanasov.

FEBRUARY 6, 1990: Bulgaria's interior minister announces that the secret police have been disbanded.

FEBRUARY 8, 1990: Premier Lukanov appoints an all-Communist cabinet.

FEBRUARY 11, 1990: Thirty reformists quit the Communist party and form an independent Alternative Socialist party.

FEBRUARY 25, 1990: More than 80,000 people demonstrate in Sofia against Communist rule. Some 20,000 stage another prodemocracy demonstration on March 2.

APRIL 3, 1990: Parliament adopts constitutional amendments creating an executive presidency and removing the words "Communist" and "Socialist" from the Constitution; Mladenov is elected president. Bulgarian Communist party changes name to Bulgarian Socialist party.

JUNE 10, 1990: The ex-Communists score a decisive victory in free elections for Parliament.

JULY 6, 1990: Mladenov resigns as president amid ongoing student protests against the ruling Socialist party.

AUGUST 1, 1990: Parliament elects opposition leader Zhelyu Zhelev president. New director of the Bulgarian arms export business "Kintex" offers to share with Western governments information on Bulgarian arms transfers to terrorist groups.

About the Author

JEANE J. KIRKPATRICK was the first woman to serve as the United States Representative to the United Nations and, concurrently, as a member of the Cabinet. She is now Leavey Professor at Georgetown University and a senior fellow at the American Enterprise Institute.

In 1985 she was awarded the Medal of Freedom by the president of the United States. In 1984 she received the French Prix Politique for political courage. She has received honorary degrees from Georgetown University, the University of Pittsburgh, Bethany College, Franklin and Marshall College, St. John's University, the Hebrew University (Jerusalem), Tel Aviv University, and other institutions. Her M.A. and Ph.D. degrees are from Columbia University, and she also studied at the Institut de Science Politique at the University of Paris.

Her principal publications include *Dictatorships and Double Standards: Rationalism and Reason in Politics* (AEI and Simon and Schuster, 1982), *The Reagan Phenomenon* (AEI, 1983), *Legitimacy and Force: National and International Dimensions* (Transaction Books, 1988), *Dismantling the Parties: Reflections on Party Reform and Party Decomposition* (AEI, 1978), *The New Presidential Elite* (Russell Sage Foundation, 1976), *Political Women* (Basic Books, 1974), and *Leader and Vanguard in Mass Society: A Study of Peronist Argentina*. In addition, she writes a syndicated column and has published articles in *Commentary*, the *Journal of Politics*, the *American Political Science Review*, and the *New Republic*.

A NOTE ON THE BOOK

This book was edited by Dana Lane of the
publications staff of the American Enterprise Institute.
The text was set in Palatino, a typeface designed by
the twentieth-century Swiss designer Hermann Zapf.
Coghill Composition Company, of Richmond, Virginia,
set the type, and Edwards Brothers Incorporated,
of Ann Arbor, Michigan, printed and bound the book,
using permanent acid-free paper.

The AEI PRESS is the publisher for the American Enterprise Institute for Public Policy Research, 1150 17th Street, N.W., Washington, D.C. 20036: *Christopher C. DeMuth*, publisher; *Edward Styles*, director; *Dana Lane*, editor; *Ann Petty*, editor; *Cheryl Weissman*, editor; *Susan Moran*, editorial assistant (rights and permissions). Books published by the AEI PRESS are distributed by arrangement with the University Press of America, 4720 Boston Way, Lanham, Md. 20706.